THE BIBLE FOR THEOLOGY

Ten Principles for the Theological Use of Scripture

by

Gerald O'Collins, S.J., and Daniel Kendall, S.J.

Paulist Press
New York/Mahwah, N.J.

Cover design by Tim McKeen

Library of Congress Cataloging-in-Publication Data

O'Collins, Gerald.
    The Bible for theology : ten principles for the theological use of Scripture / by
Gerald O'Collins and Daniel Kendall.
        p. cm.
    Includes bibliographical references and indexes.
    ISBN 0-8091-3743-7 (alk. paper)
        1. Bible—Hermeneutics. 2. Bible—Use. 3. Catholic Church—Doctrines.
I. Kendall, Daniel. II. Title.
BS476.038   1997
220.1—dc21   97-26623
                                                                    CIP

Published by Paulist Press
997 Macarthur Boulevard
Mahwah, New Jersey 07430

Printed and bound in the
United States of America

Contents

Introduction

In leading readers into this book we should state, right at the onset, what we do not intend to do. We are not attempting to write a history of modern biblical interpretation, nor are we promising to take up all the major issues that enter contemporary debates about interpretative theory. Others, in particular A. C. Thiselton, have already done this well. We have chosen as our theme the use of the Christian scriptures in Christian theology, or rather the way the scriptures should put theology "on the move"—something which has always been challenging but for different reasons. For much of Christian history theologians and biblical interpreters were identical; the same persons faced the task both of exegeting the whole Bible and translating it into their theology. In the last century or two scriptural scholars and systematic theologians have normally belonged to distinct specializations. When using the Bible, theologians need to ask among other things: What are the exegetes saying? Without indulging fanciful pretensions, we recognize that our training and academic life have given us a foot, or at least a toehold, in both camps. It is out of this experience that we wish to develop our joint work.

We are tackling the appropriation of the scriptures in one professional sector of Christian activity, not in the whole life of the church. Obviously we should not, and, indeed, cannot, separate what goes on in the lecture hall, library, and private study from the whole existence of Christians at large. Nevertheless, we want to focus on the vital role of the Bible for theology, and, in particular, for systematic theology. In doing so, we plan to avoid, as far as possible, esoteric code words and tortuous self-legitimizing forms of discourse that at times give philosophy and theology a bad name among intelligent and cultured nonspecialists.

1

Some contemporary writing on scriptural interpretation can strike the educated, general reader as either impenetrable or sterile.

At times this book will critically confront some contemporary views on the theory and practice of biblical interpretation. But our aim is not that of surveying and evaluating all the major present approaches to the use of the scriptures in theology. We wish rather to ask directly: What effects should biblical texts produce in theology? What does it mean for theologians to read, understand, interpret, and apply the scriptures? Attention to those questions will allow us to elaborate our views on how the Bible should ideally work in Christian theology, so as to come up with some guiding principles. Subsequent chapters will apply and test these principles by applying them to some key issues in Christology (the preexistent divinity of Jesus Christ, and the primacy of love in his redemptive work), the doctrine of the trinity (naming the first, second, and third persons "Father," "Son," and "Holy Spirit" respectively), and ecclesiology (the foundation of the church and the Petrine ministry). We end with some cautionary remarks about the ministry of Jesus and with some suggestions about theological use of texts, translations, and commentaries. In carrying through this task, we are not claiming that the scriptures (with appropriate interpretative principles) should have a monopoly in theological argument. Data for theology also come from history and human experience. Without ignoring that, we aim, nevertheless, to concentrate on the appropriate role of scripture in theology.

From what has already been said, it is obvious that we write out of a Christian faith-stance. Among other things this means assuming articles of that faith (like biblical inspiration) which relate specifically to the scriptures. Some of our readers may not share this faith-stance or may not share it completely. We invite those in that situation to try a mental experiment by imagining that they do share our faith-stance so that they can concentrate on the viability or otherwise of our ten principles. To try out these guiding principles we have deliberately chosen some central and controversial issues. The main aim of this book is to test our ten principles (which we propose as mainline Christian and not distinctively Roman Catholic ones) and to do so in dialogue and debate with our readers. We propose our principles at a time when few seem clear about how the scriptures might be used in practicing theology, and no one else, as far as we know, has been proposing a set of guiding principles to achieve that end. The literature on general and biblical hermeneutics is enormous, but there appears to be very little precise help and direction being offered in moving from the biblical texts to discuss and reach conclusions about particular theological questions.

For years we have enjoyed working together. It may be quaintly out of fashion to say so, but we believe that in research, discussion, and writing, our gifts complement each other. The sum of our work, we hope, is greater than the parts each of us brings to it. We warmly thank Raúl Biord Castillo, Norris Clarke, Paul Gwynne, William Henn, Megan Maloney, Earl Muller, Hilary O'Shea, James Puglisi, Frank Sullivan, Roland Teske, David Tracy, Jared Wicks, and Donald Brophy. They have helped to sharpen our case at many points. We are very grateful for their expert advice, but together take full responsibility alone for the positions developed in this book. Several audiences in Australia, Italy, and the United States (especially the twelve members of a doctoral seminar at Marquette University) have helped to improve our arguments through many questions and observations. We thankfully acknowledge this help as well. One of us (Gerald O'Collins) wishes to express his deep gratitude to Marquette University (Milwaukee) for the honor of being the Wade Distinguished Professor of Theology (1994/95), an appointment that provided the facilities and time for some of the work on our common project.

This book is dedicated to the memory of many Jesuits who, since the Second World War, have been killed in Bolivia, Lebanon, Rwanda, El Salvador, Zimbabwe, and other parts of the world. Through their ministry and death, they witnessed to their faith in the One, who as the way, the truth, and the life forms the heart of the biblical story. We know ourselves to have been blessed by these companions and by a host of other twentieth-century Christian men and women who have given their lives in witness to what they read and treasured in the scriptures. Their heroic example interprets the biblical text with a power that far outstrips any theories and principles that we might develop. But if our words can throw a little light on the integrity of their deeds, we will be more than satisfied.

In a postmodern world of institutionalized pluralism, uncertainty, and ambivalence, it is tempting to think that old, comforting certainties are gone forever about the scriptures and many other things. With life, including much academic life, largely lacking shared standards, values, and truths, it may seem countercultural and downright quixotic to write a book proposing normative principles for the theological appropriation of the scriptures. But the commitment to heroic ideals lived to the end by those to whom we dedicate this work has encouraged us to go ahead with our project.

Gerald O'Collins, S.J.   *Daniel Kendall, S.J.*
Gregorian University, Rome   University of San Francisco
31 July 1996

Abbreviations

ABD   Anchor Bible Dictionary
CSEL   Corpus Scriptorum Ecclesiasticorum Latinorum
NAB   New American Bible
NEB   New English Bible
NIV   New International Version
NJB   New Jerusalem Bible
NRSV   New Revised Standard Version
NT   New Testament
OT   Old Testament
PG   J. Migne. Patrologia Graeca
PL   J. Migne. Patrologia Latina
REB   Revised English Bible
RSV   Revised Standard Version
TRE   Theologische Realenzyklopädie

1

Ten Principles

You search the scriptures, because you think that in them you have eternal life; it is they that bear witness to me.

—John 5:39

In the present state of theology, it is painfully obvious that the scriptures are often being used incoherently or at least inconsistently and inaccurately. This book aims at improving the passage from the Bible to systematic theology, a passage that is not always being negotiated skillfully. In particular, we want to elaborate ten principles for the use of the scriptures in theology and illustrate their application in several key areas of doctrine.

Our ten principles run as follows:

1. *The Principle of Faithful Hearing.* The scriptures require theologians to be faithful and regular hearers of the inspired texts.
2. *The Principle of Active Hearing.* Responsible theologians are active interpreters of the scriptures, appropriating them within the contexts of prayer, study, and action.
3. *The Principle of the Community and Its Creeds.* The scriptures call for a theological interpretation and appropriation within the living community of faith and in the light of its classic creeds.
4. *The Principle of Biblical Convergence.* Convergent biblical testimony can bear on the theological questions being examined.
5. *The Principle of Exegetical Consensus.* Where available, the consensus of centrist exegetes guides systematic theology.

6

6 *The Principle of Metathemes and Metanarratives.* Theological appropriation of the Bible takes account of metathemes and meta-narratives.

7. *The Principle of Continuity within Discontinuity.* Various disconti-nuities within continuities affect the theological "taking over" of the Bible.

8. *The Principle of Eschatological Provisionality.* Their eschatologi-cal provisionality regulates the theological role of scriptures.

9. *The Principle of Philosophical Assistance.* The passage from the Bible to theology takes place in dialogue with philosophy.

10. *The Principle of Inculturation.* The task of inculturation helps to shape any theological appropriation of the scriptures.

These are ten principles we wish to elaborate and recommend as guide-lines in moving from the scriptures to theology. Before explaining them in detail and arguing for their relevance, we need to sketch what we presuppose about the genesis of the scriptural texts, about their past interpretation, and about their claims on present interpreters. Hence, the opening section of this chapter summarizes our major presupposi-tions about the origins of the scriptures and their interpretation in the past and in the present. We can then proceed to explain our ten princi-ples and (in subsequent chapters) to apply them.

The Scriptures in the Past and Present

Even though the identity of their editors and/or authors is often unknown, the work of all those who played a part in the formation of our biblical texts anchors these texts firmly in the foundational past: the orig-inating tradition which remembered the story of Israel, the unsurpassable and definitive presence of Jesus, and the coming into being of the church. These writers, under the special impulse of the Holy Spirit, witnessed to and interpreted the divine revelation, as well the human living out (and also at times the sinful rejection) of that revelation. It is not our intention to explore in detail here once again revelation, tradition, the charism of biblical inspiration, its relation to and distinction from the larger reality of God's self-revelation, the formation of the biblical canon, and the salvific nature of the truth which follows as a consequence from the bib-lical inspiration, and which obliges readers to ask constantly: What do these normative texts reveal and do for our salvation? The seventy-two books that Catholic Christians recognize as sacred scriptures form the literary mirror of the special revelation and salvation history which reached its absolute climax with Christ's incarnation, life, death, and resurrection, along with the sending of the Holy Spirit.[1] What Christians maintain about the Bible rests squarely on their faith in Jesus Christ.[2] Their fidelity to the scriptures is inseparable from their fidelity to their origins in Jesus Christ as absolute Revealer and Savior.

Apart from that faith, the authority of the interpreting community has no validity, and the scriptures themselves cannot credibly claim any normative value, becoming little else than "mere" historical sources, the earliest records of the origins of Christianity and—religiously—an anthology of more or less edifying religious texts from the ancient Middle East. With a full christological faith, however, believers, theologians included, acknowledge the scriptures as holy, sacred, and as embodying mysterious, transcendent authority.[3] It is because the revealing and inspiring God speaks through all these texts that they constitute the authoritative account and interpretation of Israel's history and the formation of Christianity through Jesus Christ and his earthly followers. The official collection of foundational books witnesses to that special history of revelation and salvation which remains not merely the general interpretative framework but also the decisive point of orientation for all subsequent believers (and theologians). Their attitude toward the authority of the whole Bible provides a litmus test of how theologians consider authority to function in and for their work. This calls for some account of how we understand canonical authority.

Why should the canonical scriptures legitimately function as scriptures—that is to say, enjoy acknowledged authority for the church in general and theologians in particular? In forming the biblical canon (on the basis of such criteria as orthodox content, constant usage, and apostolic origin), the church recognized certain texts coming from her foundational history as inspired *and* normative: that is to say, texts acknowledged as rightly commanding her permanent allegiance, as promising to preserve indefectibly her self-identity by constantly illuminating and enlivening her faith and practice, and as never failing to witness in every situation to the divine Truth that is Jesus Christ. This *de iure* authority is exercised *de facto* over those who voluntarily accept it and recognize that the Bible in and of itself is entitled to command this kind of loyalty, elicit these expectations, and function as standard or norm for determining the church's faith and practice. It is important to insist that the authority of the scriptures is not merely *de facto* and based simply on the way they effectively function now in shaping life and teaching for the community of faith. They have a *de iure* authority that legitimately commands permanent loyalty and is derived from a foundational and authoritative past.

The legitimation of the Bible comes from outside itself; neither any single book of the scriptures nor the entire canon of scriptures contains its own self-justification. Biblical authority is derived from the period of foundational tradition and the foundational revelation that reached its climax with Christ and his apostles. The Holy Spirit guided biblical history and tradition, an activity which included special guidance to all those involved in the production of the scriptures. After the foundational period the same Holy Spirit has continued to guide the community of faith and individual believers in being enlightened and enlivened through the scriptures. The authority of the scriptures derives also from the divine identity of Christ and his authoritative and definitive revelation. He extended his authority to all the apostles (not just the twelve) and to their collaborators, authorizing their foundational mission and what it essentially entailed. This authorization from Christ comes through powerfully in what Paul wrote in the two opening chapters of the Letter to the Galatians. Paul and the other founders, called by Christ to share in his climactic revelation of God and creation of the church, maintained the unquestioned authority of their inherited scriptures, as Christ had done in his own earthly ministry. The Letter to the Hebrews spectacularly illustrates how NT Christians viewed these inherited scriptures as divinely inspired and authoritative. Citing the OT thirty-seven times, the Letter to the Hebrews attributes all the passages to God, Christ, or the Holy Spirit, mentioning only two human authors, Moses (Heb 8:5; 12:21) and David (Heb 4:7), and referring even then twice to the divine "author" (Heb 4:7; 8:5). Paul and the other apostolic founders understood their inherited scriptures to witness prophetically to Christ; they then added (directly or through collaborators) the Christian scriptures. Thus the bipartite Bible came into being and remains not merely a linguistic medium for religious truth but the unique and authoritative linguistic medium of God's self-communication. The uniqueness of the Bible's authority derives from its historical origins in the mission of the Holy Spirit, a mission invisible in itself but visible in its effects, and the visible mission of Christ (with the passage of authority from him to his apostolic collaborators). In brief, the authority of the scriptures is pneumatological, christological, and apostolic. It derives from persons (the Holy Spirit and Christ with his apostles), and neither from itself nor, as is sometimes asserted, from the events to which it witnesses. Authority is vested in persons rather than in events. Through the scriptures (and in other ways) Christ and his Spirit remain present authoritatively. The authority of the apostles — to the extent that the foundational authority extended to them could be transmitted to their successors — remains present in the official ministry of bishops.

The missions of the Spirit and of Christ establish the theological unity of the (otherwise very diverse) scriptures, a unity without which such authority would be lost. Christ and his Spirit make the whole of the scriptures authoritatively greater than the sum of its parts. Through the use of the Bible in the liturgy, preaching, theology, and whole life of the church, the Holy Spirit authoritatively communicates life and light to the community of believers. By witnessing to Christ through the scriptures (and in other ways), the Spirit makes him the normative Presence who speaks to us today through these texts (as well as in other ways). The written word of the Bible becomes thus the proclaimed Word, authoritatively incarnated by the Spirit into every human situation and enabled to be truly the Word of God for us now. One might speak here of an *epiclesis*. Just as the *Holy* Spirit is called down upon the eucharistic elements in petition for the fruits of communion, so the Spirit can be called upon to open up the historical words and make them a living Word here and now.

We are well aware that those who do not share our high view of Christ, the Spirit, and the apostles' foundational mission will not be in a position to accept our *de iure* version of biblical authority.[4] They will find this account of the Bible's *de iure* authority incredible, just as they find belief in Christ's divinity, for instance, incredible. At best they endorse a merely functional, *de facto* interpretation. The Bible is "authoritative," not because of any inherent quality derived from its historical origins, but because of what it powerfully continues to do by providing a friendly language of faith for those who use it in their worship and teaching, shaping the lives of communities and individuals, and mediating God's presence to them. In a word, the Bible is "authoritative" only because, at least in part, it proves itself helpful and has the power to influence profoundly the lives of people. This functional view of scriptural authority, as has been frequently pointed out, is obviously prey to current fashions and ideologies. It would mean letting the Bible speak to us "authoritatively" only when it legitimizes and conforms to what we have already decided are useful or even true positions on Christian belief and practice, allowing it no independent authority to challenge and judge us and our society, and even reading it with a radical suspicion that leads to alienation from and even rejection of the biblical text.[5]

Many resist any sense of biblical authority and do so for several further reasons. How can the scriptural texts stemming from the origins of the Christian movement be and remain normative? These documents are thoroughly culture-specific and historically dated; they contain, for instance, not a few obsolete and even inhuman ethical directives, and consistently betray patriarchal features. Second, the origins of Christianity, including all that happened and all that was written down, were exposed to the contingencies of history. Things could have gone otherwise—for instance, in the ministries of Jesus and Paul. Why should a contingent past, even a quite extraordinary one, continue to control authoritatively our present life and belief? Third, as commentators on the post-modern situation have pointed out, in many cultures or subcultures insistence on autonomy and self-direction has caused an almost total eclipse of authoritative structures. The (often authoritarian) spirit of total personal autonomy is incompatible with the authority of the Bible.

Some have suggested the analogy of classic texts: the scriptures function "authoritatively" for Christians in a way that parallels the "authority" of recognized classics in Western culture. In her *Metaphorical Theology* Sallie McFague writes: "The Bible is not absolute or authoritative in any sense except the way that a 'classic' text is authoritative" (19). (In parenthesis we note that we ourselves do not use "absolute" and "authoritative" as synonymous alternatives. The Bible is authoritative but not "absolutely" and in itself; its authority is derived from and relative to the Holy Spirit, Christ, and his apostles.) Francis Schüssler Fiorenza has drawn attention to the major flaw in this "classic" interpretation of biblical authority which hardly distinguishes the Bible from "inspired" and "inspiring," classic works of art and literature. The classics exemplify in an outstanding way the deepest truths about human existence; in these books generation after generation have recognized "the truth of their own identity." But it is "the identity of Jesus" that is the basis for scriptural authority rather than the power of the scriptures to elicit from one generation to the next compelling truths about the human condition. Schüssler Fiorenza rightly recalls Krister Stendahl's observation that "it is because of their authority as scripture that the Scriptures have become classics," and it is not that "they have authority because they are classics."⁶ One might add to Schüssler Fiorenza's argument by pointing out that the great literary classics do not necessarily belong to the origins of a given culture: the works of Goethe, for instance, came long after the establishment of the German culture. No "canon" of the literary classics can be declared to be closed; outstanding writers may emerge today and in the future; their works will merit "canonization" and inclusion among a people's classic texts. The inspired scriptures, however, belong to the foundational period of Christianity. The biblical canon is closed; it cannot be enlarged, even by a lost psalm, a lost letter from Paul, or some other such text from the origins turning up in an archaeological dig. Such texts would obviously lack an essential characteristic used by the church as one criterion for accepting books into the canon: constant usage in liturgy and teaching.

All in all, it is clear that the account we have offered of biblical authority will ultimately be assessed on prior grounds. Does Christ, for example, enjoy the personal identity and authority of the incarnate Son of God? Did and does the Holy Spirit operate as we have claimed? Our intention here was only that of responding fairly briefly to the question: Why ought Christian theologians accredit the Bible not only with *de facto* authority but also with *de iure* authority? The ten principles that we expound below will sketch an answer to the questions: *How* should the Bible work authoritatively for theologians? *How* should their assertions conform to the Bible?⁷

Hence we challenge, for example, proposals for evaluating the authority of the Bible not on the basis of the central role of the Holy Spirit in the formation of the scriptures but in the light of human experiences of oppression and liberation. Unquestionably the Bible has been repeatedly misused as a tool for oppression and, in particular, for the patriarchal oppression of women. But we part ways with those who react to this by "granting" revelatory authority *only* to those texts that critically break through patriarchal culture,⁸ excluding all scriptural texts that do not—or do not obviously—promote the present-day liberation of women and other oppressed groups. This is to use an exclusive norm for ultimately inclusive purposes. This is also to locate the seat of normative authority outside the Bible—in those readers whose experience of oppression and liberation allows them to discern (that is to say, authoritatively decide) which texts can convey revelation from God. This procedure is at times "justified" as the hermeneutical principle of the oppressed. Is one expected then to marginalize or even excise passages deemed theologically unworthy? This view, to say the least, minimizes the force of biblical inspiration. What that charism essentially meant was recording in writing all that the Holy Spirit wanted to be recorded for the sake of our salvation. Many biblical texts reflect deficient and even appalling human beliefs and behavior; many other texts record words and events that mediated divine revelation. But all the biblical texts were inspired by the Spirit; any of those texts—and not just the promising, liberating passages—can speak to people today and become the vehicle of divine revelation and grace. "Hateful" and "oppressive" texts from the Bible do just that, by warning against shutting ourselves to the divine grace and by showing how much we all depend on God's loving initiatives toward us. We should be grateful for the *full* biblical record. Under divine inspiration it authoritatively and realistically mirrors God's dealings with sinful men and women. All its passages can generate for us today moments of revelation; we should not try to limit God or ourselves to those passages that patently speak words of liberation. When commenting on the *Diatessaron,* St. Ephraem (d. 373) expressed the spiritual potentiality of the entire Bible: "Lord, who can grasp the wealth of *just one of your words?* What we understand is much less than what we leave behind, like thirsty people who drink from a fountain....The Lord...has hidden many treasures in his word so that each of us is enriched as we meditate on it. The word of God is a tree of life that *from all its parts* offers you fruits that are blessed" (1.18; italics ours).

The divine authority and revelatory power imparted to the scriptures through the charism of inspiration in no way, however, exempts interpreters from the serious task of establishing the meaning intended by the human authors. The special grace of inspiration did not violate the natural talents and limits of the biblical writers. The Holy Spirit acted in and through the actions of these finite agents, without destroying their individual characteristics and relative autonomy. We hear the voice of God through their voices; the Word of God came and comes to us in and through the words of human beings: that is to say, in a medium that is historically and culturally conditioned. The scriptures are wholly human as well as wholly divine. While recognizing the divine authority of the scriptural texts, Christian believers need some competence as readers and must still labor at understanding the biblical sense: the meaning(s) intended by the human authors of these texts— that is to say, what they intended to communicate and "fixed" in their texts when they chose to write this and not that for the specific audiences and situations they had in mind. Their meaning was generated and expressed by their choice of genre (e.g., by composing letters, hymns, or popular history), the goals to which they directed themselves, the judgments they made, the responsibility they assumed in asserting certain truth-claims, the invitations they conveyed, and the commitments in which their texts involved them. Obviously their meaning did/does not coincide in a simplistic way with the explicit wording they adopted. The literary and religious conventions of the whole thought-world of biblical times, as well as what we know about their particular life-setting, are indispensable guides in recovering, with greater or less success, what the biblical authors wanted to say when they used the words they did.[9] Even the most "successful" exegetes and interpreters must make allowance for a certain imprecision built into the "original" intention and audience. There is no reason to presuppose that the original meaning was always sharply defined as if it could be clearly recovered and paraphrased. The original audience likewise was often not a single, clearly demarcated group, made up of hearers and readers of uniform convictions and needs.

The "past" of the scriptural texts includes not only their original genesis but also their life after the apostolic age ended: for instance, in the privileged period of reception that was the patristic age. Besides being "canonized" or acknowledged as belonging to the normative list of inspired scriptures,[10] the biblical texts gained a life of their own, a "reception history," as they distanced themselves from their human authors, entered new contexts, and found later readers (and hearers). Any written document enjoys such a dynamic, natural potential for developments in meaning. Originally graced in their formation by a powerful input from the Holy Spirit, the scriptural texts have been richly graced as bearers of subsequent illumination and redemption, mediated through their use in the liturgy, preaching, catechesis, theology, and the whole life of the church. Despite the human sin, corruption, and ineptitude that disfigure the post-NT dependent phase of revelation and salvation, the Holy Spirit has continued to guide the interpretation and use of the scriptures which the same Spirit had once and for all inspired in the foundational phase of revelation and salvation which closed with Christ and the apostolic church.[11]

The many centuries of biblical interpretation[12] have been marred by periods of sheer neglect and decadent formalism. Yet the patristic witnesses, the Desert Fathers, the best of the medievals, the *devotio moderna,* the Reformers' return to the scriptural sources, and mystics in every age show the enduring vitality and deep richness of the inspired texts. The history of the church and her tradition have been shaped by and are to be evaluated by the interpretation of those texts. One might even describe tradition as the church's collective experience of the Bible. Undoubtedly, the rise of historical consciousness and the growth of literary criticism and other disciplines opened new, valuable, and henceforth indispensable methods of exegesis. Both in scriptural studies and beyond we now "know" much more, at least in the sense of having vast amounts of information at our electronic disposal. But, despite all our journals, biblical commentaries, concordances, dictionaries, and translations, dare we claim that we understand and interpret the scriptures better than Origen, Augustine of Hippo, Cyril of Alexandria, Hildegard of Bingen, Thomas Aquinas, Martin Luther, and Teresa of Avila? They had memorized by heart vast stretches of the biblical texts, related them to one another, and through prayerful contact with those texts found in them light and life for their journey. It would be foolhardy to assert that twentieth-century Christians have clearly progressed beyond all previous generations in their personal study, understanding, and interpretation of the Bible. Let us cite one among countless examples to illustrate the living, graced power of the biblical texts. Around the year 270 a wealthy landowner in Egypt heard read in church two verses from the "first" Gospel (Mt 19:21 and, shortly thereafter, Mt 6:34). Matthew's texts entered a new context and proved their potential when they inspired the young Egyptian to do something never envisaged by the first evangelist: he gave up his wealth, retired to the desert, and entered history as St. Anthony the hermit, one of the greatest figures at the origins of Christian monasticism,

What finally do we hold about the appropriate and legitimate interpretation of the scriptures today? Here the intention of the reader *(intentio legentis)* comes into play in activating the potential meaning(s) of the
text *(intentio textus)* produced by the sacred writer(s) *(intentio auctoris)*.
Over and over again meaning occurs as readers discover, liberate, and
re-create the sense of the text in (and to some extent from) their own
contexts. By being able to talk about the text in a variety of ways (without, of course, aspiring to establish any definitive interpretations) readers show whether and how they have understood it. Death has long ago
taken away the original authors, but their communicative intentions created normative texts which have enjoyed a long history of fruitful interpretation and actualization before reaching present-day interpreters. In
attributing to the writers, the texts themselves, and contemporary readers the same term (communicative "intention"), we recognize analogous, not identical, functions. The difference remains among the
original creators, their dynamic products, and contemporary re-creators.
Yet the ideal convergence between their communicative perspectives
allows us to apply to the writers, their texts, and their readers, one and
the same term ("intention"). Such communicative convergence excludes
theories that attribute radical indeterminacy (or lack of intention) to biblical and other texts. We return shortly to the issue of unchecked "reader-
freedom" which would clearly exclude the biblical texts from ever
yielding objective norms of judgment over against their readers.

What then do we expect from contemporary readers of the scriptures—in particular, from theological readers? In seeking to appropriate
biblical texts by establishing their meaning and truth, they should do this
theologically in the spirit of "faith seeking understanding": that is to say,
they do their interpretation within the faith community and out of a faith
that the one Holy Spirit, despite endless human limitation and failures,
both inspired the writing of the scriptures and has guided their living
interpretation. Exegesis apart from the community means exegesis apart
from the Spirit that gave the community their scriptures, indwells the
community, and facilitates the never-ending appropriation of the scriptures. Such interpretation breaks the continuity between the Bible and
theology. Many biblical commentators, however, take their distance from
any such confessional approach. They do their work in the name of the
merely descriptive, impartial, independent, and scholarly work proper to
disengaged reason, which is alleged to have normative authority in their

academic world. Their ideal practitioners are thoroughly free, rational, and enlightened spectators who are emancipated from all authority, open to a true and "objective" grasp of things, and promise to provide us with the assured results of scholarship. What are their results like? Barbara Thiering's *Jesus the Man: A New Interpretation from the Dead Sea Scrolls,* by spectacularly misusing both the NT and the Dead Sea Scrolls, is an offense not only to Christian faith but also to critical, historical reason.[13] What of such less extreme examples as the *Five Gospels: The Search for the Authentic Words of Jesus,* edited by R. W. Funk, R. W. Hoover, and the Jesus Seminar?[14] The work purports to take a neutral, unbiased, and properly skeptical stance in treating the four canonical Gospels and one noncanonical Gospel (the Gospel of Thomas). It presupposes that a religiously neutral, independent, and nontraditional interpretation of the scriptures will prove a more reliable guide to the biblical origins of Christianity than any interpretations coming from those who are confessionally committed and interpret the scriptures within a living tradition. The radical difficulty with this methodology derives from the fact that it expects far too much from merely "objective" procedures, which can yield detailed results but no valuable insights into the life of text as a whole. Let us take an example from another discipline, literary criticism. "Scientifically objective," disengaged methods might establish the date of *Macbeth*'s composition and the various sources used by Shakespeare. But only a responsive, imaginative, and participatory approach that invests our own being in the act of appropriating the text will give us a perspective on the whole play and appropriate insights into the heart of the tragedy. Those who study great dramas in libraries but steadily refuse to attend the theater and share in the living tradition of acting and production are hardly likely to prove superior dramatic critics. Without a love for literature and a living affinity with it, we cannot expect to relate to the great texts and expound them in any worthwhile way. It is precisely such loving affinity that provides the proper and privileged conditions for understanding and assessing literary classics. In a similar fashion, merely "objectifying" knowledge that refuses to let participatory knowledge also come into play when interpreting the scriptures might produce some historical and other detailed findings. But it cannot take us very far, because this "merely objectifying" method chokes the voice of the biblical texts and declines to face them for what they are on any showing: extraordinary ecclesial, religious, and theological works. To

ignore as an irrelevance the spiritual message of the scriptures is a little
like reading Shakespeare while sedulously ignoring the poetry and
drama. This inappropriate method reminds us of works by scholars who
used Homer's *Iliad* as a guide to the archaeology of Troy and steadfastly
refused to face and read the first and perhaps greatest epic of Western literature for what it primarily was/is: a richly illuminating masterpiece on
the enduring human themes of life, love, breakdowns in relationships,
violence, and death. Likewise, a religiously neutral, disinterested, and
"objectifying" interpretation misuses the scriptures by taking them up as
presenting us with mere puzzles and problems rather than as setting us in
front of interpersonal mystery: the encounter between God and the
human readers, two ultimately incomprehensible infinities. The knowledge of God and ourselves is available only by personal participation and
through relationship. The scriptures are in the business of furthering such
self-knowledge and knowledge of God.

Nothing of what we have just written should be construed as
attacking the historical-critical method as such; that concerns itself
with the genesis of our biblical texts. To aim, however, at making historical judgments from a wholly detached, "scientific" perspective not
only is a technique for abandoning the real thrust of the texts but is also
an illusion. Biblical scholars are always doing much more than merely
describing what some text(s) meant. After the work of Albert Einstein
and others, natural scientists have come to terms with the fact that the
observers (along with the instruments they choose) belong to the
process of investigation. All human knowledge, including knowledge
in physics, chemistry, and the biological sciences is participatory and
personal. There is an inevitable relationship between the observer and
the observed. Even more in historical study, including historical study
of the scriptures, the subject is necessarily and properly involved—
with his or her questions, beliefs, values, inherited traditions, and presuppositions. Historical understanding and interpretation are always
also "subjective," even when (or especially when?) historians and biblical scholars deny that this is so.[15] This search for the meaning of biblical and other texts is essentially conditioned by the situation of the one
doing the searching.

Such then, very briefly, is our view of (or perhaps the ideal we
propose for) contemporary readers of the scriptures and, specifically,
theological readers. They participate already in the inspired text; their

reading and interpretation form a further act of self involvement. What specific principles then do we propose for receiving and appropriating the scriptures in theology?

Ten Principles for Using the Scriptures

More than twenty years have elapsed since David Kelsey published *The Use of Scripture in Theology.*[16] He developed his own view in critical dialogue with notable theologians of the twentieth century. We prefer, however, another approach: stating our own positions and principles in this opening chapter and then in subsequent chapters testing their value by applying them to major theological questions. We propose ten principles that inevitably overlap somewhat with each other and perhaps need to be supplemented by further principles.

First Principle. Theologians are faithful hearers of the Word, oriented primarily toward the scriptural texts rather than toward themselves, and primarily responsive to the meaning they discover and receive rather than to the meaning they construct and create for themselves. In doing so, they respect the divine revelation's absolute priority over all human opinions and judgments. They read the whole Bible with consent (and not suspicion) and with the anticipation that, being imbued with the hidden presence of the infinitely true, good, and beautiful God, it may say something to them that they have never heard before. They come face to face with the biblical text, and are "answerable" to that text. St. Augustine of Hippo exemplifies supremely the exposure to the scriptures all theologians need: in his extant writings he quotes about two-thirds of the Bible. His example calls on theologians to hear again the voice crying out: "*tolle et lege* (take and read)." Our first principle opposes the practice of those theologians who take little notice of the scriptures, or submerge the scriptures in their closed orthodoxies and systems, or else make biblical (and other) texts mean just about anything they want them to mean. They draw from the texts what they have already decided to say. This is to risk turning the scriptures almost into a series of Rorschach inkblots that call up merely individual, purely projective interpretations.[17] This also raises the question of ethics in biblical reception and moral categories that are relevant to our meeting with the Bible. May we remake the text and invent its meaning in our own image? Some build such practice into theory, claiming that texts of unavailable authors (and of available authors?) have no rights, belong absolutely to readers, and may be used (misused?) in whatever ways biblical interpreters, theologians, and other readers choose. In the name of excavating for the hidden subtext, some critics dismantle biblical and other texts, let meanings proliferate, and come up with an uncheckable range of alternative interpretations.[18] Any such total reader-freedom that dominates the texts turns its interpretations into mere reflections of a particular community's or individual's interests and experience. It espouses an extreme form of reader-response that simply constructs meaning without being in any way rooted in the text it reads; meaning is simply what the reader makes of the texts. These approaches not only worry such a secular literary critic as Umberto Eco,[19] but also can be readily turned against the contemporary writers who espouse such freedom. If we may always interpret the meaning of texts quite independently of those who produced them and if meaning in no sense inheres in the texts themselves, we readers can give free reign to our projective interpretations of the modern critics, allow our experiences to dominate, and make *these* texts mean whatever fits our purposes. Pure reader-freedom is a self-destructing theory, as well as an unethical one. We may neither arbitrarily manipulate the meaning of texts nor do violence to what the authors intended to communicate. Theories of reader-oriented and reader-creative meaning that almost inevitably become reader-manipulative are even less appropriate in the case of the scriptures. There, if anywhere, readers should be listening and "corresponding" to the texts, through which come the voices of the original authors, the voices of interpreters down through the ages, and, above all, the voice of the Holy Spirit. Letting themselves be encountered by the Bible, and expecting something new from their reading, especially from those sections which have the closest relationship to God's self-revelation, theologians allow the scriptural texts in all their strangeness and otherness to convey meaning, disclose truth, correct theologians "from beyond," and so authoritatively transform theological ideas, interests, and practice.[20] Only those who let themselves be addressed and judged by the Bible will notice, for instance, where their routine appeals to certain scriptural texts enjoy no more validity than ingrained habits fostered perhaps by some merely doctrinaire and inadequate tradition. Only those theologians consistently open to revelatory encounters effected by the Bible will cherish their work as a process in which their interpretations can never enjoy definitive and final status (see principle seven below).

Second Principle. Along with such openness, we expect, however, theologians to be active, responsive, and "answerable" interpreters of the scriptures, and not merely passive, purely receptive hearers of the Word who woodenly reflect biblical texts in a purely formal way and do not "give" them anything or "complete" them in any way. Hearing the scriptures lets these texts preserve the self-identity of Christian theology; yet these same texts must be constantly and freshly reappropriated as the living Word of God for today. This second principle calls for creativity, coherence, choice, and a self-awareness about one's experiences, presuppositions, questions, and interpretative framework. Theology, like art, dies in the hands of those who are content to simply turn out the motifs already explored by their predecessors. His inventiveness let Albrecht Dürer break through to something new in the story of Western art. His innovative woodcuts depicting Christ's birth, life, death, and resurrection give him an honorable place in the history of Christian spirituality and theology. With his genius Dürer illustrates admirably another aspect of great innovation, be it artistic or theological: developing particular themes, he sets out a coherent whole. In using the scriptures, theologians must inevitably allude to specific texts and themes. Brilliant creativity shows through when the particular biblical items are coherently related to the whole.

Theological activity requires appropriate choices among the methods suited to the different books and texts of the Bible. Narrative criticism can illuminate, for example, historical books of the OT; rhetorical criticism has its value in interpreting the Pauline letters.[21] The divergent nature of parables, hymns, prophetical texts, apocalyptic texts, and wisdom texts — to cite some major examples — must obviously affect the methods used for interpreting and appropriating them in theology. Some texts like NT kerygmatic passages about Christ's death and resurrection (e.g., 1 Cor 15:3–5) convey a meaningful message that calls for the response of faith. Other texts like parables and apocalyptic passages, right from the outset, aim at generating the meanings partly by stimulating their readers or hearers to react. In a special way readers interact with these texts to create fresh meaning, which, while not unconnected with these texts, is not simply objectively "there" waiting to be uncovered. Active interpretation of the scriptures by theologians also entails critical awareness of three items that largely coincide: one's *interests, contexts,* and *audiences*.

The audiences that constitute the social and cultural contexts in which theologians work and which they address, likewise elicit and measure the interests that activate theological practice. The reading purposes of theologians will vary according to their particular specialization in, for instance, systematic, moral, fundamental, or pastoral theology. Their audiences help relate the biblical texts to the shifting experiences, thought, and realities of current human history and contemporary culture. Meaning is always, at least in part, a cultural and social phenomenon. Any given cultural tradition, including its language, will persistently help to shape a community's perception and interpretation of reality. This is not, however, to accept that the criteria of the theologians' own culture, age, and interpretative community should have sole, or even decisive, authority in their appropriation of the scriptures.

In *God Encountered* Frans Jozef van Beeck notes, but rightly cautions against overstating "the characteristic differences between the language of the sanctuary" and "the idioms of the study."[22] Writing fifty years after the martyrdom of Dietrich Bonhoeffer, we recall once again that the contexts for theological interpretation of the scriptures move beyond (1) personal prayer and the liturgy of the worshiping community and (2) the library and the lecture hall. Theologians also discover the meaning and truth of the biblical texts in (3) prison and other situations of cruelty, injustice, and death. In all three contexts theologians act *and* are acted upon, even if study can support the illusion of being simply in charge of the subject matter, and liturgy, as its name suggests, can come across as "the work of the people." The cross and suffering cast their shadow across all three contexts, bringing deep spiritual struggles to theologians. They have to deal with "sacred" scriptures that communicate the holiness of God and aim at achieving a threefold result: (1) the holiness of people gathered for grateful praise of God in liturgy, (2) the intellectual integrity and morality of the mind manifested by holy theologians and other teachers/writers, and (3) the practical holiness of those whose faith "does justice" by striving to eliminate oppression and alleviate human suffering. Like musical scores the scriptures remain incomplete if they are merely studied and not performed in liturgy and in life. With faith, expectation, and thanksgiving, they need to be heard eucharistically and "practically." Theologians encounter and interpret the Bible in several appropriate ways: adoring on their knees, maintaining theoretical integrity at their desks, or being committed to practical action in the mud of overcrowded slums and refugee camps. Their interpretation of the biblical texts constitutes both (academic) theory and (prayerful and effective) practice. In the case of the first and third contexts (worship and practice) the scriptures remain, more or less, rooted in their native linguistic environment, whereas the desymbolizing, abstracting, and universalizing mindset of academic theology moves the scriptures into a different environment. Yet the biblical texts make truth claims about reality — a truth to be, respectively, prayed over (or worshiped as the Truth), explored and known, or practiced with steady commitment. These truth claims need to be examined in light of a universal context of worship, common concerns for truth, and worldwide experiences of suffering and injustice. They will not yield their meaning to a closed community of interpreters who indulge vested interests (1) by manipulating biblical texts to illuminate their own experiences, legitimate their own programs, and further their own particular aspirations, and (2) by steadily ignoring the hopes and dreams of the young, the experiences of exploited women and children, and the voices of the marginalized everywhere.

Third Principle. The Christian public as a worshiping, studying, and acting/suffering *community* brings to mind our third principle for theological use of the scriptures: they are read and interpreted within the living community of faith and in continuity with undivided Christianity's creed and with the vast progression of ways in which the vital potential of the scriptures for faith and practice has been actualized down through Christian history within the church. Primarily formed and fashioned from the scriptures, the Apostles' Creed and the Nicene-Constantinopolitan Creed normatively summarize the history of salvation and illuminate the biblical texts by highlighting the central truths they communicate about the tripersonal God and human destiny. Since the time of St. Irenaeus, who insisted that valid theological understanding is possible only within the hearing- and reading-community of faith, creeds have been taken not as substitutes for the scriptures but as essential and normative frames of reference guiding theological understanding and interpretation within the mainline tradition. In his *Catecheses* St. Cyril of Jerusalem explained to his baptismal candidates the credal faith: "The faith which the Church hands down to you has all the authority of the scriptures behind it.... This summary of our faith is not a merely human composition; the more striking sayings of the scriptures have been assembled together to form the comprehensive statement" (5.12–13). Beyond question, particular traditions have at times expounded the biblical texts in a bizarre and sinful manner. A monstrous and tragic case in point is the way many Christian leaders and writers, from the time of St. Melito of Sardis, encouraged popular anti-Semitism by their misinterpretation of the cry put in the mouths of the Jews present for Jesus' condemnation by Pilate: "His blood be on us and on our children" (Mt 27:25).[23] But sad misuse never justifies trying to wrench the scriptures out of their traditional and credal frames of reference with the aim of elaborating a nontraditional and noncredal Christianity or theology.[24] Religious truth-claims are essentially related to a religious way of life. The truth-claims of the scriptures cannot be systematically clarified unless they are also related to the Christian community's cumulative tradition of interpreting and "performing" the scriptures.

In divided Christianity this continuing tradition, which sets the context for interpreting the scriptures, also involves confessional elements that can diverge and in some cases seem intractably irreconcilable. The history of biblical interpretation, when taken in the broad sense of exegesis for worship, knowledge, and action, coincides with the whole history of the church. But disunity has marred and continues to mar this history. Hence Christians need a hermeneutic of unity, a common listening to the scriptures that will heal divergence and end separation. In short, the scriptures can powerfully transform traditions having undergirded separation, as well as being appropriately read and interpreted within common traditions that already exist. The hermeneutic that respects tradition should also foster a unifying consciousness and communion where particular traditions lean in the opposite direction.

Fourth Principle. We name next our fourth principle: biblical convergence. Far from endorsing a biblical positivism that is content to pile up allegedly clear "proof" texts, the principle of convergence entails letting the broadest and most varied amount of biblical witness come to bear on the theological question at issue. The opposite approach would build a position out of an isolated scriptural text. Some have taxed Eastern Christians in particular, and Roman Catholics in general, for doing just that by basing themselves on 2 Pt 1:4 and explaining the life of grace to mean partaking in the divine nature. In this case we believe the testimony from Paul and John converge with the deification-talk from 2 Peter. We will, however, use other examples to illustrate the convergence of biblical testimony. Obviously the principle of convergence emphasizes the unity of the canonical scriptures more than their diversity, that unity effected by the Holy Spirit over against the diversity due to the human authors and the complex differences between the OT and the NT. To expect convergent biblical testimony presupposes that one takes the Bible to exhibit, in and through its diverse witnesses and the tension between their perspectives, much more unity than a mere anthology of ancient, religious writings held together by the covers of one book. Ultimately it is the divine authorship by the one Holy Spirit that forges the christological unity of the Bible in the convergence of its many witnesses. To quote Rupert of Deutz, "the many words" of the scriptures are really "only one Word," Christ himself (*In Ioannem*, 2. 7).

Fifth Principle. By "contemporary consensus" we intend a very different principle: namely, the willingness of theologians to prefer, all things being equal, the line taken by widely respected, centrist biblical scholars or at least the majority of them. In reflecting on the scriptural texts, theologians ought not plunge forward by themselves and ignore what professional exegetes have to say. However they cannot remain stuck on major questions, waiting for a universal consensus to emerge in biblical studies; experience shows that such a consensus on some questions may never emerge. It is also obviously ill-advised to take over into theology adventurous, even maverick, theses advanced by individual biblical scholars or a small group with its own particularist agenda. One might dub this practice rushing to apply in theology the latest thesis from the banks of the Seine or the Neckar. To some extent, Edward Schillebeeckx did just that in his 1974 Christology.[25] At the same time, theologians need to know whether certain interpretations have come to win or lose a broad spectrum of support in eminent biblical circles. James Barr and others have put an end, for instance, to Joachim Jeremias' original proposal to interpret "Abba" (Mk 14:36; Rom 8:15; Gal 4:6) as "Daddy" or baby talk.[26] Yet this interpretation enjoys its afterlife in Jürgen Moltmann's *The Way of Jesus Christ*.[27] Theologians must respect the work of their professional colleagues in biblical studies. They may not maintain interpretations that exegetical arguments have shown to be false or implausible. But in the spirit of *"caveat emptor,"* they must also learn to adjudicate between competing interpretations and discern what they buy and continue to buy on the exegetical market. The call for innovation in theology (principle two above) does not exclude shrewdly testing the material taken on board from the distinct, if closely related, field of exegesis as such. Here some suspicion can well be exercised toward those who easily and blandly appeal to "the assured results of biblical scholarship."

Furthermore, theologians need to be alert to four factors that affect the making of any biblical consensus and what they can draw from exegetes. First, in their pursuit of the "literal" meaning of scriptures those who practice the historical-critical method may at times presuppose that in all cases there is only one unique meaning to be established: what Paul, Luke, or some other biblical author intended to communicate in a given text directed toward their given readership. But the intended meaning need not have always been merely single and solitary. Especially in hymnic and poetic passages (e.g., Phil 2:6–11) intended meanings cannot always be precisely paraphrased, as if Paul and others meant "just this" and nothing else. Right from their historical origins at the hands of a given author, some texts could bear differing shades and even differing levels of meaning. In such cases it is folly to expect only one "correct" answer to the question: What did the author mean? Second, not all exegetes have made their peace with the fact that, while being valuable and necessary, the historical-critical method needs to be supplemented by further methods and approaches that encourage readers to recognize (1) that texts can bear meanings that go beyond the original authorial intentions, and (2) that, once composed, texts begin to enjoy a life of their own and yield further meanings, particularly as they are read in different and later contexts. A theologian has to be on the lookout for what exegetes envisage themselves as doing: merely clarifying the original, authorial intent or else allowing for more-than-literal meanings. Third, about fundamental matters (e.g., the expiatory value of Jesus' death) some measure of biblical consensus is clearly more important than would be the case with less fundamental issues (e.g., the "best" title or image to use when summing up Jesus' earthly ministry). Fourth, even on fundamental issues theologians may at times have to allow for considerable differences between exegetes—a kind of "differentiated" consensus, if you will.

We have an example of this situation in the post-Rudolf Bultmann and Joachim Jeremias debate from the seventies and eighties about Jesus' intentions when faced with death. Among the numerous biblical scholars like Martin Hengel, Xavier Léon-Dufour, C. F. D. Moule, E. P. Sanders, and Heinz Schürmann who contributed to the discussion, some (e.g., Anton Vögtle) argued for a rather minimalist interpretation, others (e.g., Rudolf Pesch) argued for a stronger, even maximalist interpretation of Jesus' precrucifixion intentions and expectations. Nevertheless, the exegetical community in the seventies and eighties broadly agreed at least that Jesus anticipated a violent death and somehow prepared himself for it.[28] Systematic theologians have to be content with this differentiated consensus, since the salvific, expiatory value of Jesus' death should never be alleged to depend simply from his conscious intentions when faced with a violent end. His death drew its meaning also from what came before (his utter dedication to the preaching of the kingdom and the service of those in need) and from what came later (the resurrection and outpouring of the Holy Spirit).

Sixth Principle. Metathemes and metanarratives furnish a sixth principle for guiding theological appropriation of the scriptures. These are single themes and extended narratives that rise above their original settings and recur, with appropriate developments and modifications, in new contexts. We can measure a given theology by its success at incorporating metathemes that pervade the Bible like covenant, creation, faith, law/gospel, liberation, life, love, mercy, prophecy, sin (in particular, idolatry), and wisdom. Love as *agapē* already surfaces in the Greek Septuagint and then, as we shall see in Chapter 3, is massively used in the NT. Such a metanarrative as the exodus from Egypt, constantly celebrated in the Passover feast and then reenacted once and for all in the resurrection of the crucified Jesus, provides an overarching scheme for theological interpretation. In particular, the story of the first Good Friday and Easter Sunday conclusively and once and for all (Heb 1:3; 5:9; 6:19–20; 7:11–28; 8:5–6; 9:11–14:26; 10:12, 14; 11:1) condemns all idolatry (1 Cor 8:4–6) through the "spiritual" wisdom of the cross (1 Cor 1:18–2:16), reveals God as the effective God of resurrected life (1 Cor 15:15), relativizes all "normal" human differences (Gal 3:26–28), and reinterprets the history not only of Israel but also of the whole world (Rom 8:18–11:36). As the central metanarrative of the Bible, the resurrection of the crucified Jesus binds the scriptures together, intersects with our history, and holds theology together for all those who consciously align themselves with the Easter mystery. They acknowledge that the crucifixion and resurrection (along with the lesser metanarratives) stand in judgement on all historical efforts and achievements. Linking Job, Jeremiah, Isaiah's Suffering Servant, Jesus, Paul, and others, stories of cruel suffering cast their shadow over the scriptures. But a thread of trust stubbornly maintains that the divine power will change the situation for God's "weak" ministers and servants (2 Cor 12:9–10). These metanarratives and metathemes make the Bible into one cumulative story. Respect for them allows us to satisfy something of the desire expressed by the Reformation's call to interpret the scriptures in the light of the scriptures.[29] Earlier themes and narratives in the Bible recur (in new and modified ways) to illuminate and interpret what comes later: for instance, the yearly ceremony of the Day of Atonement (Lv 16:1–34) helps to interpret something greater and definitive that occurred in the once-and-for-all sacrifice of Christ (Heb 9:1–10:18). This sixth principle does not aim to repeat the naive appeals to "authoritative" biblical concepts that James Barr, Brevard Childs, and others rightly criticized years ago.[30] It simply aims at noting the existence of patterns of divine activity and promise that recur in the Bible, yield an overall picture, evoke varying human responses, and throw light, above all, on Jesus' activity and identity. Any adequate theology will be sustained by the biblical metathemes and metanarratives.

The sixth principle, like the fourth, is not intended to deny the momentum of the new, which the scriptures consistently attest. Talk of convergence and metathemes/narratives is not to be dismissed as a mental straightjacket or crypto-ideology that tries to make everything biblical count in the same way, as if after all there was nothing new under the scriptural sun. Our fourth and sixth principles are to be understood flexibly, as allowing for discontinuity within continuity, our seventh principle.

Seventh Principle. This seventh principle may be best exemplified by the classic shift from Jesus to Paul.[31] If we lay the synoptic Gospels alongside Paul's letters, it may seem that nothing is changed—except for the fact that Paul's rhetorical, theological, and autobiographical style has replaced Jesus' unique storytelling style and that Paul does not include (or deliberately leaves to others) the teaching of the earthly Jesus, even if at times his parenesis echoes Jesus' words. Both are deeply Jewish, even if they express in different ways and through different concerns their Jewishness. Both accept their inherited scriptures (our Old Testament) as normative literature that enjoys divine authority. Jesus calls God "Abba (Father)," and the apostle not only maintains this distinctive usage, especially in his opening greetings, but also cites "Abba" as entering into Christian prayer (Rom 8:15; Gal 4:6). By drawing together Dt 6:4–5 and Lv 19:18, Jesus teaches that the whole Mosaic Law should be understood in terms of love (Mk 12:28–31). He extends love for one's neighbor to include love for one's enemies (Mt 5:43–48; Lk 6:27–36). Paul likewise sees love as the "fulfillment" of the Law (Rom 13:8–10; Gal 5:14), and urges his fellow Christians to show love for their enemies (Rom 12:14, 20–21). Jesus denies any absolute religious significance of food laws (Mk 7:14–23), and so too does Paul (Rom 14:13–23) who flatly declares: "The kingdom of God is not food and drink, but righteousness and peace and joy in the Holy Spirit" (Rom 14:17). This example also brings to mind a change that goes beyond mere habits of speech. Unlike Jesus, Paul rarely speaks of the (present and future) divine kingdom—only eight times in all. Jesus presents his exorcisms and miracles as signs of God's powerful rule breaking into the world to free men and women from the spirit of evil (e.g., Lk 11:20; see 10:18; 13:16). Paul associates his own mighty works with his apostolic ministry (Rom 15:18–19; 2 Cor 12:12) in the service of "the Gospel." Replacing "kingdom" talk, "the Gospel" runs as a leit-motif right through Paul's masterpiece (from Rom 1:1 to 16:25), as it does in the case of Mark's theology (1:1, 14; 8:35; 10:29; 13:10; 14:9). One might argue that, behind the different terminology, both Jesus and Paul are saying substantially the same thing. For Jesus the kingdom or reign of God has broken powerfully into the world (e.g., Lk 11:20) and is to be received as sheer gift with childlike simplicity (e.g., Mk 10:20) and great joy (e.g., Mt 13:44–46). Paul agrees that there is no self-redemption: we cannot reach the goal of life through our own efforts. For the apostle faith "comes" (Gal 3:23, 25), God's justice is revealed and imparted (e.g., Rom 1:16–17; 3:24), and the apostolic ministry is the gift of God's grace (e.g., 1 Cor 15:10; Gal 1:15–16). Jesus' language about his being "sent" (e.g., Mk 9:37; 12:6) or having "come" (e.g., Mk 2:17; Mt 11:19) is mirrored by Paul's talk about the Son being "sent" (e.g., Gal 4:4) or taking the initiative in assuming the human lot (e.g., Phil 2:7–8). The case seems similar with Jesus' Son of man language, it drops away, but a major function of that self-description (his role as the judge to come) is maintained (e.g., 1 Thes 2:19; 3:13). One could press also the similarity between the "already" (e.g., Lk 11:20; see Mt 12:28) and the "not yet" (e.g., Mt 6:10 = Lk 11:2) in Jesus' preaching of the "kingdom" and Paul's message of an adoption that has already taken place (Rom 8:14–17) and is yet to be completed in the future (Rom 8:18–25). The perspective looks the same, even if thematized differently. Indeed, it is not always thematized differently. Paul's talk about inheriting the kingdom (1 Cor 6:9–10) displays the same "time frame" as Jesus' language about the future kingdom, while the apostle's assurance that believers can experience here and now some of the kingdom's benefits (Rom 14:17) matches Jesus' proclamation of the kingdom's present power.

In a sense nothing seems changed, and yet with the resurrection of the crucified Jesus nothing is the same. Revelation and salvation are now thoroughly personalized in the Easter proclamation (e.g., 1 Cor 1:23; 15:1–11); redemption has come through Christ's sacrificial death (e.g., Rom 3:24–25; 1 Cor 5:7; 11:23–26). The "Lord" Jesus, who now stands with "God our Father" as the source of "grace and peace" (e.g., Rom 1:7), is announced and worshiped as Messiah (Christ), Lord, and Son of God (e.g., Phil 2:9–11). The fullness of salvation history, summed up in terms of grace, love, and fellowship (2 Cor 13:13), has been enacted through the Father, the Son, and the Holy Spirit. Where Jesus had called to conversion, offered forgiveness, and invited his audience to participate now through love in the coming reign of God, Paul proclaimed the liberating and reconciling love released through the saving events of Christ's crucifixion and resurrection. Christ's death and resurrection (with the associated gift of the Holy Spirit) form the most crucial watershed in the history of revelation and salvation, being the instance *par excellence* of discontinuity in continuity. Some deny the resurrection, push discontinuity to the extreme of a complete break with Jesus' ministry, and misrepresent Paul as the real (and misguided) founder of historic Christianity. But if we argue that the crucified Jesus rose from the dead, we face an Easter mystery which neither replaces *tout court* all that went before, nor is to be reduced to the situation of Jesus' ministry. The uniquely new event that has taken place does not invalidate what has preceded it, but it does entail newly interpreting everything prior to it and recognizing the great Easter gift (the Holy Spirit) and new family created by Christ's resurrection and the power of divine love (the church). Thus the Easter-event, with the move it brought from the situation of Jesus to that of Paul, stands as the classic exemplification of our seventh principle.

Eighth Principle. A sense of the discontinuity within continuity characterizes the theological appropriation of the scriptures above all in handling the shifts from the OT to the NT and from the situation of Jesus to that of Paul. In close association with this seventh principle we introduce an eighth: the eschatological provisionality of everything the biblical texts yield for theology. The future-oriented nature of God's self-revelation has impressed a similar characteristic on its biblical record and interpretation. The divine promise controls the way we understand the present; we dare not let everything revolve around the contemporary situation of the church and the world. The promised consummation of all things has not yet arrived. At the same time, no biblical and no theological words can give more than the faintest idea of the shape of things to come. As we observed above (second principle), theological interests, contexts, and audiences are open to a threefold classification: in terms of worship, knowledge, and action. At the end of all things, action will blend with worship and knowledge to bring the vision of God in a transformed universe. The mysterious fullness of glory to come invites us to acknowledge steadily the partial, provisional, and anticipatory nature of even the best insights to be drawn from the scriptures about the tripersonal God and the world of grace in which we live today. When appropriating the biblical evidence, theologians enjoy no special exemption from the never-ending search for understanding that characterizes their discipline. Reflecting in faith on the meaning and message of the inspired scriptures, they pursue a goal that will be fully realized only in the final vision. Here and now they know only "in part" (1 Cor 13:12).

Ninth Principle. Principles three through eight, which elucidate various aspects of the active hearing of the scriptures (principle two), call for the fine-tuning and use of historical reason. Our ninth principle states that theology will remain low on clarity and substance unless it puts the scriptures into dialogue with philosophy. From the time of St. Justin Martyr, philosophical views of God, the created world, and the divine interaction with the world have assisted the interpretation of the Bible. In general, philosophical reason sharpens the questions to be asked, helps to organize the methods and the material, partly illuminates the condition of human beings and their world, and brings conceptual clarity to bear on the biblical texts, which by and large are prephilosophical.[32] One question, for example, that calls out for dialogue with philosophy is that of Jesus' personal preexistence. In his review[33] of K.-J. Kuschel's *Born before All time* (London: SCM Press, 1992) E. Krasevac took issue with Kuschel's assurance about the collapse of classical metaphysics (503), but missed the larger lacuna: the absence of dialogue with philosophy in this book. It is puzzling how a work on Jesus' eternal, personal preexistence could ignore what philosophers have been arguing, both recently and earlier, about personal being, time, and eternity.[34] The debate about Jesus' intentions when faced with death (reported above under our fifth principle) would have been sharpened by introducing the philosophical distinction between event and act: that is to say, by distinguishing between the language of causality, which asks how the agent contributed to some occurrence, and the language of intention, which asks why the agent acted in this way. By developing insights into the nature of knowledge, meaning, and truth, philosophy can elucidate that spiritual dynamism that affects our reading and hearing of the scriptures.

Philosophy copes also with questions about the status of religious language. Does such language merely reflect and express our inner experience? Or can both literal and metaphorical statements about God yield true knowledge? If we agree that God's being is too mysterious to be caught in a net of descriptive language, are we necessarily condemned to a Neo-Kantian agnosticism? St. Augustine drew from philosophy when he wrestled with such questions as, How do words in the Bible (and elsewhere) relate to the things they purport to describe? Philosophy has also something to offer about the kind of certainty we should expect in biblical interpretation. In short, over the centuries the best of its enduring contributions to theology and exegesis have shown that philosophy does not "leave everything as it is."[35] We may distinguish faith and *philosophical* reason (principle nine), just as we distinguished faith and *historical* reason (principles two through eight). But in neither case is there a separation: theological reason, whether philosophical or historical, should work in, with, and through faith and the faithful hearing of the biblical word (principle one).

Such valid collaboration becomes, however, impossible when philosophy replaces the voice of revelation, assumes control, and allows dubious convictions to take over. A deistic-style cosmology that *a priori* rejects any special divine interactions with the world dictates, for example, the way Maurice Wiles interprets NT texts about Christ's preexistence, incarnation, and virginal conception. Instead of being "particular divine acts ensuring the birth of the particular person, Jesus," he understands all three beliefs "as a retrospective way of expressing the totality of his [Jesus'] commitment to and fulfilment of the will of God for the world."[36] The same deistic-style philosophy likewise firmly controls the way Gordon Kaufman is ready to interpret NT texts about the virginal conception of Christ: "It is not possible for us to think [of] an 'event' as simply, supernaturally caused."[37] The debate here concerns the validity of "our" preconceived notions of what could or could not have occurred. Those who maintain a "higher" view of divine activity, on the one hand and acknowledge the incompleteness of scientific "explanations" on the other, leave open the possibility of thinking and speaking literally of such a divine action as the virginal conception. *Pace* Kaufman, modern science does not render impossible belief in such divine interventions. After the insights and discoveries of Planck, Bohr, Heisenberg, and others, the clockwork universe is dead. Even if the closed Newtonian model of the natural order still prevailed, the impossibility of such events as the virginal conception would be, "at most, an impossibility within the natural order, not an unqualified impossibility."[38]

Tenth Principle. Lastly, theologians need not only some philosophical expertise but also the intellectual and spiritual courage to inculturate the biblical testimony and let their theology become enriched by different cultures—in traditionally Christian countries, in lands where for centuries Christians have remained a tiny minority, in lands where Christian majorities became minorities centuries ago, and in recently evangelized lands. There is one Christ and one Bible, but there are many cultures. Translating scriptural thought into contemporary languages and cultures (so that every generation can appropriate and "inhabit" the biblical narrative) calls for a deep knowledge of cultural experiences and for innovative fidelity. Inculturation could be listed with our second principle; in fact, we noted under that principle how meaning is always, at least in part, a *cultural* phenomenon. But the task is so important that it deserves to be named separately and, preferably, in close proximity to philosophy. Through its dialogue and debate

with contemporary thought, philosophy offers invaluable help both
toward understanding the spiritual experiences, ethical values, theological perspectives, and symbolic expressions of other religions (including indigenous religions that do not have written traditions) and toward
articulating and spreading the biblical message through all cultures. Let
us insist, however, that we understand "culture" to include but not to be
limited to the religious sectors and dimensions of life; culture concerns
the totality of life. Hence culture (and with it the task of inculturation)
goes beyond language and is also not merely about language and differences in language; it spans a whole complex of secular and religious
value-systems, ways of thinking, orientations toward God, traditional
lifestyles, and ways of celebration. The fact that any given culture will
have such subcultures as those formed by the urban proletariat, the
young, and the farming communities reminds us of further complexi-
ties in the reality and notion of culture. Nor should we ignore multicul-
tural and multiracial societies like Australia, where one nation
embraces and fosters many cultures. What is it to inculturate the scriptures in such a society? Finally, we do well to recall two further items.
Each culture, expressing as it does one and the same human nature,
enjoys a potential universality. But not every inherited culture is sufficiently open and dynamic to develop and even be transformed when it
encounters fresh knowledge and experience.

The thorough inculturation of the biblical message depends, at
least in part, from the success or failure of theologians in discerning the
potential of their own culture (including the literature and visual arts) to
be illuminated by the scriptures and to serve as a means of expressing
the great metanarratives and metathemes of the Bible. This capacity to
discern requires a mastery of what one's own culture and biblical faith
within that culture mean. Such mastery can grasp, to some extent, how
the scriptural message has been, or at least can be, embodied in a particular culture. Such attention to inculturation implies both faith and
reason: both (1) a faith to believe that, as the Word and Wisdom of God,
Christ is present at least seminally and anonymously in all human cultures, and that, as centered on him, the Bible is a book for all cultures,
and (2) a sensitive mind to discern and fashion the way inculturation
should function for any given period, people, and language.

Asia summons theologians to reflect deeply on its ancient religions (with their sacred writings, ways of life, and forms of worship),

to enable the Christian scriptures to be appropriated not only theologically but also spiritually, pastorally, and liturgically. A respectful dialogue with Asia's cultures will mean seeking and finding God in the religious traditions of its peoples, a mutual teaching and learning that can shed fresh light on the Christian scriptures and on the whole Christian message. Such an inculturating dialogue, if it is going to be integral, involves the three contexts we expounded above (principle two). First, it calls for a theological exchange that attempts to know and understand "the others" (in their culture and religion) as they wish to be known and understood. Such an academic dialogue includes both (1) the courage to hear painful truths about our Christian theology and lives, and (2) a love that is open to find God and Christ everywhere and in dialogue. Apropos of (1), it may take "others" to show us how conditioned, parochial, or ideologically captive our theology and use of scriptures really are. Second, any inculturating dialogue also involves encountering and experiencing each other's practices of personal prayer and public worship. Third, such dialogue also requires common action with those of other religious traditions, in order to overcome racism, sexism, genocidal intolerance, irrational fundamentalism, and cultural prejudices of all kinds. Every continent, and not just Asia and Africa, suffers from its ideologies of hatred that arouse nationalistic, racial, economic, and sexual violence. Any interreligious, inculturating dialogue remains empty unless and until it brings a shared commitment to transform cultural and social life through promoting truth, human rights, the transmission of spiritual values to the rising generation, harmony among all, and our common responsibilities toward the poor, the handicapped, the sick, the old, the defenseless, and God's creation. In short, interreligious dialogue in the service of inculturation demands practice and worship, as well as theological thinking and sharing. For such a dialogue the scriptures are to be practiced and celebrated, and not merely interpreted academically.

The Western world presents its theologians with a special challenge. Without wishing to contrast speech and writing too sharply, we observe that it is within a writing, reading, and visual culture that we Westerners struggle to interpret and inculturate the biblical message. The Bible itself came out of largely oral cultures that were trained in memorization and rhetoric. When coping with this challenge, inculturation calls for fidelity to the Bible, not a capitulation that simply interprets the scriptures according to the standards of contemporary society and the passing "certainties" of one's culture. As with every other situation our Western culture sets the initial horizon for our theology and our theological appropriation of the scriptures. While letting the riches of our cultural heritage illuminate the scriptures, we will also find the scriptures in collision with some aspects of our culture. What is it to inculturate the scriptures in societies scarred by the sins of abortion and euthanasia? In many ways Western societies lack a moral and spiritual basis for their existence, and often seem to be disintegrating morally and spiritually. Genuine inculturation of the scriptures must not bring capitulation to sick aspects of our societies, which can seem obsessed with material "success," possessions, and health. In any case the eschatological provisionality of everything (principle eight above) touches not only theological reflections but also our entire cultural existence. No culture can be considered perfect and definitive.[39]

The task of inculturating the scriptural witness entails relating to each other the Bible's metanarratives, metathemes, and images (in particular, key metaphors), and at times paraphrasing them in forms of speech that are both accurate and communicative. It is theology's characteristic work in seeking fresh understanding and a new, lively, and experiential language. To call such organizing of the scriptures and restating them theologically a work of "translation" — as we did above — does not presuppose that there is consistently only one meaning to be transferred relatively simply from a biblical to a theological text. The "reception history" of the Bible (see above) bears ample witness to the rich, polyvalent significance of its texts, which St. Gregory the Great describes as waters in which lambs may walk and elephants may swim.[40] Moreover, "translation" may fail to do justice to the way theological activity constitutes part of the church's life; by inculturating scriptures that recorded and interpreted foundational revelation, this activity also aims at triggering dependent revelation now. In its own modest fashion, the inculturating work of theologians serves to proclaim the good news, rouse faith, encourage discipleship, and effectively criticize social and political injustice. It appropriates the scriptures in ways that enrich the identity and welfare of the Christian community.

The Principles Summarized. Our ten principles require: listening to the scriptures (principle one), doing so creatively (principle two), within the framework of tradition and the rule of faith (principle three), looking for convergence in the biblical witness (principle four), possible consensus among the exegetes (principle five), important meta-themes and metanarratives—above all, the critical role of the Easter mystery—(principle six), continuity in discontinuity (principle seven), and respecting the eschatological provisionality of all interpretations (principle eight), the contribution of philosophical reason[41] (principle nine), and the broad and demanding task of inculturation (principle ten). Christocentrism binds together these principles like a golden thread. They invite theologians to be active hearers (principles one and two) of the scriptures that converge on Christ (principle four) and find their enduring frame of reference in the historic creeds built around Christ's death and resurrection (principle three). The classic metath-emes and metanarratives of the Bible (principle six), illuminated by various forms of exegetical consensus (principle five), find their heart in the radical continuity-in-discontinuity of Christ's death and resurrec-tion (principle seven). The eschatological provisionality of the scrip-tures refers us to the final consummation of all things in Christ (principle eight). Inculturation (principle ten) proceeds from the faith that as divine Word and Wisdom Christ is present through his Spirit in all cultures, and from the conviction that philosophical reason (prin-ciple nine) can support a biblical message about Christ, the light of all nations. Martin Luther encourages this scriptural Christocentrism as follows: "Think of the Scriptures as…the richest of mines which can never be sufficiently explored, in order that you may find that divine wisdom which God here lays before you in such simple guise as to quench all pride. Here you will find the swaddling cloths and the manger in which Christ lies…. Simple and lowly are these swaddling cloths, but dear is the treasure, Christ, who lies in them."[42]

By drawing his central image from Christ's activity, Luther also recalls here the need to maintain steadily the historical reference when appropriating the scriptures in theology. Philosophical reason-ing (principle nine) and inculturation (principle ten), for example, are to be brought into play, but not in a one-sided fashion that would sup-press the historical origins and reference of the scriptures which the traditional creeds (principle three) and the central metanarratives (principle six) properly maintain. A concern for inculturating trinitar-ian belief through Hindu philosophy can recommend, for instance, professing faith in "Being, Consciousness of Being, and Enjoyment of Being." But when we discuss analogous examples in Chapter 4, we shall argue that a-historical translations of trinitarian belief must not be allowed to take over in an exclusive way. The more historically oriented principles (principles one through eight) in our list of ten suggest otherwise.

This chapter, in elaborating ten principles for the theological use of scripture, has not developed much detailed argument for the positions we hold. But we hope that their validity will emerge more clearly when we see how they work in practice when applied to a number of key questions in systematic theology. Various conditions for the possibility of the valid role of the scriptures in theology cannot be simply assembled *a priori* but show up simultaneously as biblical texts enter theology. We turn now to this task, conscious of the fact that theology like the life of faith itself is a common pilgrimage (Heb 11:1–12:2). We can never hope to finish hearing the biblical texts and letting them constantly renew our theology in the light of what we read.

To help readers, let us conclude this chapter by formulating our ten principles in the style of theses:

1. Theologians are *faithful hearers of the scriptures,* responsive to the meaning and truth they find in the whole Bible.
2. Theologians are *active, critically self-aware interpreters* of the scriptures, appropriating them within the context of prayer, study, and action.
3. Theologians interpret and appropriate the scriptures *within the living community of faith* with its classical creeds.
4. Theologians allow *convergent biblical testimony* to bear on the questions at issue.
5. Recognizing that even a strong majority need not guarantee truth, theologians normally prefer *the consensus of centrist exegetes.*
6. *Metathemes* (e.g., covenant, prophecy, and wisdom) and *metanarratives* (above all the resurrection of the crucified Jesus) that help make one cumulative story out of the scriptures also guide their theological appropriation.
7. Theologians recognize in the scriptures recurrent *discontinuities within continuities*—a phenomenon classically exemplified by the shift from the situation of the earthly Jesus to that of the apostle Paul.

8. A sense of *eschatological provisionality* characterizes the theological appropriation of the scriptures.
9. When appropriating the scriptures, theologians need to be *in dialogue with philosophers* and draw help from them.
10. When appropriating the scriptures, theologians also make their contribution toward *inculturating the biblical testimony.*

2

The Divinity of Christ

*To the extent that you are crucified to the world, you will be able
to grasp what the holy Scriptures are saying.*
—A. H. Franke

It is a commonplace to remark that many modern writers in their anxiety to vindicate the humanity of Christ have jettisoned his divinity. In such revisionist Christologies the "true man" of the Chalcedonian teaching has often prevailed at the expense of the "true God." Some do not argue the point directly; others like John Hick openly aim to correct previous christological interpretations which they hold to be mistaken. Thus Hick dismisses belief in Jesus' literal divinity as a gradual apotheosis promoted by early Christians that reached its climax at the Council of Nicaea in 325.[1] The NT's "merely" poetic language about Jesus and his "divine" sonship gradually hardened into the prose of Greek metaphysics and claims about God the Son who is "consubstantial" with God the Father. What do we see as an appropriate scriptural approach to the issue? How might our ten principles apply to the topic of Jesus' divinity?

Our first principle invites theologians (and others) as disciples (who share in the NT's faith, are consciously open to the workings of grace, and let the Holy Spirit mediate Christ to them) to hear the biblical witnesses before drawing their conclusions. This entails listening with the attitude of "what are they saying and why?" This also entails avoiding the "it-can't-possibly-be-so-or-mean-that" reaction when encountering high claims in what the scriptures report and proclaim about Jesus. The synoptic Gospels recall, for example, how Jesus presented himself as the Son of man to come as final and divine judge. At the end of a learned article on "Son of Man" in the *Anchor Bible Dictionary,* George Nickelsburg

40

declares it to be "problematic" to accept as "genuine sayings of Jesus" any of the sayings which "identify Jesus as the son of man," and, in particular, those which concern the final stage of human history. To agree that these sayings go back to Jesus himself, "one must posit" that Jesus "believed that his vindication from death would result in his exaltation to the unique role of eschatological judge."[2] Prior convictions seem firmly in control here in rejecting as genuine these sayings, without offering any convincing alternative account of their provenance.

Something similar turns up when some writers deal with the NT's language about an event that carries its own significance for the question of Christ's divinity: his resurrection from the dead. In *Christology* one of us drew together the various idioms deployed by the NT in pointing to the personal transformed life Jesus enjoyed after his death.[3] In the spirit of "the first Christian authors can't possibly have meant that," some recent writers have created for themselves various versions of the Easter message. An excessive reader-freedom allows them to project onto the NT texts interpretations that, if true, would indicate that Paul, the evangelists, and other early Christian writers were either deliberately deceptive or else extraordinarily obtuse.[4] Using the tools of historical-critical research, theologians and other readers should be ready to hear what the NT authors intended to communicate when they wrote what they did about Jesus' resurrection and other matters closely connected with his divine identity.

Authentically hearing the scriptural testimony about Jesus' life, death, and resurrection (or other themes in the history of revelation and salvation) is not possible without being religiously attuned to the scriptures and open to their spiritual dimension with a connatural knowledge that opens one up to their spiritual dimension. According to St. Paul, only a "spiritual" person will grasp the "spiritual things" (1 Cor 2:10–16). The Bible proclaims and witnesses to spiritual things—not least, for instance, in Paul's own christological message.

Active hearing (principle two) invites the theologian to go beyond merely passively taking in the biblical data relevant to the question of Christ's divinity. Active hearing entails consciously situating myself and reflecting on where, when, and with whom I am hearing the christological texts. Such subjective awareness should make theologians attentive, for example, to what their worshiping communities and other dedicated Christians (especially those heroes and heroines who give their lives away in serving suffering people) make of scriptural texts that bear on Christ's death, resurrection, and personal identity. How do those who worship, sacrifice themselves, and suffer interpret and apply the NT passages that bear on the divinity of Christ? Such self-conscious attention implies that theologians, above all when facing Christology, should scrutinize their own performance as honest thinkers, devout worshipers, and generous imitators of Jesus' own self-sacrificing love. In Christology the whole person of the theologian is involved.

The liturgical aspect of our second principle leads to the historic creeds (principle three) that illuminate and guide biblical interpretation. Both the Apostles' Creed and the Nicene-Constantinopolitan Creed single out three christological titles from the NT to play the role of master-titles ("Christ," "Lord," and "only Son of God"), two of which ("Lord" and "only Son of God") as "high" titles express Jesus' divine identity. "Christ" and "Lord" bulk large in the Pauline epistles; "Son" enjoys a rich background in the Letter to the Hebrews and in the Gospels of Matthew and John. Our two Creeds do not overload themselves with other such high titles as Word and Wisdom, but the Nicene Creed, with its statement "through him all things were made," does introduce a divine function that the Bible links up with those two titles: the Word (e.g., Jn 1:3) and Wisdom (e.g., Prv 8:22–31) as agent(s) of creation. As the scriptures also associate the work of creation with the "Son" (e.g., Heb 1:2; Col. 1:13, 16–17) and our "Lord" (e.g., 1 Cor 8:6), we may understand the role of creator to be implied by these two titles which occur in both Creeds. Without adopting the pertinent NT language about the coming Son of man and the day of the Lord,[5] both Creeds confess that Christ "will come again to judge the living and the dead." Lastly, the Nicene Creed names Christ in an even more directly divine fashion as "eternally begotten of the Father, God from God, Light from Light, true God from true God, begotten, not made, one in Being with the Father." Except for the last phrase (Christ as "consubstantial" or *homoousios* with the Father), these six Nicene phrases enjoy a rich biblical pedigree. They represent a common discernment about the way to use, understand, read, and relate christological affirmations, some of which, as the Arian controversy richly illustrated, could suggest that the Son is less than the Father (e.g., 1 Cor 15:28) or could stand in seeming contradiction to each other, as "I and the Father are one" (Jn 10:30) stands over against "the Father is greater than I" (Jn

15;28). Not only the six Nicene phrases but also the choice of the high titles of "Lord" and "only Son of God" (used by both Creeds) show the Apostles' Creed and the Nicene Creed privileging certain biblical texts and titles as yielding a glimpse of the central truth about Christ: his divine identity.

Revisionists like Hick have no choice but to acknowledge that the Nicene and other historic creeds professed faith in Jesus as God the Son. But they regard this development as a deplorable decline and a gross mistake. If they are right, however, the overwhelming majority of Christians, by maintaining these creeds, have been and remain guilty of idolatry. Their official professions of faith lead them to worship as fully divine someone who should not be identified as God the Son.

Through the creeds the interpretative community set up patterns and standards of the reading of the biblical texts pertinent to Christology. On the key question of Christ's divinity very many biblical texts present themselves for examination. Here any christological discussion will remain rootless unless it begins by reflecting on those OT personifications of the divine activity: the Word and the Wisdom of God. These and further Jewish images and notions provided the language which the first Christians appropriated and transformed to express Jesus' divine identity. The first Christians enjoyed the same stock of images in their rich Jewish inheritance as Jesus did. But they made different choices in the images they used and transformed to express their experience of him. In the NT itself there are numerous images and texts theologians must read and account for: from the pre-Pauline material (e.g., Phil 2:6–11; 1 Cor 16:22), through Paul (e.g., 1 Cor 8:6; Rom 10:13), the synoptics (e.g., Mt 11:27; Lk 12:8–9), the Letter to the Hebrews (e.g., Heb 1:1–3, 10–12), the Pastoral Epistles (e.g., Ti 2:13), and on to the Book of Revelation (e.g., Rv 1:17; 5:12–14; 22:20) and the Gospel of John (passim). From its earliest to its latest writings the NT offers, in a rich variety of ways, convergent testimony to the divine identity of Christ.[6] The authors of the NT believed this to be revealed and true. Profession of this belief comes in many idioms and from a chorus of NT witnesses, some known (e.g., Paul) and many unknown (e.g., the authors of the pre-Pauline traditions). This biblical faith in Christ's divinity exemplifies admirably our fourth principle, that of convergence, a principle that obviously does not function in John Hick's *The Metaphor of God Incarnate*. He charges Paul and later Christian writers with having gradually divinized Jesus as God the Son, claiming that genuine clues to Jesus' identity and mission are to be found only in what the synoptic Gospels record or rather in what Hick wishes to draw from them.[7]

The principle of convergence involves appealing to a wide range of witnesses, phrased in different idioms, and checking scholarly opinion and possible consensus (principle five) concerning the various items that constitute the convergent testimony. Questions such as the following need to be asked: How strong is the case for holding that Jesus presented himself as the Son of man to come at the end to judge all people? What conclusions about Jesus' self-awareness may be drawn from the antithesis ("Of old it was said to you, but I say to you") through which he took it upon himself to modify the Law as understood to be given by God (Mt 5:21–28)? How strongly supported is the interpretation of Phil 2:6 as referring to Christ's divine preexistence?[8] What are the implications when NT authors apply to Jesus OT texts that refer to God (e.g., Rom 10:13; Heb 1:10–12)? Would a broad spectrum of exegetes consistently recognize a divine meaning when the pre-Pauline tradition (e.g., 1 Cor 16:22; Phil 2:11) or Paul himself (e.g., Rom 1:7) names the crucified and risen Jesus as "Lord"? How strong is the case for assigning the doxology in Rom 9:5 ("God who is over all be blessed forever") to Christ?[9] In short, appeal to convergent testimony about Jesus' divine identity involves one in doggedly checking the consensus (or lack thereof) about all the individual pieces of testimony supposed to contribute to the convergent case.

To the extent that we establish some consensus, Christology, on any showing, pulls in metathemes and metanarratives from the Bible (principle six). It must, for instance, make the connections and account for the contrasting elements between OT messianic expectations and what Christians chose to say (and write) when they called Jesus "the Christ." What engages our attention in this chapter, however, are such personifications of the divine activity as "Word" and "Wisdom,'" which went on to become high titles for Jesus. Whether we deal with these and their divine titles for Jesus (e.g., "Lord" and "Son of God") or with such "low" titles as "Last Adam" or "Suffering Servant," any adequate Christology must incorporate such metathemes that bind together in dynamic tension both Testaments. When explaining metathemes in Chapter 1, we remarked on ways in which they can undergo remarkable modifications when they recur in different contexts, "Word" and "Wisdom" exemplify this spectacularly — in their shift from being OT *personifications* for God's activity to becoming titles for the divine *person* of Jesus. The great christological and biblical metanarrative is, of course, the resurrection of the crucified Jesus, "the paschal event" which "has established a radically new historical context."[10] His resurrection from the dead brought the Holy Spirit, revealed that Jesus was right in calling God "Abba," vindicated his high claims to personal authority, and showed him to be the climax of the OT story, the Jewish Messiah who is also the definitive, divine Savior and source of eternal life for all men and women of all times and places. The salvific function and divine identity of the risen Christ embraces the past (Jewish and human expectation), the present gift of the Spirit, and future and final overcoming of death. Christology needs to face some vexed questions about the resurrection of the crucified Jesus. But it remains true to say that any given Christology will stand or fall by the way it handles the biblical metanarrative that holds together not only the Bible itself but the whole of Christian faith.

Easter effected the shift from the situation of Jesus' ministry to that of the church, the classic biblical case of continuity within discontinuity (principle seven). The Preacher of the kingdom became the One preached by Paul and other missionaries. To echo Rudolf Bultmann, the Revealer became the Revealed One. The implicit, indirect Christology of the ministry developed into the explicit, direct Christology about Jesus as "Christ," "Lord," and "Son of God." The previous chapter has illustrated how the shift from Jesus to Paul worked.

Some writers maintain here the thesis of overwhelming or even total discontinuity. They claim that within twenty years from his death, the followers of Jesus had blunted the thrust of his countercultural, aphoristic message, gone back to the apocalyptic modes of thought they had learned from John the Baptist, credited Jesus with claims about his own central role in the coming judgment, and turned him into a dying and rising God. This "reconstruction" coming from the Jesus Seminar, or at least from their leaders, makes Jesus out to be an incompetent teacher who failed to convey to his first followers the difference between his enigmatic, wisdom-style teaching and the apocalyptic message of his precursor. As soon as Jesus was gone, they reverted to what they had previously been taught by John the Baptist and then left us in the Gospels a Jesus who is their "imaginative theological construct."[11] Even though they were brought up in Jewish monotheism, the first disciples were apparently so obtuse that they neither noticed nor complained about what Paul and the pre-Pauline tradition were doing in attributing to Jesus the divine work of creation (1 Cor 8:6), setting him on a par with the OT's Lord God (e.g., Phil 2:9–11), and placing Jesus side by side with "God the Father" as the source of salvation ("grace and peace"—e.g., Rom 1:7, 1 Cor 1:3). The Pauline correspondence reflects debates and even sharp polemics among early Christians about such matters as the end of the world, justification, the works of the law, and apostolic authority. Yet right in his first letter (1 Thes) Paul called Jesus "Lord" twenty-four times and never had to argue that he merited this divine title. The apostle expanded the *Shema* or central Jewish confession of monotheism to include Jesus and produce a christological monotheism (1 Cor 8:6). He did not pause to argue for this conviction but took it for granted that his readers would agree with him. Undoubtedly arguments from silence must be treated with caution. But, given the strictly monotheistic origins of Christianity, the explicit, high Christology of Paul and the pre-Pauline tradition would have triggered loud protests if many or even some early Christians reckoned it to be an unjustified and blasphemous development. The NT records such protests but only in one of its later books, and they are violent protests coming from outside, not from within the Christian community (e.g., Jn 5:18; 8:59).

The Jesus Seminar is by no means alone in questioning the validity of the interpretation of Jesus that arose after his ministry. John Hick, for instance, does not reject the apocalyptic thrust of Jesus' message. But he denies authority to the post-Easter interpretation of Jesus.[12] In challenging and even rejecting the apostolic response to the events of Jesus' life, death, and resurrection, Hick and others take a position against the apostles and the apostolic generation as empowered by Jesus and the Holy Spirit to be normative mediators of revelation. Where James Mackey maintains that "the faith of Jesus" is "still determinative of how we acknowledge him,"[13] Hick follows Schleiermacher in attributing to Jesus an "immensely powerful God-consciousness."[14] Terminology differs but the result is the same: any valid revelation of Jesus' identity and mission comes only from his earthly history, so that post-Easter, apostolic interpretations of him have no binding weight and can be set aside as merely human, culture-conditioned, and even deviant evaluations. In this way history (= the history of Jesus) is held to overcome the early christological doctrines of Christianity on which later creeds and conciliar definitions subsequently based themselves. Apart from ignoring and distorting data from the synoptic Gospels to reinvent the history of Jesus,[15] such a position erodes the force of the divine revelation. Jesus, while being the primary Revealer, associated with himself others (above all the twelve and the wider group of Easter witnesses) to be empowered by the Holy Spirit as interpreters and mediators of revelation. He stands or falls with those men and women whose testimony and preaching set Christianity going. Either we accept their authoritative account of what was revealed in Jesus or we reject Jesus along with them. The apostolic proclamation and interpretation of the climactic revelations in Christ belong essentially to all that God disclosed in Christ and about Christ. Our seventh principle rests on a "high" view of the revelatory function of the apostles and the apostolic generation.

Talk of revelation leads naturally to our eighth principle, the eschatological provisionality of all our christological thinking and affirmations. The NT repeatedly recalls that the fullness of divine revelation is not yet here but to be consummated still (e.g., Rom 8:19; 1 Pt 1:5, 7, 13; 1 Jn 3:2). In Christology, and specifically for the question of Christ's divinity, the scriptures encourage a lively sense of expectation. The synoptic Gospels present him as the Son of man to come at the end in divine judgment. This will be the "day of the Lord" (e.g., 1 Cor 5:5), when Christ's divine glory will be revealed (e.g., 1 Pt 4:13)—what the Letter to Titus calls "the appearing of the glory of our great God and Savior Jesus Christ" (Ti 2:13).[16] This lively hope for Christ's final coming in glory expresses itself in a prayer that names him in terms of his divine identity: "Come, Lord Jesus" (Rv 22:30; see 1 Cor 16:23).

Nowadays one no longer needs to overcome that fateful legacy from post-Reformation Christology—of being too "knowing" about Christ's divinity and how it is personally united to his humanity. A latter-day stress on his humanity threatens not only to submerge his divinity but even to exclude it altogether. Our principle, the partial and provisional nature of all christological thinking, applies, however, to both sides of the mystery. Here and now we enjoy no more than glimpses of what it meant and means for Christ to be simultaneously fully human and fully divine. Without dialogue with philosophy (principle nine), Christology cannot hope to achieve much clarity about Christ's being divine or about doctrines very closely associated with it, his personal preexistence and incarnation. Right from the time of St. Justin, theologians have picked up clues from various philosophers about ways to translate the symbolic language of the Bible and express the divine. What makes God to be God? What is it to be divine in the proper sense of the term? Through events, theophanies, and prophetic oracles the Bible supplies a range of attributes for God as the all-powerful, ever-living, all-holy, merciful Maker of heaven and earth, who as the God of Abraham, Isaac, and Jacob is the Lord of human history and will come in judgment at the end. God is the One from whose presence we can never flee (Ps 139:7–10), the one in whom "we live and move and have our being" (Acts 17:28). The biblical narratives enable readers to identify the divine presence and purposes. Often this prephilosophical language is thoroughly anthropomorphic and richly symbolic as when God is said "to ride upon the clouds" (Ps 68:4), to be the loving husband of two unfaithful wives (Jerusalem and Samaria in Ez 23:44), to live "in unapproachable light" (1 Tm 6:16), and to be revealed in a bush that burns without being consumed (Ex 3:2–6). These symbols enjoy an inexhaustible depth of significance, and can never be adequately and definitively restated in philosophical or semiphilosophical language. Such secondary language may, in part, live off the primary scriptural images, narratives, and rituals; yet even its clearest concepts can never hope to convey everything, let alone to replace the biblical texts. Because of their profound depth the scriptural narratives can never be exhausted, their mystery never fully captured. Rudolf Otto's version of "the Holy" as "the awesome and fascinating Mystery" *(Mysterium tremendum et fascinans)* interprets and illuminates the call-experience of Isaiah in the Jerusalem Temple (Is 6), but the rich imagery in the story of the prophet's encounter with the all-holy God cannot simply be reexpressed once and for all in second-order, academic language. Following St. Thomas Aquinas in naming God as Subsistent Being and the First Cause[17] or using reflections from Gabriel Marcel to express God as "the Absolute Presence" (or "Absolute Closeness") serves clarity and precision, and (in the case of Marcel-style terminology) catches something of the mysterious, spiritual character of personal existence, both God's and ours. Yet such terminology loses the vibrancy of the first-order, religious language: "Maker of heaven and earth," and the One "in whom we live and move and have our being." Something similar happens when theology draws on philosophy to speak of God as the ineffable, incomprehensible divine mystery, or as the Totally Other, the Utterly Transcendent One who is above, beyond, and over everything and everyone. For its part the Bible tells of Moses climbing a mountain and entering into darkness as he goes to speak with God (Ex 20:21), or of God as dwelling in "unapproachable light" and beyond all human sight (1 Tm 6:16). In its "God-talk" philosophy domesticates this scriptural imagery and symbolism. Its generalizing talk of divine attributes also differs markedly from the narrative style of the Gospels in recounting the personal history of Jesus and describing how his divine (and human) identity unfolds through his life, death, and resurrection. These narratives invite their readers to enter their world and share their identification of Jesus. The strategy is worlds apart from the abstract, argumentative style of philosophy.

Nevertheless, philosophy's hard-edged jargon has proved essential whenever theologians move from merely repeating biblical language, and attempt to respond to key christological questions. What is required and sufficient to recognize in Christ full and proper divinity? That he is eternally preexistent (e.g., Jn 1:1–2), that he is agent of creation (e.g., 1 Cor 8:6; Col 1:16), that he forgives sins with his own authority (e.g., Mk 2:5–12), that with the Father he gives the divine Spirit (e.g., Jn 15:26; 16:7; Acts 2:33), that he merits the worship due to God (e.g., Phil 2:10–11; Rv 5:12–14), and that as Lord he will come in judgment at the end (e.g., Phil 1:10; 1 Thes 2:19; 3:13)? How are these scriptural claims to be translated philosophically? In particular, what account can we give of his eternal preexistence and being a divine person? Generally speaking, theologians have been properly alert to the shifts and changes that have taken place in the philosophical notion of a person since the days of Boethius, as well as the impact of these developments on the possibility of maintaining and rereading the Chalcedonian doctrine of one (divine) person in two natures. But far less attention has been paid in Christology to philosophical discussions of time and eternity, and the fact that they are asymmetrical in their relationship. The prefixes of "pre-existence" and "in-carnation" subtly slide over this by inserting into Christ's eternal existence a sense of temporal "before and after." While present to all times, the "now" of eternity is altogether "outside" time, excludes any temporal distinctions between past, present, and future, and hence excludes any prior "will be" and posterior "has been."[18]

Philosophical versions of God vary. Is there a tension or even a conflict between the version we have elaborated (or, more likely, accepted) and the massive divine "intervention" claimed by the doctrine of the incarnation or "the Word becoming flesh" (Jn 1:14)? What are the conditions for the possibility (or at least for the seeming non-impossibility) of the incarnation, by which the eternal Word assumes a temporal created nature and begins to act through it in a temporal universe?[19] Did and could the Word literally give up divine attributes by assuming a human existence and history? Or was it simply a matter of largely renouncing the use of them during his earthly existence? Since the incarnation entails taking on a human mind and will, other questions force themselves on theologians: How might one person enjoy simultaneously a divine consciousness and a human consciousness? Can we say anything at all about the conditions for one person functioning freely through two wills? Obviously philosophy may be expected to offer some help in struggling with the questions raised by Christ's two minds and two wills. Philosophy comes into play as well when reflecting on causal conditions and difficulties about the particular way the incarnation took place: through the virginal conception. Is it true that this belief is incompatible with a genuine incarnation: that is, with the assumption of a genuine humanity? Since human beings uniformly come into existence through the agency of two human parents, a virginal conception would throw grave doubt on Christ's being truly human. A philosopher could properly reply here that possessing a genuine humanity does not necessarily entail any given conditions for its origin, *unless* one adds the claim that everything in this world happens within an absolutely closed system of causes and effects. That assertion would rule out the virginal conception as being incompatible with Christ's genuine humanity: the effect (his genuine humanity) must have been produced by the uniform and universal cause (sexual intercourse between two human beings). But is that additional assertion warranted?

When dealing with the incarnation, some writers, such as John Hick in *The Metaphor of God Incarnate,* prefer the categories of action over those of being—that is to say, verbs replace substantives. Jesus "incarnated" the divine purposes for human life rather than being the incarnate God the Son. He lived a life of unselfish love that "embodied" the ideal human response to the divine reality rather than being himself divine. Verbs like "lived," "revealed," "embodied," and "incarnated" replace noun-talk (especially that of one person in two natures) to describe how Jesus behaved historically and how he continues to make God real to those who are inspired by him. The substitution of action-categories for being-categories amounts to the attempt to replace an ontological Christology with one that is purely functional. Yet no amount of functional talk can banish the question: Did Jesus reveal the divine love and claim because he belonged in person to the divine reality? If Jesus functioned and functions in that way, who and what was/is he?[20]

Finally, appropriating the scriptural texts for Christology calls on theologians to grapple with the task of inculturation (principle ten). They engage themselves in an act of dialogue which should never assume that they improve on and substantially supplement the christological texts of the Bible, let alone render them obsolete or even invalid. Simultaneously they must cope with situations of rupture between faith and culture when finding a new language for the christological truths. We often "do" Christology today in a cold climate. More than ever, theologians need a poetic, creative imagination when moving from the scriptures and tradition to state the truth of Christ today.

Inculturating biblical witness to Christ's divinity involves drawing on the available "God-talk" of a given culture and the resources of an age. We are both of the Western world. Where might we turn for a language that could successfully capture and communicate today a sense of God and of Christ's divine identity? The extraordinary complexity, diversity, and lawfulness of the world that modern scientific culture has decoded offer one possibility. The ingenuity of the laws of physics, the amazing intelligibility of our physical environment, and the sense that we inhabit a wonderfully interesting universe yield some glimpses of the mind and might of God. That is all at the macro-level. What of our personal, inner lives? We have experiences that take us to the limit or depths of our human existence. Sickness confronts us with our radical fragility, the death of a close relative with our common mortality, grave injustice with the absurd unfairness of life's lottery, and cold indifference with the savage selfishness that seems to rule much of our world. Yet in and through these experiences we also glimpse the "Beyond in our midst," the hidden God who is utterly strong, eternally reliable, totally truthful, and completely, if mysteriously, just, fair, and caring. By "graciously" ministering to us when we face such limit-experiences of death, absurdity, and hatred, men and women can evoke the presence of One who is the fullness of life, meaning, and love. The living God makes all things possible for us, even eternal life. As Truth and Meaning in person, the incarnate Son of God proves to be the Word of God and the Light of the World; together the Father and the Son send the Holy Spirit, who is Love in person. In short, deep experiences of life, meaning (truth), and love yield possible ways of thinking and speaking of God in our Western culture and perhaps in other cultures.

This choice of language for Christ's divinity has the advantage of illustrating the relational aspect of his divine identity—something repeatedly expressed in Paul's opening greetings that pray for "grace and peace" from "God our Father" and "the Lord Jesus Christ." When the Nicene-Constantinopolitan Creed confessed Christ's divinity, it did so in relationship to the Father and the Holy Spirit. Our suggestion for an inculturated Christology follows suit. By revealing himself as the supremely meaningful Truth, Christ revealed also the limitless life of the Father and the supremely worthwhile love of the Spirit.

This chapter has brought our ten principles to bear on the use of scriptures in elaborating theologically Christ's divinity. Our next chapter takes up the challenge of articulating his redemptive "work" in conjunction with the Bible.

3

Redemption Through Love

How is it we are saved by you, O Lord, from whom salvation
comes and whose blessing is upon your people, if it is not in
receiving from you the gift of loving you and being loved by you?
—William of Saint Thierry, *On Contemplating God*

Alongside the question of his personal identity, the other central concern about Jesus is the nature of the redemption he has brought. How should theologians appropriate the scriptures in tackling the questions: What are we saved *from* and *for?* How should the salvific role of Christ be best described? What does he do as Savior or Redeemer? What is the salvation, redemption, or atonement (the terms are practically interchangeable) that he brings? There are questions that theologians want to wrestle with when they take up the issue of Christ's redemptive role. But this chapter would have grown into a book if we attempted to show how one might use the scriptures in responding to *all* these questions. Let us narrow matters down to one question to be answered in the light of the scriptures: *How* did/does Christ perform his redeeming role? Is it primarily by liberating us, by expiating our sins, or by loving us?

Both the scriptures and the post-NT Christian tradition offer these three differing, if complementary, responses to our question. Redemption takes place as victorious liberation from various oppressive and evil forces—in particular, from sin, death, and diabolic powers. Or else redemption has been understood and interpreted to come through the expiation from defilement and purification from sinfulness that Christ has effected in his role as priest and victim. Third, the transforming power of love has been acclaimed as the focal point for a biblically based account of redemption. All three responses have been legitimated by appealing to scriptural witness that has shaped post-NT liturgies, theologies, and other sectors of the Christian tradition. Should theologians give these diverse biblical (and traditional) voices equal time? Is the choice between liberation, expiation, and love simply a matter of personal preference that should be encouraged, so long as one's option does not pretend to disregard the biblical and further evidence that justify the two alternate responses? Do the scriptures give us the authority to "grade" the three versions of how redemption takes place or only to present them as *there* in the great, mysterious richness that is the biblical record? Having identified the problem, we want to maintain the preeminence of love as the premier statement of the "how" of redemption—a position that can be tested and verified by applying our ten principles.

Some might detect a switch of levels in the way we have set up the choice. After all, "liberation" and "expiation" express the "mechanisms" of redemption or salvation attested by the scriptures, whereas "love" suggests the (divine) motivation for these "mechanisms" coming into play. However, as we shall see, the gift of love clarifies powerfully the very "mechanism" or "how" of redemption. It is the "motive force," in the sense of being both *the* motive and the force at work in redemption (and in creation, for that matter).

What we wish to argue in this chapter is not always so obvious when we journey through an assortment of contemporary theological landscapes. Whatever reservations we have about the way Hans Urs von Balthasar treats Christ's death and "descent into hell," he does at least expound Jesus as the "manifestation" and "proof" of the tripersonal God's love for the world.[1] The theme of God's loving self-communication in history shapes the heart of Karl Rahner's Christology and, indeed, entire theology.[2] Gustavo Gutiérrez expounds the gratuitous love of the God of life revealed in the liberation of the poor.[3] Once we leave von Balthasar, Rahner, and Gutiérrez behind, what do we find in late twentieth-century theology? Recent works on the redemption by such outstanding scholars as Colin Gunton, John McIntyre, and Bernard Sesboüé have scarcely a word to say about love.[4] When he speaks of the saving action of Christ in the second volume of his *Systematic Theology*,[5] Wolfhart Pannenberg develops the theme of "reconciliation" (397–464). The divine love as such makes no appearance; there is one reference to "the new commandment of love" given to human beings (461). But we do not feel completely comfortable, to put it mildly, with this playing down of love. We harbor more than a nagging feeling that the scriptures, if examined in the light of our ten principles, will support the attempt to retrieve and reaffirm love as the major way to understand and interpret the "how" (and the "why") of Jesus' salvific role. Love is not merely one of three ways for articulating salvation, but the very key for appreciating how and why it takes place. Love provides a mysterious coherence for the whole drama of redemption, and—one should add— for the "prior" work of divine love, creation. Liberation from evil and, even less, expiation from sin do not hold together creation and redemption quite so easily as love. Furthermore, the divine and human love deployed in Jesus' saving "work" incorporates the central truths expressed by the other two, major responses to the "how?" of redemption. His powerful love "conquers all" (liberation; "amor vincit omnia"), as well as purifying and sanctifying all (expiation). Unquestionably, human beings find it easy to corrupt such words as love. But no decay of language should allow "love" to be called into question, let alone become a casualty of theological nervousness. When justifying the centrality of love for the theology of redemption, we will invoke our first eight principles. But we must have an ear for the voice of philosophy (principle nine) and the claims of inculturation (principle ten) if we hope to set the record straight about redemptive love and how it works. In this chapter we want to show that these last two principles enjoy a peculiar importance in moving from the scriptures to a theological version of how Christ saves us. But first let us briefly check how the first eight principles bear on our account of redemption.

Principles One Through Eight

Familiar, yet always lively, language from such OT prophets as Hosea, Jeremiah, Ezekiel, and Second Isaiah speaks eloquently of the loving concern of God to deliver and enrich a sinful and suffering people. Yahweh protests that even if a mother were to "forget her nursing child or show no compassion for the child of her womb," he will never forget Jerusalem and her people (Is 49:15). God assures Israel: "I have loved you with an everlasting love" (Jer 31:3). Marriage imagery is adopted to express what the divine love wishes to do for sinful and exiled Zion (Is 54:5–8; see Jer 2:2). No infidelity on their part to the covenant prevents God's loving desire to renew his nuptial relations with the people in a kind of fresh betrothal (Hos 2:14–23). Over and over again in the psalms and elsewhere, *hesed* expresses God's merciful love and loyalty toward weak human beings (e.g., Jon 4:2). When we move to the NT scriptures, a responsive ear (principle one) will discover even more testimonies to the divine love and its redemptive impact. In Luke's Gospel Jesus' image of himself as mother hen (Lk 13:24) and parables of the lost sheep, the lost coin, and the lost son (Lk 15:3–32) do not explicitly mention love but certainly pose vividly the question: Is this message of divine mercy and forgiveness intelligible unless it strongly presupposes the active presence among us of God's searching and saving love? What remains largely but clearly implicit in the synoptic Gospels becomes forcefully explicit in John's message of "God so loving the world" and initiating a mission of redemptive love (Jn 3:16), and in the way that Jesus' last discourse to his disciples begins with love being affirmed (Jn 13:1) and ends with a prayer of love (Jn 17:26). Paul's masterpiece interprets redemption as the effective revelation of God's love "for us" (Rom 5:8; 8:31–39) and "for me" (Gal 2:20), a love that cannot tolerate the absence brought by death and that has changed death into the gateway to everlasting, risen life (Rom 8:11; 1 Cor 15:12–57). The apostle also eloquently presents redemption in terms of "reconciliation" (Rom 5:10; 2 Cor 5:18–20), a theme that makes sense only if subsumed under love.

How would our second principle of active interpretation work here? Here, as when applying the other principles from one through eight, we do not pretend to answer this question in anything like a thoroughgoing way. Otherwise this chapter would turn into a book in its own right. Let us limit ourselves to one observation. "Answerable" interpretation entails a critical awareness of the social and religious contexts which shape in part the reading purposes and practice of theologians as they appropriate the biblical texts. As we saw in Chapter 1, a church, a library, and a prison serve to symbolize three different "loci" for reading and interpreting the scriptures. Theologians, at least in the North Atlantic world, normally encounter the Bible in an academic context of study, lecturing, and writing. There they need the love that makes knowledge possible or at least more accessible—a point to which we return below. But they need also to keep an eye on the way the redeeming love of God works and is appreciated in the liturgy of the community and in situations of suffering and injustice.

Our third principle for the theological use of the scriptures, reading and interpreting them in the light of the community's "rule of faith" and mainline tradition, does not promise to illuminate decisively the issue of this chapter. The classic, early creeds of Christianity do not disentangle various approaches to the mystery of redemption but are content to affirm that Christ came "for us and for our salvation." Unlike the case of Christ's person and natures, no major controversies have ever directly arisen about his saving "work" to force general councils of the church to take a stand. Debates on matters like original sin, justification, and the sacraments brought up the issue of salvation, but as such it has never directly been a central issue for conciliar interpretation and teaching. The Christian tradition, as expressed in a great variety of liturgies, ranges over the three major biblical fields of imagery for redemption. It strikes us as extremely difficult to defend the priority of love when all three approaches to redemption and its impact (as liberation, expiation, and love) have been extolled liturgically over the centuries.

Biblical convergence (principle four) looks more promising. As we noticed above, prophetic imagery, the historical recollection of the synoptic Gospels, and the theological reflections of John (e.g., 1 Jn 4:7–12) and Paul (e.g., 2 Cor 13:11, 13) converge on love as central to the shape taken by God's salvific dealings with human beings. Do we enjoy here a consensus on the part of biblical scholars (principle five)? Ceslas Spicq's *Agape in the New Testament* presents a strong case for the new covenant being centered on the saving revelation of the divine love that calls forth the response of human love.[6] Covenanted love as the major line for articulating redemption can appeal to a good number of exegetes and biblical theologians for support. Principle six (metathemes and metanarratives) also allows us to position ourselves in favor of the preeminence of God's redemptive love. That liberating and transforming love found prophetic expression as God's spousal love for Jerusalem; this nuptial imagery fed into the NT's presentation of Christ's redemptive work (e.g., Mk 2:18–21; Eph 5:21–32), right through to the closing vision of the new Jerusalem adorned as a bride for her loving Redeemer who is to come (Rv 21:1–22:21). The central metanarrative of the scriptures, the Easter mystery of Jesus, who dies and rises to save all, is repeatedly phrased in terms of love (e.g., Gal 2:20). John is second to none in appreciating how the redemptive events of Good Friday and Easter Sunday aim at nothing less than

enabling all believers to participate in the inner life of the tripersonal
God, that is, in the most profound fellowship of love (Jn 17:20–26).

Our seventh principle (continuity within discontinuity) describes
the shift from Jesus' redemptive ministry to the situation in which John,
Paul, and other NT authors (e.g., Ti 3:4–7) directly articulate redemption in the language of the divine *agapē* and philanthrōpia toward us.
Although the synoptic Gospels never report Jesus as saying that his
Father has *agapē* for human beings and rarely attribute to Jesus himself
the explicit attitude and language of love (in Mark only at 10:21 and
12:30–31), the universal kindness and mercy of God (e.g., Mt 5:45; Lk
6:35–36) and Jesus' compassionate care for the sick, the sinful, and the
lost make no sense if we do not recognize how love motivates and
empowers the whole story in the synoptics. Yet the articulation of
redemption in terms of love remains largely implicit. The crucifixion,
resurrection, and outpouring of the Holy Spirit render salvation in and
through Christ even more personal, at least in the sense of its being now
expressed explicitly in terms of the Father's love for human beings
(e.g., Jn 16:27; 1 Jn 4:9; 1 Thes 1:4; 2 Thes 2:13, 16), the Father's love
"in Christ" for human beings (e.g., Rom 8:39, Eph 1:3–10), and
Christ's love for human beings (e.g., Jn 13:34; 15:9, 12–15; 2 Cor
5:14–15; Rv 1:5), for the church (e.g., Eph 5:2, 25), and for specific
individuals (e.g., Jn 11:5; 13:23; Gal 2:20). Without claiming an
unquestionable superiority in this regard over faith and hope, love illuminates the eschatological provisionality (eighth principle) of everything that the biblical texts yield for a theology of redemption.[7] The
promised consummation of salvation has not yet arrived. We hope for
the mysterious fullness of redemption (see Rom 8:24) which the divine
love has in store for us. Love grounds all our hopes.

Thus far this chapter has set itself to secure at least a prima facie
case for considering love to be the leading way for interpreting the way
God's redemptive activity in Christ looks and works. Our first eight
principles yield an initial plausibility for such a conclusion. But any
version of redemption as motivated by and working through divine love
will remain low on clarity and substance until it puts the scriptures into
dialogue with philosophies of love (principle nine) and tackles under
principle ten the challenges of inculturating the message of God's
redemptive love in our apocalyptic times. To these tasks we now turn,
while insisting once again (see Chapter 1) that one should not make too

much of the difference between philosophy and theology and allege a hard-and-fast separation between the two disciplines.

A Philosophy of Love

To appropriate the scriptural witness and construct a theologically coherent account of redemption as starting from and coming through divine love cannot be done without a reasonably deployed philosophy of love. At the end of the twentieth century it is impossible to claim much if any originality. What more is there to say about love and friendship after Plato, Aristotle, the Song of Songs, Augustine, Abelard, Bernard, William of Saint Thierry, Aquinas, Bonaventure, Dante, Julian of Norwich, Sören Kierkegaard, Max Scheler, Martin Buber, Simone de Beauvoir, Viktor Frankl, Rollo May, Denis de Rougemont, Anders Nygren, those who debated his views (e.g., M. C. D'Arcy), C. S. Lewis, Maurice Nédoncelle, Gabriel Marcel, the Bhagavadgita, the classic novels from Spain, Russia, and elsewhere, the works of great mystics, Italian opera, and lyric poetry from every culture? Our aim is not as such to make some startling new contribution but rather to retrieve the best insights of our Western heritage, reflect on love in its most exemplary forms, and set out some workable philosophical themes that can help to structure a theology of how God's redemptive love expresses itself and operates.[8] At least ten points enter into such a scheme.

Approval has good grounds for being named as the initial characteristic of love wherever it is found. To love others is to accept, approve, wonder at, and rejoice in these persons. It is to affirm these others as they are in themselves, particular and mysteriously unique manifestations of reality and goodness. It is to value them for their complete personal totality and not merely for this or that characteristic they possess. It is to wonder at their existing, rejoice in their being what they are, and prize the individuality of each one of them. Love as "amor complacentiae," to use the medieval term, gratefully delights in the object of its love. The voice from heaven at Jesus' baptism discloses exquisitely love as approval: "You are my beloved Son; with you I am well pleased" (Mk 1:11; see 9:7). Later in the same Gospel Jesus himself conveys this primary dimension of love when he gazes with loving approval on a rich young man (Mk 10:21). God's redemptive love means the fundamental divine approval of our "being there," each in one's own unique, personal reality. Every "beloved" enjoys intrinsic, incomparably different value for God as an irreplaceable individual.

Second, such loving approval entails identification with the other and taking the initiative in making the interests of the other my own. Love is more than some vague, even passive good will; it calls for active good will toward "the other." Here love shows itself the opposite of apathy, that uninvolved and unfeeling indifference which simply does not care about others. Love invites me to reach out beyond myself and put myself, so to speak, in the place of the ones I love. This benevolent concern, practical action to advance the welfare of others, or "amor benevolentiae" is love as it shares, gives, forgives, reveals, and creates. What Colin Gunton calls the "prior and redeeming act of God in Jesus Christ" (*The Actuality of the Atonement,* xi) becomes specified here as the prior and redeeming *love* of God. Under this second heading we place those observations about the divine love that lies behind creation and redemption as the self-sharing, self-giving love. To echo the words of the dying priest in Georges Bernanos' *Diary of a Country Priest,* all is gift. Yet one must add that here the gift brings the divine giver. In lovingly bestowing on us what is good and valuable, God comes with the gift. All divine giving is self-giving. The "agapeic" activity that flows in spontaneous abundance from the divine goodness communicates nothing less than the divine reality. Dionysius the Pseudo-Areopagite disseminated the theme of *bonum diffusivum sui:* the good—above all, the divine Good—shares itself (*Divine Names 4).*[9] Often called "gift-love," this divine *agapē* would be more accurately styled as "self-gift-of-love." None of the NT writers appreciated more keenly than John and Paul how this "amor benevolentiae" of God entailed nothing less than the self-gift of God's Son in person and then the divine self-gift that is the sending of the Holy Spirit (e.g., Jn 3:16; 20:22; Rom 5:5; 8:32). In Jesus' own extraordinary parable, the father of the prodigal gives himself in love to both his sons. His love for the younger son, in particular, does not express itself merely through gifts like clothing, a ring, and a family feast (Lk 15:22–23). It is the father's self-gift to the returning prodigal that transforms the situation and makes all the difference (Lk 15:20).

In the last paragraph we listed forgiveness and revelation among the aspects of love as "benevolentia" or "beneficentia." It is matter of human experience that the real "for-giving" (as opposed to mere forgetting) calls for a kind of giving to the power of *n*—a fact reflected in several lan guages by the way "to forgive" is a strengthened form of the verb "to give" (e.g., "vergeben" in German, "pardonner" in French, "perdonare" in Italian, and "perdonar" in Spanish). Sometimes, as here, such linguistic phenomena clearly hint at the way things are: the love required to forgive real personal offenses against ourselves requires much, even an heroic act of "amor benevolentiae"—love "in spite of" what has been done. God's loving activity toward sinful human beings includes such "loving-in-spite-of" as it redemptively undoes the consequences of sin, takes unlovable sinners and makes them lovable, effects a lasting reconciliation, and brings about a new and transformed relationship, not merely the restoration of a broken relationship to its original situation (e.g., 2 Cor 5:17–21; 1 Jn 1:9). No scriptural passage catches this aspect of salvific love more brilliantly than Jesus' parable of the prodigal son, or—as it would be more accurately entitled—the parable of the merciful father (Lk 15:11–32). In pardoning and loving sinful enemies, God clearly goes beyond what might be rationally expected in merely human terms (e.g., Rom 5:6–11).

Love as gift covers also that trusting disclosure of ourselves which comes naturally with those who already are or are becoming our closest friends. It is not a question of indulgent self-congratulation that prattles on about one's successes and strengths. Nor is loving self-disclosure simply a matter of having faith that those others will not betray our confidences. We make a gift of ourselves and do so also by revealing ourselves to those whom we love. In her love Beatrice manifests herself and leads Dante to the ecstatic vision of God's presence. Love means revealing oneself and one's God. John's Gospel captures nicely this dimension of love: Jesus' deep friendship leads him to disclose to the disciples his life's greatest treasure, the eternal relationship with his Father (Jn 15:15). It is love that prompts the self-revelation of the trinity (Jn 14:21, 23, 26).

Lastly, love as gift does not merely bless and bestow value on those who already exist; it brings them into existence. God's "overflowing" goodness and love brings about the original creation and the new creation of grace (e.g., Jn 3:3–8; 2 Cor 5:17). Human procreation and its analogues in other "creative" activities provide only faint hints of what the divine *agapē* does in calling into existence those whom God can then bless with further gifts of love. The creative, redemptive love of God bestows our identity upon us—a point to which we return shortly.

Freedom, vulnerability, reciprocity, and union sum up the next four characteristics of love. Any form of slavery, whether external and social or internal and psychological, destroys love and the possibility of love. Authentic love exists only in freedom and respects freedom, as God's appeals in Hosea make clear. Jesus' teaching and miraculous signs aimed at dismantling all that stopped people from hearing the message of the kingdom and the invitation to become his disciples. With all his powers of language, he never misused this capacity as communicator to dominate and coerce agreement. He summoned his audience to believe and love (Mk 12:29–31)—freely and courageously—albeit the synoptic Gospels never represent him as explicitly eliciting the free response of a disciple's love (as in Jn 21:15–19) or even naming freedom as the essential condition for the possibility of such a response. It was left to Paul and John to express the role of freedom for love. Paul celebrates the freedom of God's redemptive love in Christ (Rom 8:31–39), that love which freely identifies with us and wants to endow us with every blessing. The human love that responds to the divine initiative becomes possible for those who have been set free from the slavery of sin (Rom 6:17–18) through "the Spirit of life" (Rom 8:2). To be set free is to be liberated for love (Gal 5:1, 6, 13–14). The apostle's use of fifteen verbs (in the original Greek) at the heart of his hymn to *agapē* lets the dynamically free quality of love come through (1 Cor 13:4–7). The fullness of the Father's love for human beings (Jn 3:16) and for his Son (Jn 3:35; 10:17) allows John to identify God with love (1 Jn 4:8, 16). The divine love toward us is clearly free, faithful, and unforced (1 Jn 1:9; 3:1; 4:9–11). Like Paul, John recognizes that the human response in love to God's saving overtures cannot be coerced but can come only in freedom, a freedom effected by knowing the truth that is Christ himself (Jn 8:32, 36; 14:6). God's love saves us but not by suppressing our moral freedom and (relative) autonomy. No modern novelist appreciated this better than Flannery O'Connor. In "A Good Man Is Hard to Find" she builds the story around a grandmother, whose contriving selfishness leads to the murder of her whole family but who finally chooses to love and freely brings Jesus' love to bear on a brutal, serial killer.

Love, wherever it is authentically active, puts those who love at risk, and not at war—as is sometimes mistakenly professed. Love does not sponsor the active aggression suggested by the words from a once-popular song: "You always hurt the one you love." On the contrary, love produces vulnerability, the fourth characteristic in our analysis of love. In the Middle Ages the exponents of courtly love, whether found in fiction or practiced in "real" life, certainly appreciated suffering and the risk of suffering that love entails, especially when the lover is separated from the beloved.[10] Generous, self-sacrificing, and unconditional love risks being exploited, rejected, and even murderously crushed. Loving service to those in terrible need can turn oneself into a target. The last decades of our century have witnessed thousands of Good Samaritans paying with their lives because they stopped for wounded travelers. In less dramatic but very real ways those who love constantly make themselves vulnerable by reaching out in their concern for others. No parable from the Gospels evokes more poignantly the risk of love than the story of the merciful father (Lk 15:11–32). His love leads him to face and endure the insulting behavior of his elder son (Lk 15:29–30) as well as the deep pain over the moral and spiritual death of his younger son (Lk 15:24, 32). Love cost Jesus himself much (2 Cor 8:9) and put him at mortal risk, as Paul (e.g., 1 Cor 1:13; Gal 2:20), the Deuteropauline Letters (e.g., Eph 5:2, 25), and John (e.g., Jn 13:1; 15:13) vividly recognized. In the midst of pagan selfishness, cruelty, and despair, Jesus' self-sacrificing love shone through from his cross. In various languages a wise choice calls Jesus' suffering and death his "passion"—a term that combines intense love with the mortal suffering it brought the lover. Second to none in its dramatic intensity, Mark's passion story tracks the steadfastness of Jesus' commitment that made him vulnerable right to the end, while one of his male disciples betrayed him, another denied him, and the rest fled in fear. Readers sense that they can count on the unconditional steadfastness and "folly" of his self-forgetful love in a way that they cannot count on their own. His self-sacrificing love figures in the appeal for love made by 1 John (e.g., 1 Jn 3:16).

"Reciprocity" comes up as the fifth item in our account of love. Without such reciprocity love remains radically incomplete, a "disinterested" love that is at best a kind of unilateral generosity or outgoing beneficence. A giving without receiving, even more a giving that deliberately excludes any possibility of receiving and reciprocal transformation, can hardly be deemed love, which seems to us essentially a relational reality. Love of its nature aims to establish and maintain in mutual freedom a relationship.[11] To express love is, in effect, to hope that this love will be returned, but not in a selfish fashion that simply exploits the other to fulfill my needs and yield me some desired benefits. Without the openness and desire for a reciprocal relationship and a mutual giving and receiving, one must wonder whether the lover wishes to deal with the beloved as a personal agent and respects the integrity of the other. As Vincent Brümmer observes, we find our very identity in the mutual relationship of love: "Our identity as persons" is not determined by ourselves alone but is "bestowed on us in the love which others have for us.... Our identity is equally determined by the love we have for others. In both senses we owe our identity as persons to others."[12]

The reciprocity that belongs essentially to God's redeeming love repeatedly surfaces in Micah's call "to walk humbly with your God" (Mi 6:1–8) and in Jesus' invitation to committed discipleship. When John associates love and the mutual relationship involved in "following" Jesus (e.g., Jn 21:15–19), that Gospel builds on a similar association already present in the more historical record of the synoptic Gospels (e.g., Mk 10:21). Jesus' ministry consistently respects the personal integrity of his hearers. Nothing reveals better the way in which God, while creating human beings with the personal autonomy to accept a loving relationship, granting them in the order of redemption the grace needed to enter and maintain such a relationship, and desiring their reciprocal love, nevertheless treats them all as free, personal agents and "waits" with infinite patience and fidelity upon their response of love to be expressed in adoration and discipleship. Here, above all, our lasting, redeemed identity as persons is bestowed upon us in the love which the tripersonal God has for us and by which we respond and relate in loving fellowship with God.

This leads naturally to the sixth point in our analysis: love as "union." Love joyfully[13] breaks down barriers and goes beyond boundaries that isolate individuals and entire groups. It unites, but without a smothering absorption, fusion, and loss of identity. A forceful case in point is the ecstatic union of erotic love. St. Bernard and other Christian writers have frequently drawn on the magically fresh and vivid language of the Song of Songs; it has supplied nuptial terminology in which Christian mystics could express their loving union with God. The desire to be united with the beloved may well be fueled by libidinal energy. But it was an overbelief in the universal relevance of sexual interests and instincts (along with the self-preservative instincts and the death instinct) that led Sigmund Freud to evaluate sexually all human relationships: in particular, every desire to see or be in the presence of another person. He related all love to sexuality, arguing that psychic mechanisms often disguise the sexual origins of all love and friendship. Without repeating here the criticisms already brought against Freud's expanded concept of sexuality,[14] let us simply remark on the fact that love realizes itself in being with the beloved, whether or not sexual interests are involved. Love approves, enriches, and identifies with the good of the beloved—but not from a distance. Love wants to be present to and to be one with the beloved. In the OT the temple and the ark of the covenant, among other things, figured forth God's faithful and loving presence with the people—a theme continued by Matthew's sense of Christ as "God with us" (Mt 1:23; 28:20). The three great theologians of the NT all highlight the personal presence brought about by God's loving desire for human salvation (e.g., Jn 3:16; 15:23; Rom 5:8; 8:3; Heb 1:1–2). Paul's letters, in particular, testify to the powerful presence of divine love at the heart of the new community created by God's love (e.g., Rom 5:5) and summoned to conform to God's love (e.g., 1 Cor 12:31–14:1). The apostle reaches for the image of marriage when recalling the community's graced and loving union with Christ (2 Cor 11:2). Revelation portrays the final stage of redemption as God "dwelling with" human beings (Rv 21:3). A compassionate love for wounded humanity provides the reason why Jesus "has come" to be with the sick and sinful (e.g., Mk 2:17). Both here and hereafter this unifying, redemptive love of God does not entail an annihilating dissolving of oneself into God; such an outcome could never be dignified with the name of love. Human union with God reflects infinitesimally the way the three persons of the trinity give themselves to each other in selfless, living communion but do not lose themselves in one another.

"Knowledge" and "eternity" evoke two further properties of love which leave their imprint on the divine drama of redemption. A modern prejudice holds that love distorts reality, inevitably prevents lovers from understanding the beloved's reality, is essentially deceptive, and necessarily produces false idealizations based on fantasy. In *A Midsummer Night's Dream* Shakespeare presents love as fostering illusions, seeing beauty that is not there, and leading us away from the real world. At the start of the final act, when Theseus equates lovers with poets *and madmen* one is left wondering what the "seething brains" of lovers can apprehend of reality. In a later play *(As You Like It)* Shakespeare has Rosalind dismiss love for being "merely a madness" (3.2.420). One might entertain such a comment on the split between the intellect and passionate, romantic love. But otherwise it seems a rather befuddled view of things, a view that runs clean contrary to the link that John's Gospel, Augustine, Bernard of Clairvaux, William of Saint Thierry, and many others have recognized between knowing and loving. His special love allows the beloved disciple to leap to the truth about the resurrection (Jn 20:8) and to identify the mysterious stranger on the beach at dawn (Jn 21:7). "Show me a lover and he will understand,"[15] exclaimed Augustine. In *The Nature and Dignity of Love* William of Saint Thierry championed the role of love as enlightening reason and making reality intelligible (e.g., 15, 21). The eyes of love let us see,[16] whereas the eyes of hatred are sure to lead us astray. It is hatred rather than love that is blind. Love between persons opens the way to knowledge, and recognizes the real values in the beloved, even if it may disapprove of some deficient characteristics. The loving father in the parable of the prodigal son is only too painfully aware of the sinful situation of his younger boy but love makes him also aware of his potentiality for growth—a point lost on the elder son who can see nothing good in his sibling. Jesus' parable not only evokes the truth seen by the merciful eyes of divine love but also rings true in common human experience. Those who love perceive the meaning and truth in people and things; love enables us to see meaning and catch sight of truth. In love God knows what we can become through the grace bestowed on us, just as Jesus' love saw the goodness of the rich young man and the further greatness into which he might grow (Mk 10:17–22).

This same redemptive love is not short-lived, but eternally faithful—our eighth point. In *Twelfth Night* and elsewhere Shakespeare represents love as being subject to "devouring time" which brings decay and death to everything. Yet popular sayings (e.g., "Diamonds are forever") and popular songs (e.g., Irving Berlin's "I'll Be Loving You Always") acknowledge that love is a long-term pledge and a lifetime commitment, or it is nothing. The lover cherishes and is unconditionally committed to the beloved, come what may. The details of this commitment cannot be spelled out in advance, but the lover is prepared to cherish the beloved, whatever the future brings. The Song of Songs claims that not even the strongest forces of nature can quench love (Sg 8:6–7). Gabriel Marcel sees love as maintaining that not even death itself can take away the beloved: "To love someone is, in effect, to say 'You will not die.'"[17] In his own way Plato appreciated how love may not be qualified by temporal limitation. In the final section of the *Symposium* Diotima declares: "Love is the desire for the *perpetual* possession of the good" (206a; italics ours). The OT repeatedly testifies to the divine fidelity toward the people who have been loved and chosen. Christ's love, manifested supremely on the cross, continues forever in his heavenly intercession (e.g., Rom 8:34, 35, 37). The loving union through which he became "the bread of God" (Jn 6:26–58, at 33) will bring nothing less than "eternal life"; whoever is open to this union "will live forever" (Jn 6:27, 40, 47, 51, 54, 58). Here and elsewhere (e.g., Mt 25:46) the NT promises that God's redemptive love will embody what authentic human love cherishes as its ideal: consistent, eternal fidelity and permanent union.

Finally, two further features of love call for some attention: the desire-dimension of love and the status of those who love each other. As yearning desire, *amor concupiscentiae,* or *erōs,* love seeks fulfillment and longs to possess forever what is supremely beautiful and good.[18] Plato's view had an enormous influence on Western views of love and is preserved in Augustine's understanding of love as the longing for ultimate happiness, which will consist in enjoying forever the infinitely true, beautiful, and good God. We need God, and only God will fill our hearts in every way we can possibly desire. As Augustine addresses God, "Our hearts were made for you and will not rest until they rest in you."[19] This leaves us with the questions: Is human love finally reducible to the desire to know, love, and "possess" God and be "possessed" by God? *Pace* St. Paul, is our love self-enhancing, or even should it be, and does it seek the things that are ultimately to our own advantage (1 Cor 13:5)? Is love really a one-way street, with God as the supreme, all-powerful, and self-sufficient Good who "moves the sun and the other stars,"[20] rouses the deepest desires of the human heart, and draws us all home to the utterly worthwhile happiness of the face-to-face vision of the tripersonal deity? The truth is rather that even here the receiving and giving of love obtains: when "the perfect comes" (1 Cor 13:10), human *erōs* will receive what it desires from God but in *agapē* human beings will praise and worship God with unconditional love and obedience forever. Eternal enjoyment of God will coincide with an eternal glorifying of God. *Erōs* and *agapē,* need-love and gift-love, will be totally reconciled forever in a give-and-take relationship of loving and being loved as *agapē* gives and *erōs* takes.

Before leaving the *erōs/agapē* issue, something has to be added about God. We need God, need to be loved by God, and need to find in God our greatest and utterly fulfilling treasure. We experience God's *agapē* or pure gift-love toward us. Can one also speak of the divine *erōs* toward us? Or is divine love totally and simply a perfect, outgoing "self-sacrificing" *agapē* that spontaneously gives but never acquires? God desires our love, loyalty, and worship (see Hosea passim), knowing that our loving worship is supremely to our advantage. But does God need our love? Is there even here a reciprocal need? The incarnation suggests a qualified yes. By assuming a human existence, the Son of God deigned to need our love, to long for intimacy, and to need to be needed by other persons. His life and ministry among us repeatedly exemplified these needs: for tender care and nourishment from Mary and Joseph, for loving responses when he called people to discipleship (e.g., Mk 1:16–20), for material support (Lk 8:1–3), for loving service (Lk 7:36–50), for a penitent response from Jerusalem (Lk 13:34–35), for consolation on the eve of his death (Mk 14:32–42), and—in short— for loving solidarity toward him in his mission. This need for love signifies a real, non-Docetic incarnation. If the Son of God merely appeared among us without assuming an authentic human existence (as Docetists of various kinds have claimed), he would not have needed or even have been able to receive our love. Christ's "need-love" should figure in any non-Docetic account of the incarnation.

Does this need for our love disappear with Christ's resurrection and exaltation? Not so, since (as should be argued) his history and humanity rise with him. The glorified humanity of Christ remains eternally relevant for our full and final redemption; among other things that means that the risen Christ has gathered up the love he has received and eternally needs our love. Some sense of this comes through the image of the glorified Christ's marriage to the community of the redeemed (Eph 5:25; Rv 21–22). Mutual love, as both gift-love and need-love, will remain forever, transformed by the resurrection from the dead. This claim automatically raises the question: If his "need-love" rose with him, what of his sufferings? Did they also rise with him? Does he remain eternally the "Man of Sorrows," needing comfort in his pain? He rose as one whose human history had been shaped (in part) by need for our love and by the sufferings we brought on him before he was gloriously transformed. What was "given" to be so transformed was a human life of (among other things) need and suffering. It was *that* life which God's love re-created and transfigured. Hence we believe ourselves justified in holding that Christ's need-love and suffering rose with him and for all eternity will affect our relationship to him as the One through whom final salvation comes.

Our ninth point grappled with the challenge of reconciling *erōs* and *agapē* in the loving drama of human redemption. The challenge emerges from the unequal status of those who reciprocally love each other: the all-perfect God and very limited human beings. Does such inequality and lack of affinity rule out love? After all, popular wisdom declares that "birds of a feather flock together." When Aristotle called a friend "a second self," he supposed that we recognize friends as kindred souls, substantially like ourselves and equal to ourselves.[21] How can this situation be verified between the tripersonal God and created human persons? A fundamental abyss—what Kierkegaard called "an infinite qualitative difference"—separates even rational creatures from God. Nevertheless, despite the infinite difference, God did make men and women in the divine image and likeness (Gn 1:27). Redemption entails dwelling with God (e.g., Jn 14:23), receiving the gift of the Holy Spirit (e.g., Rom 5:5), and becoming, to the extent that this is possible, "partakers of the divine nature" (2 Pt 1:4). By making and remaking us in the divine image, God enables mutual friendship to take place. Through the Holy Spirit we are empowered to replicate the Son's loving relationship with the Father. God can look upon us in friendship and see in us "other selves." God wants to love us. Any divine likeness that we manifest does not as such fully account for and explain, let alone merit or necessitate, God's love for us. Nevertheless, without at least a minimal divine likeness bestowed on us, God's love for us would seem strangely unfounded and unmotivated.

Such then are the ten points that we would draw from a philosophy of love and transform when appropriating the scriptures to reflect theologically on how divine redemption primarily expresses itself and operates. We understand love to entail joyful approval, active concern for others, freedom, vulnerability, reciprocity, union, knowledge, eternal fidelity, a reconciliation between *erōs* and *agapē,* and that likeness which enables love to occur. Such clarification from philosophy is vital if one is going to produce a biblically based account of salvation in the key of love. Here, as much as anywhere, philosophy performs its ministry to theology. Our final principle (inculturation) must also be applied in some detail.

Inculturation

How might we inculturate the biblical testimony about God's universal redemptive love effectively revealed in Jesus Christ? The task calls for real courage in facing two challenges, the first being the destructive hatred and pervasive evil that the divine love overcomes.

In "On Not Neglecting Hatred" we reflected on the curious reluctance of theologians (and many philosophers) to address the ugly but very real theme of hatred.[22] Government agencies, lawyers, social workers, and others gather statistics on hate crimes, and struggle to develop strategies for curbing irrational, destructive violence. The daily press constantly reports episodes of cruel hatred that strike individuals, ethnic and religious groups, and even whole nations. Genocidal hatred flourishes somewhere in almost every continent. Any library search will turn up books with such titles as *Free to Hate, The Tyranny of Hate, The Hate Virus, Hate on Trial, Hate Mail, The Masks of Hate,* and *Bigotry, Prejudice and Hatred.* Nevertheless, modern theologians, including the very great ones, have by and large ignored the theme of hatred that daily experience must constantly confront. Without dealing with hatred, theologians can hardly expect to inculturate very convincingly the biblical message of God's saving love. The coming of Christ meant salvation from hatred (Lk 1:71) and victory over it (Lk 6:22–23, 27–29). The opposition between love and hate plays a key role in Johannine theology, with its series of symbolic polarities. Whoever does evil hates the (divine) light and refuses to "come to the light" (Jn 3:20) that brings life. The (evil) world hates Jesus (Jn 7:7; 15:18), God (Jn 15:23–24), and the disciples (Jn 15:18; 17:14); it will not enter the sphere of light, love, and life. In the Middle Ages Thomas Aquinas drew partly on Aristotle to develop a treatise on the emotions or "passiones animae" in the *Prima Secundae* of his *Summa Theologiae.* He associated love with hatred as its contrary, while examining both dispositions. In the

Secunda Secundae, while considering the vices opposed to love, Aquinas spent question 34 (six articles) discussing the sinfulness of hatred—appealing to the scriptures and the Fathers rather more than to Aristotle. Centuries after Aquinas "related" love to hatred and angry aggression, Melanie Klein (1882–1960), in pioneering the psychoanalysis of children, developed ideas about the struggle between love and hate.[23] The example of the NT, Aquinas, Klein, and many others who work in therapy and education should encourage a robust realism among theologians. In translating the biblical message of love into contemporary language, they must face up to the enormous sufferings that hatred, fueled by greed and fear, continues to inflict on our world.

To announce that the love of Christ saves and unites the whole world rings false if we refuse to acknowledge the pain that hatred has inflicted on the living and the dead. Even less than other teachers and leaders, theologians should not, of course, be promoting historical bitterness and spurring on their audiences to relive hatred and let it define them. At the same time, to suppress bitter memories and ignore the massive presence of hatred robs theologians of their credibility, even if they want to join Dante and other great voices in the Christian tradition in proclaiming the divine love as the universal force of redemptive union. The *Divine Comedy* celebrated that love effectively because it also unflinchingly looked at the world of hatred and evil. A few decades earlier Thomas Aquinas did not fail to put hatred and evil into sharp focus, and so could argue believably that love is stronger than hatred, just as the good is stronger than evil.[24] Primarily, sin is not guilt to be expiated, a state of corruption to be wiped out, or oppression to be overcome; rather it is an unloving alienation from God, a hatred toward God and others that requires the reconciling intervention of divine love.

A second great challenge for theologians who seek to express God's redemptive love at work in Christ comes from those like John Hick who sponsor "democratic" views of the divine goodness. The Sermon on the Mount pictures God as indiscriminately good, benevolent toward all, and guaranteeing to all the essentials of life (Mt 5:45). If God has no favorites, how can one maintain any special, redemptive self-communication of God in Christ? As Hick says in *The Metaphor of God Incarnate* (London: SCM Press, 1993), such a claim seems "incompatible with a universal divine love" (159). J. J. Rousseau made a similar point more than two centuries ago in *Émile.*[25] But, in the matter of salvation, must God behave in an equal, "democratic" way toward all people? The parable about the laborers in the vineyard (Mt 20:1–15) and Paul's reflections on Israel and the Gentiles in the divine plan (Rom 9–11) suggest otherwise. Interfaith dialogue has led Hick to decry any talk about "an important religious advantage to a person's being a Christian" (158); such talk seems to him an unwarranted claim to a head start in the matter of salvation. He never reckons, as far as we can see in *The Metaphor of God Incarnate,* with Christian faith in Jesus (and the salvation he has brought for all) entailing an awesome religious responsibility to announce and live up to this uniquely good message. The debate with Hick, Rousseau, and others touches also the nature of love and, in particular, our seventh point above. Good human beings love others differently because they know them to be different. *A fortiori,* God loves all people and loves them all differently, because the "eyes" of divine love know them to be incomparably different. Those who ascribe an "equal," "democratic" love to God forget that love cannot be measured and qualified as being "more" or "less," "equal" or "unequal." The relationship of love between two particular persons is simply incommensurable with any other loving relationship. Once again, this is true *a fortiori* of the loving divine relationship between God and any human being. Hick and his predecessors have created an important challenge for those bent on translating into contemporary terms the biblical message of redemption. The appropriate response is to ponder the nature of God's unconditional and inclusive *agapē,* not to belittle the unique, definitive, and effective disclosure of that love in Jesus Christ.

This chapter has applied our ten principles to the *redemption* effected by Christ, paying particular attention to the relevance of the ninth and tenth principles. We have put the scriptural case for describing salvation primarily in terms of love. Just as all commands are summed up by love (Gal 5:14; Rom 13:8–10), so the divine love "sums up" best and draws together what is to be said about *how* redemption primarily operates (and, for that matter, why it occurs). The previous chapter and coming chapters illustrate the importance of philosophy in moving from the scriptures to systematic theology. But on the issue of the "how" of redemption, philosophical analysis (principle nine) enjoys a special importance in negotiating the passage from the Bible to theology.

Rereading our attempt to set out and inculturate a workable philosophy of love so as to facilitate some insights into the functioning (and motivation) of God's redemptive love has made us more aware than ever of the complex, multifaceted, and inexhaustibly mysterious nature of human and *a fortiori* divine love. In and through their experience of redemption the first Christians knew God to be love (1 Jn 4:8, 16). But how should we best interpret and articulate this biblical truth at the end of the twentieth century? We draw encouragement from the classical struggles with our theme that we find in the poetry and sermons of John Donne (1571/2–1631). Retreating from the unstable world around him, he longed to fashion with his wife a "little world" of perfect love that would boldly assert its immortality: "all other things to their destination draw, only our love hath no decay."[26] Then Donne found a new center in Christ's love which has transfigured our fragile, mortal world and can be experienced as that fullness and life that satisfies all our yearning for union with "the other."

Where Donne drew some of his most striking images from introspection, the love-literature of the Middle Ages with its public world of idealized chivalry provided courtly commonplaces for depicting and honoring the heroic, extravagant love of the redeeming Christ. The intense feeling of love-poetry illuminated the message of the divine love at work through Christ, the knight-lover *par excellence*. Love songs like "Love me brought" were put in the mouth of Christ to express what he had been about as Savior. Another love song, known by its refrain *quia amore langueo* ("because I faint with love"), blends the Song of Songs with medieval images of Christ-the-Lover. He speaks as the lover who constantly seeks and will suffer any pain in the hope of being finally united with his beloved.[27] Christians have never articulated more exquisitely their faith in the redeeming love of God efficaciously revealed through Christ. In our troubled, postmodern society, however, it may be too much to hope that we could retrieve the delicate intensity of the Middle Ages. John Donne may serve as a more efficacious model for those who seek to translate the biblical message of God's redemptive love into contemporary idioms.

4

Father, Son, and Holy Spirit

We are bound to be baptized in the terms we have received and to profess belief in the terms in which we are baptized, and as we have professed faith in, so to give glory to the Father, Son, and Holy Spirit.

—St. Basil, *Epistle* 125.3

Having tested in Christology the worth of our ten principles as steering mechanisms in the move from the scriptures to systematic theology, we turn now to the doctrine of the trinity. What if we bring those principles to bear on current proposals for renaming the Godhead as, for instance, "Source, Word, and Spirit," "Creator, Redeemer, and Sanctifier," "Creator, Liberator, and Comforter," "Creator, Redeemer, and Sustainer," "God, Christ, and Spirit," "The Creator, the Christ, and the Spirit," "Parent, Child, and Paraclete," "Mother, Daughter, and Spirit," "Mother, Lover, and Friend," "Spirit-Sophia, Jesus-Sophia, and Mother-Sophia," "Father, Child, and Mother," or "Mother/Father, Child, and Paraclete?" All of these proposals avoid the masculine name of "Son" for the second person of the trinity, and all but the last two avoid talking of "the Father."

With terms for sovereignty now often played down in many cultures, such names for God as "Lord," "King," and "Ruler" seem threatened. In any case, pressure for inclusive God-language would rule out the first two names as irreducibly masculine. What future should the more personal, more intimate, but gender-specific name of "Father" enjoy? Has the language of divine Fatherhood, by fostering a male-related image of God, legitimated male domination, underpinned the power structure of patriarchal religion, supported idolatrous androcentrism, helped to produce a false fixing of roles between the sexes, and proved a major (if not the major) cause of women being oppressed and excluded in the Western world (and beyond)? Can we assume that in the biblical traditions about God "Father" necessarily presupposed an antiwoman social orientation? Can or should we rename God as "the God of Sarah, Rebecca, and Rachel," or even as "She Who Is"? Should "Father" be abandoned, because calling God by that name inevitably encourages sexist disvalues and chauvinist attitudes? Was the predominantly "Father-language" historically appropriate (or, given the religious and social structures of the time, simply inevitable)[1] in Jesus' ministry and the time of the early church, but this is no longer the case now? Do we need a Nietzschean shaking of the foundations, a kind of linguistic death of God, as "the Father" and its correlative, "the Son," are expunged from Christian liturgy and teaching? Or is this proposal partially or even largely another case of wanting to be "on the side of history"—that is to say, to jump onto the latest, popular bandwagon? Let us try to *listen* to what is being said, but without abandoning critical evaluation and leaping into mere credulity.

The Case for Change

While recognizing that the biblical language for God is predominantly masculine (e.g., "King," "Husband,"and "Father"), even if not completely so (e.g., "Rock," "Shield," and "Fortress"), many writers have urged the need to hear all the scriptures (our principle one) and to respect the feminine terminology applied to God by the OT, Jesus himself, Paul, and other NT writers. Second Isaiah compares God's interventions in history to a woman crying out in labor (Is 42:14; see 45:10), insists that the divine love for Israel surpasses even that of a mother for her child (Is 49:15), and portrays God as comforting the people in the way a mother comforts her child (Is 66:13). God is seen as the midwife in the rebirth of Jerusalem (Is 66:9; see Ps 22:9–10). The psalmist likens a group praying for deliverance to servants utterly attentive to their master *and mistress:* "As the eyes of servants look to the hand of their master, as the eyes of a maid to the hand of her mistress, so our eyes look to the Lord our God" (Ps 123:2). Jesus himself compares God's saving activity to a woman searching for lost money (Lk 15:8–10) or baking bread (Lk 13:20–21 = Mt 13:33). By applying to God such feminine images, Jesus showed that he never intends to depict God in exclusively masculine terms. Conscious of the authority bestowed on him by God the Father (Gal 1:1, 15), Paul, nevertheless, interprets his ministry in a motherly (Gal 4:19; 1 Thes 2:7–8) as well as a fatherly (1 Cor 4:15) fashion. John's Gospel pictures "the hour" of Christ's death and resurrection as birth pangs (Jn 16:21; 17:1) and the piercing of his body in a feminine way (Jn 7:37–39; 19:34)—as some medieval Christians appreciated.[2] Reclaiming biblical (and traditional) feminine language for God also entails recognizing the Holy Spirit's mothering role (Jn 3:6; see 1:12–13; 1 Jn 4:7). Thus attention to the full scope of the NT (and the tradition) shows that all three persons of the trinity are depicted through feminine as well as masculine imagery, and that Israel's God was not portrayed in exclusively masculine terminology.

The case "against" the Father image might appeal to our second (innovative hearing), sixth, and eighth principles. The sustaining and sheltering wings of a mother eagle provided a recurrent metatheme in the OT for representing the divine activity (e.g., Dt 32:11–12; Pss 17:8; 36:7; 57:1; 61:4; 63:7; 91:4).[3] Jesus took up this image but gave it a homely twist when he spoke of himself as being like a hen gathering her chickens under her wings (Mt 23:37 = Lk 13:34). The eschatological provisionality of the biblical language and revelation (principle eight) can also be pressed into service. In some ways both the OT and the NT opposed prevailing patterns in the male-dominated societies of the ancient Middle East. The Ten Commandments inculcated equal honor for mothers and fathers (Ex 20:12; Dt 5:16). Jesus broke with tradition and prevailing standards by including women among his disciples and in his entourage (Lk 8:1–3), opposing divorce (Mk 10:2–12 par.), and repeatedly showing his sympathetic regard for women (e.g., Mk 12:41–44; 14:3–9). There is no trace of misogynism in Jesus' mission and message. Even so the patriarchal structure of his culture left him little choice but to invoke and picture God as "Father" but never as "Mother."[4] While Jesus knew God to be the personal, loving, intimate God *par excellence,* "Father" or "Abba" was the only practical way for him to say that. In brief, the choice—it is argued—was at least partly conditioned by the contemporary culture and remains open to revision. To innovate (principle two) and call God "Mother" would not seem to be alien to what Jesus intended.[5] The content of his message about God can be separated from its container, the dispensable male-related image of God the Father.

The revisionary proposal also claims help from philosophy (principle nine). The attributes of the Absolute Being exclude bodiliness and the specific limitations of human sexuality; God is beyond gender, quite beyond maleness and femaleness. The scriptures speak of God in fatherly and motherly terms. To the extent, however, that we hearken to philosophers who stress that God in all respects is ultimately unknown and unknowable, feminine language will do just as adequately, or rather just as inadequately, to refer to and represent what we mean by "God."

It is, however, probably inculturation (principle ten) that presses most for a revisionary "translation" of the NT language about God as Father. Here we must juggle with a vast amount of material from psychology, cultural anthropology, history, and other disciplines, as well as facing central questions for which unqualified, clear-cut answers are hardly available. Does "Father" necessarily evoke a masculine image for God that inevitably reinforces male dominance and devalues women? Is "God the Father" inevitably used to justify social domination by men and the subjugation of women? Or can cultures and peoples that have female God-images prove no less androcentric, so that the inferior status and oppressive treatment of women seem largely unconnected with any dominant use of masculine image for the divine? Is Rosemary Ruether, who has to recognize the fact that "not all patriarchal societies have male monotheist religions," correct in her assertion that "in those patriarchal societies which have this view of God, the God-image serves as the central reinforcement of the structure of patriarchal rule"?[6] What has been clear for several decades in the Western world is the alienation many (how many?) women feel from the onesidedly masculine references to God that have characterized the Judeo-Christian tradition (as opposed to the Judeo-Christian scriptures). They have sent scholars back to Gn 1:27 and its obvious implication: the male Adam is no more godlike than the female Eve; he has no special advantage as an image of God. While biologically and perhaps psychologically different, women do not form a second (inferior) human nature and are equally reflective and representative of God. Talk of differences raises, of course, difficult questions. How far are the nonbiological differences between men and women also due to culture and nurture and not simply to nature? What is specifically masculine and feminine or specifically fatherly and motherly? What do people mean when they speak of a "fatherly mother" and a "motherly father"? Do women *qua* women experience God in a distinct way?[7] In her *She Who Is* (New York: Crossroad, 1992) Elizabeth A. Johnson writes of women's "love of connectedness" (62; see 252–53), "solidarity with each other" (63), "capacity to exercise moral agency" (67), "ways of knowing," "loving" (68) and "being in the world" (69; see 253). But is she talking of "the female reality" (56) as such, or is she rather naming some of the noblest features of the *human* reality as such?

Inculturation of biblical language always calls for sensitivity to current experience. Naming God as "Father" in the Western world (and often elsewhere) happens today in a situation in which the instability of marriage prevents many families from being places of genuine security and care. Fathers (and mothers) betray their children, who experience themselves as fatherless (and motherless). Or else many fathers stay with their families but prove themselves to be strict and punishing, self-ish and uncaring, weak and incapable, even ready to abuse sexually their children, especially their daughters. In such circumstances how often does relating to God as "Father" express an unsatisfied yearning to experience an "omnipotent" father who will provide unqualified love and security? Or, to switch the question in another direction, how believable for many damaged and deprived men and women today is the proclamation of God as the only almighty, all-wise, all-just, and all-loving Father?

Keeping "God the Father"

Sheer abundance characterizes identification of God as "Father" in the NT: 254 clear references and 4 doubtful cases. John's Gospel calls God "Father" 118 times (with 2 uncertain further cases); Matthew's Gospel does so 41 times (also with 2 uncertain further cases). In all, the four Gospels contain 181 certain references to God as "Father." God is only once called "Creator" in the NT (1 Pt 4:19), although the work of creation (and new creation) is referred to through a verb *(ktizō)* 15 times and a noun *(ktisis, ktisma,* or *poiēma)* 26 times. This language of foundational Christianity recorded by the scriptures must be heard (principle one), interpreted, and not eliminated. Matthew's Gospel ends with the command to baptize "in the name of the Father, and of the Son, and of the Holy Spirit" (Mt 28:19), a point of arrival for the NT that becomes a point of departure for the creeds which will take their structure around the confession of faith in the Father, the Son, and the Holy Spirit. Naming "God the Father" forges an essential link between the NT and the church's ancient rules of faith that in their turn provide the major frame of reference for interpreting and appropriating the scriptures (principle three). The creeds and, even more broadly, the witnesses of the church's liturgies (the *lex orandi*) constantly praise and confess God as "Father, Son, and Holy Spirit." The creeds have proved central in the Spirit-assisted transmission of God's self-revelation in Jesus Christ. Undoubtedly one should treasure the feminine imagery for God and Christ endorsed by Anselm, Bernard, and other medieval writers (above all, Julian of Norwich). They remind us forcefully not only that we should go beyond exclusively masculine references to God but also, as we shall point out, that there is a metaphorical, "as" quality to naming God "Father." At the same time, however, the voices of the NT scriptures and Christian tradition harmonize in promoting "Father, Son, and Holy Spirit" as the primary way of speaking about the tripersonal God. Here, if anywhere, the scriptures and tradition work authoritatively together because the Holy Spirit is in both.

Some who agree that Jesus did speak to and about God as "Father" minimize the normative significance of this. Thus Elizabeth A. Johnson calls this only "one particular motif from among the many other things the Gospels depict Jesus saying and doing" (*She Who Is,* 79). Not having enjoyed "exclusive centrality" in Jesus' speech about God, the paternal metaphor is not to be granted "sole right" and be singled out "for absolute emulation" (79, 81). Here one should recall that this metaphor was not "exclusive" in Jesus' speech about God. To observe the obvious, Jesus at times spoke of God as "God" (Mk 12:17, 24), "Lord" (Mk 12:29–30), or as "the God of Abraham, Isaac, and Jacob" (Mk 12:26). Who has claimed or is claiming that "Father" should have "sole rights"? Johnson's unsupported accusations echo those made by McFague, to which we come later in this chapter. Here let us simply note two points. First, Johnson passes over important pieces of evidence (e.g., Rom 8:15; Gal 4:6) about the distinctive prominence of the paternal metaphor among early Christians and in their prayer-life,[8] a prominence stemming from Jesus himself. Raymond Brown endorses John Meier's assessment: "One is justified in claiming that Jesus' striking use of *Abba* did express his intimate experience of God as his own father and that this usage did make a lasting impression on his disciples."[9]

Second, in the course of her book Johnson at times detects an implicit premise in positions she opposes. Could such an implicit premise be at work in her argument—namely, the notion that whatever was not used abundantly "by the actual Jesus who lived" can be considered nonnormative, merely "a matter of theological development in the early church" (81)? This would be to join many others, both liberal and conservative, who maintain or more often presuppose that God's authoritative revelation stopped with the life and death of Jesus, and that what we hear from the pre-Pauline tradition, Paul, the evangelists, and other NT witnesses can be qualified (or even written off) as simply their developing theology. Nearly one hundred pages later in her book Johnson refers to the "biblical narratives of origin" (= the NT) that show Christian life to be "unthinkable apart from the presence and activity" of the Holy Spirit (141) and the "Spirit poured out on the circle of disciples" (158). She recognizes that the original "Christian experience of faith" was "the generating matrix for language about God as triune"; the NT's stories, narratives, and doxologies record "threefold symbols of God that arose spontaneously out of Christian existence" (198). All of this positive appraisal of the Holy Spirit's impact on the life, language, and symbols of God raises some questions: Did that activity of the Spirit at the origins of Christianity (= in the apostolic age) *also* convey normative revelation about God? (Primarily, but not exclusively, the threefold symbols of God took the form of "Father, Son, and [Holy] Spirit.") Was the Holy Spirit, without whom Christian life is "unthinkable," authoritatively active in generating that language about God?

After the NT period, Origen goes too far in proscribing any nonbiblical names for God: "The Supreme God ought not to be invoked by any name except those used by Moses, the prophets, and our Savior and Lord himself" (*Mart.* 46). What comes through clearly, however, is the centrality of the Father/Son relationship for Origen's successors, the post-Nicene writers. Their faith in Jesus as Son of God coincides with their faith in God as Father. Their respect for God *in se* (as Father/Son) takes precedence over their respect for God *pro nobis* (as Creator and Savior). Thus St. Athanasius insists that it would be "more devout and accurate" to approach God as Father through the Son "than to name

God from his works" (*Contra Arianos* 1.34). The inner-trinitarian relation of Father/Son "precedes" any relationship God has to us. St. Hilary of Poitiers calls "the very center of a saving faith" the belief "not merely in God, but in God as Father, and not merely in Christ, but in Christ as the Son of God" (*De Trinitate* 1.17).[10]

The convergence (principle four) of the OT and NT witness allows evidence to accumulate in support of naming God as "Father." Unlike pagan deities who were understood to become, through a kind of natural procreation or biological parenting, fathers (or mothers) to various peoples, Yahweh became "Father" to Israel through a free choice in history that delivered the suffering people and gave them a new, covenanted existence. Fatherhood was a metaphor for God's historical relationship to the people. On their side, this liberating election summoned the people to a life of fidelity as sons and daughters toward Yahweh, their "Father" (e.g., Jer 3:19–20; Hos 11:1; Mal 2:10). Jesus took this personal name for the biblical God and elaborated it in his own distinctive way, addressing and speaking to others about God normally as "Father." Jesus used an intimate, colloquial term (even if it was not simply children's talk) when he called God "Abba" in his own prayer (e.g., Mk 14:36). He apparently used the term frequently in his teaching.[11] Far from being One whose supreme quality is power and whose only concern is to dominate, the compassionate "Father" of whom Jesus spoke knows our needs before we ask (Mt 6:8; 7:11), cares for all (Mt 6:25–33), and forgives all, even the wickedly unjust and sinful (e.g., Mt 5:43–48; Lk 15:11–32). Jesus' Father-image subverted any oppressive, patriarchal notions of God as primarily or even exclusively an authoritarian figure. As the Son, Jesus disclosed the Father; the revelation of God's fatherhood was intimately bound up with the revelation of Jesus' unique sonship (e.g., Mt 11:27 = Lk 10:22)—a theme that was to be massively developed in John's Gospel. Drawing together the rather scattered OT references to Yahweh's "sons" (and "daughters") and the even fewer places where the OT names God as "Father," we could trace a progress and enriching of this language in the NT and defend here the existence of a biblical metatheme (principle six). This particular metatheme is given by God and not simply fashioned by human beings. The knowledge of God as Father comes through prophetic revelation and, above all, through the mediation of Jesus himself when he calls God "Father."

Our first chapter showed how we can likewise look upon the case of Father-language for God as an outstanding example of continuity between the somewhat discontinuous situations of Jesus and Paul (principle seven). But more should be added here. When risen from the dead and gloriously transformed, Jesus remained a first-century Jew; the once-and-for-all particularity of his entire embodied history was transformed, not annihilated. In a particular way that was integral to the revelation brought, he had constantly approached and preached God as loving "Father." This central relationship of Jesus' life and ministry rose with him, even as his whole earthly history was raised with him. His revelation of the ultimate divine reality as the Father to whom he stood in a unique relationship as the Son was vindicated and lived again in a new, transformed fashion. To be baptized into the risen Christ (e.g., Gal 3:27) and to live "in Christ" (e.g., Phil 3:9) means being incorporated into One who is personally and uniquely related to God as "Father." In other words baptism entails becoming "in the Son" adopted sons and daughters of God the Father, praying to God as "Abba" (Rom 8:15; Gal 4:6), and joining together in confessing the God of Israel to be not a Father in general, but, quite specifically, the Father of our Lord Jesus Christ. Jesus related to God as his Father; the crucifixion and resurrection enabled the baptized to replicate through grace this relationship by participating through the Holy Spirit in the Son's vital knowledge of the Father. Thus the personal language of "Father, Son, and Holy Spirit" is *also* participatory language in that it brings believers to share through baptism in the trinity's life. We relate to God in a threefold manner, because the persons of the trinity relate to themselves and to us in a threefold manner.

This line of argument invites the obvious question: How much of Jesus' religious history "rose with him"? He himself seems to have challenged the absolute importance of the food laws (Mk 7:14–23). But he never aimed any criticism against circumcision. Did that practice and obligation "rise with him"? Here, however, guided by the Holy Spirit the early church and its leaders acknowledge a radical discontinuity: the death and resurrection had abrogated the necessity of such an obligation of the Law. In the case of naming, relating to, and praising God as "Father," Paul, John, and others remained in rock-hard continuity with the message and practice of Jesus. He had lived his life in a profound relationship to the Father; the crucifixion and resurrection (with the outpouring of the Holy Spirit) made Jesus the eldest Son of the Father's new eschatological family (Rom 8:29), a family now empowered to share intimately in Jesus' relationship to the Father in the Spirit.

Our ninth principle leads us to several philosophical questions, in particular: How does "Father" function as a metaphor for God? Is it adequate for naming and describing God? First and foremost, let us insist that metaphors refer to and describe reality. Unlike ordinary literal utterances that refer directly to things and use terms in their primary meanings, in the case of metaphors we "speak about one thing in terms which are seen to be suggestive of another."[12] Metaphors use and build on literal utterances and literal meanings but go beyond them, at times saying things that can be said only in metaphor. Metaphors constitute a different, comparative, more vivid, and often much more effective strategy for depicting reality, contributing to our knowledge of things, stating the truth, and changing or even transforming a situation. Hence we set our faces against the slipshod talk of "only a metaphor" and "merely metaphorical" which even theologians can indulge. They make it sound as if those more in touch with the real can dispense with metaphors, or at least as if plain, literal prose has a clear-cut advantage over metaphorical language. Our high respect for metaphors entails rejecting the notion that direct, literal discourse can or even regularly should replace metaphorical discourse. Metaphors are not amenable to being literally paraphrased in an exact and exhaustive manner. At best the propositional content of metaphors can be partially restated in literal terms. Furthermore, we challenge any suggestion that one metaphor can regularly replace another without changing or losing the meaning. Switching metaphors will normally mean saying something different; in that sense one metaphor is not as good as another. Metaphors are much more than dispensable containers that can be separated at will from their meaningful content. This is especially true of root or master metaphors, which we develop in a sustained and systematic way. Lastly, literalizing metaphors or taking metaphors as if they were literal utterances may be a common enough practice, but it always misreads and misrepresents what metaphors aim at communicating. The practice turns the connotations of a metaphor into its denotations, focuses attention on the image it uses rather than on the subject matter it illuminates, and slips over the "as quality" of metaphorical speech.

To return to God, let us recall that all of our speech about God is analogical, whether we talk literally (e.g., "God is good and faithful")[13] or metaphorically (e.g., "God is the Father of Jesus Christ"). In the latter case we are not delivering ourselves of a simile that states a resemblance (e.g., "God *is like* a woman giving birth to a child") but using a metaphor to depict a relationship, state an identity, and refer to the way God really is ("God *is* the Father of Jesus Christ"). The principle of analogy highlights the differences built into the metaphor: unlike literal, human fatherhood, the eternal begetting of the Son did not entail any temporally prior existence of the Father, any temporally subsequent existence of the Son, any causation, any cooperation of a second parent (the mother), and any bodily action. At the same time, the first person of the trinity reveals authentic fatherhood by "acting as" Father within the immanent life of the tripersonal God and in the created world of human history. He relates in eternity and time as the life-giving, nurturing, and infinitely trustworthy Father toward the Son and those who through the Spirit find faith and life "in" the Son. This case wonderfully exemplifies what William Alston says about metaphor in general: the speaker presents the literal model "as a source of hitherto unnoticed insights into the nature of the subject."[14] Here Jesus and subsequent speakers present the literal model of ideal human fatherhood as the source of hitherto unknown or unnoticed insights into the characteristics of God.

Those who find this metaphor idolatrous seem to be creating for themselves and then rejecting a "straw god," so to speak: the image of God as literally a male human being. They misread the metaphor by ignoring its "as quality" and literalizing the male imagery. Right from the start the Judeo-Christian tradition has consistently indicated that "references to God as Father do not indicate male sexuality."[15] The mistake of literalism shows up clearly when faced with the "mercy seat" representation of the crucifixion, in which the Father tenderly supports Christ's dead body and the Spirit is present under the form of a dove. Repeated for centuries by European painters and sculptors, this theme finds its most impressive rendering in El Greco's *Holy Trinity* (Prado, Madrid). It would be an absurd mistake to "literalize" the first person of the trinity as really being an elderly male gentleman and the third as really being a small bird. The meanings of the metaphor that El Greco endorsed are grounded in the history of Jesus, who lovingly and obediently called God "Father" and as risen from the dead joined the Father in sending the Holy Spirit. Besides rejecting any literalistic interpretation of the "mercy seat," we need also to take notice of the fact that not all the potential meanings in such a metaphor as "God is Father" are valid. Metaphors are symbols put into sentence form, as when the primordial symbol "father" (lowercase) becomes metaphorical in the sentence "God is our Father" (uppercase). Paul Ricoeur has classically stated that symbols give rise to thought.[16] We might well add that symbols can also give rise to the wrong thoughts and to evil, even atrociously evil, actions. The case is similar with metaphor. The metaphor, "God is Father," because it refers without defining and leaves things open to the indefinitely many meanings that belong to any great metaphor, has also left things open to pathological misuse: for instance, in the long-standing vision (or should we say cruel "nightmare"?) of God the Father furiously and implacably punishing Christ on the cross.[17] One should equally disown the opposite caricature of the Father as a powerful, authoritarian but uninvolved patriarchal God; such a meaning is also alien to the OT scriptures, Jesus' teaching, and healthy Christian tradition. El Greco's rendering of God the Father, probably the greatest of its kind in the Western world, shows us not a dominant or remote "male-God," but the "powerless" God of infinite "com-passion" who holds the crucified Jesus in his arms. The central symbol of the cross as the "mercy seat," when depicted by El Greco, Masaccio (in S. Maria Novella, Florence), and other classical artists, gives the lie to those bent on dismissing "Father-language" as inevitably representing a distant, detached "male-God." The "mercy seat" representation brings to mind another classical rendering of the postcrucifixion situation, this one based roughly on Jn 19:26–42: the "pietà" or depiction of the dead Jesus lying in his mother's arms. Here we cannot help wondering whether a high regard for Mary as one who figures forth the maternal love of God would solve many problems about God the Father.

The metaphor of God the Father functions validly when we refuse to literalize it, respect its "as quality," anchor it in history, recognize the close connection between the divine Agent's identity and the narrative, and align ourselves with the meanings communicated in that metaphor by the biblical witnesses and, in particular, by Jesus himself. It is these meanings that convey true information about God. "Father" names and, to an extent, describes God; as a proper name or, if you prefer, as a kinship term that behaves like a proper name, it is shorthand for a definite description that is more than "just" an abstract set of divine attributes, and cannot be referred to any other "deity." "Father" is uniquely the God revealed experientially in Israel's history and known relationally as the "Abba" of Jesus' life, death, and resurrection. As a central, personal metaphor it organizes our thinking about God; its reliability is guaranteed by Jesus. For Christians "Father" fixes the reference when they speak of God and what they take God to be like. Jesus' resurrection from the dead vindicated the truth of his central way of picturing and naming God, something that belonged intrinsically to his preaching of the kingdom. The image and language of "Abba" emerged from Jesus' specific experience of God. Once we agree that language and experience, while distinguishable, belong inseparably to each other, we will misrepresent Jesus' experience if we insist on replacing his central language for God. Fidelity to Jesus calls on us to name God as "Father," which entails acknowledging Jesus himself as "the Son of God." Even so, not even the metaphor of "Father" can adequately represent God: while knowable as the Father of our Lord Jesus Christ, God also remains incomprehensible. Cataphatic language must always be qualified by the *via negativa* of apophatic theology: ultimately God transcends all our knowing. When naming God as "Father," we look for a middle ground between the anthropomorphic (or androcentric?) nonsense rejected above and the sheer, Kantian-style agnosticism about God exemplified by John Hick.[18]

Finally, what does inculturation (principle ten) say to the issue in hand? When all is said and done, is "Father" a "mere" metaphor for God that may be changed at will, or at least changed for the sake of more effective inculturation and communication? May we or even should we, in the name of inclusive God-language, go so far as to suppress "Father" when renaming the tripersonal Godhead? A number of considerations tell against this move. First, "Father" has worked and continues to work as a concrete, personal name for the first person of the trinity. Such alternate proposals as "Source," "Creator," "Parent," "Wisdom," and "Absolute Being" sound remote, even impersonal and nowhere near as directly relational as "Father." Unquestionably these alternatives contain or imply personal (or at least relational) elements, and are not intended to subvert Christian belief in a personal God. But when we try using "Source," "Creator," and so forth as forms of address to God, we perceive the superiority of "Father." Some of the alternative triads (e.g., "Creator, Christ, Spirit," and, even more, "God, Christ, Spirit") have a strong Arian flavor about them, as if only the first person of the trinity possessed the divine power of creation and had in fact created Christ and the Spirit. Although it may claim some kind of NT pedigree (perhaps in Acts 3:13, 26; 4:27, 30), "Child" (as in "Parent, Child, Paraclete" and "Father, Child, Mother") puts down the second person of the trinity, as if the Son were not yet properly mature. This name also seems to reveal embarrassment over the particularity of the incarnation. A child can be either male or female, whereas in fact the Word of God became incarnate as male. Renaming the first person of the trinity "Mother" (as in "Mother, Daughter, Spirit"), besides enjoying no direct warrant in the scriptures, runs the clear risk (noted in n. 5) of feminine language for God: identifying the deity with creation, it moves toward pantheism. "God is Mother" is not on a par with the statement "God is Father." "Mother" in the form of "Mother-Sophia" enters into Elizabeth Johnson's proposed triad that otherwise uses only terms for which there is massive scriptural backing: "Spirit-Sophia, Jesus-Sophia, and Mother-Sophia" (*She Who Is,* 124–87). The order of persons (which corresponds to that of 1 Cor 12:4–6) takes us from the (present) experience of the Spirit, through the historical manifestation of Jesus, to the primordial source in the first person of the trinity. The NT and early Christianity, however, settled the order as "Father, Son, and Holy Spirit," as in Mt 28:19, the order that corresponds to the "eternal processions" within the trinity and to the "economic missions" in history. "Order," incidentally, is not synonymous with something Johnson abhors, "subordination." Here triple repetition of "Sophia" has the effect, presumably desired, of playing down the inner-trinitarian "processions" and highlighting perfect equality in trinitarian relations. We cannot help wondering about moving her proposal from theology into liturgy and opening community worship "in the name of the Spirit-Sophia, and of the Jesus-Sophia, and of the Mother-Sophia." Others have suggested introducing the hybrid "Mother/Father," but it seems like returning to a Gnostic-style, androgynous female/male deity. By naming the divine Subject (the first person of the trinity) in different ways, we are not merely updating language; we are saying something different. Exchanging metaphors entails changing and/or losing meaning, and may well change beliefs about the tripersonal God and the worship of God—as Roland Frye, Colin Gunton, and others warn.[19]

Second, "Father" functions in relationship to Jesus and to us. The name expresses our dependence on God who brings us into existence and sustains us—the God from whom we come at the beginning and to whom we go at the end. We have no choice about our existence and the way it must close in death. But puzzlement and even terror over our fragile nature and fearful destiny are taken away, because the God of our life is the infinitely loving Father of whom Jesus spoke. The name of "Father" allows us to replicate through grace the relationship at the heart of Jesus' life. Third, Jesus (and his first followers) gave Christians their foundational language for God, the revealed and root metaphor for their life, liturgy, and teaching. Fidelity to foundational revelation dictates maintaining "Father" as the central (albeit not exclusive) metaphor and proper name for the first person of the trinity. The best philosophers and non-Christian religions have something, at times much that is valuable, to say in response to the question: What is God? They can provide true orientations toward the idea of the divine and the essential attributes of God. Jesus responds rather to the question: "Who is God?" and through the power of the Spirit discloses to us the name and person of "the Father."

Fourth, a crypto-modalism comes through some of the alternate proposals we listed at the beginning of this chapter: "Creator, Liberator, and Comforter," for instance can readily suggest a rigid monotheism, a monopersonal God who behaves toward us in diversified ways as "Creator, Liberator, and Comforter," but whose internal life is simply not differentiated into three divine persons. To be sure, not even the NT names of "Father, Son, and Holy Spirit" could automatically safeguard all ancient Christians from lapsing into modalism. But the triad, "Creator, Liberator, and Comforter," prepares an obvious and easy launching pad for neo-modalism.

Fifth, like the proposed triad we have just examined, "Creator, Redeemer, and Sustainer" (as also "Creator, Redeemer, and Sanctifier"), emphasizes what God does *for us* and has nothing to say about the divine relations in themselves. It offers a blatantly functional, non-ontological version of the trinity. As it stands, this triad fails to distinguish Christianity from other religions that profess faith in deities who create (or in some lesser way make), redeem, and sustain human beings.[20] "Creator, Redeemer, and Sustainer" has as such little to convey about the historical roots of Christian faith in the God revealed in history. "Redeemer" could point us to something historical by implying the questions: When, where, how, and through whom did this redemption come? But "Father, Son, and Holy Spirit" tie us much more firmly to the history that culminated in the events of the first Good Friday and Easter Sunday.

Sixth, renaming the Holy Spirit as "Mother" (as in "Father, Child, Mother") seems to convey something about the divine relations in themselves, the bond of Love in the eternal life of God. But this triad clearly risks misrepresenting the inner-trinitarian relationships. Within the trinity the Holy Spirit does not play "Mother" to the Logos, who proceeds from (and is generated by) the Father and not the Holy Spirit. The suggested replacement, "Father, Child, and Mother," could gravely distort the doctrine of the trinity *in se* or immanent life of the trinity. "Mother" may suggest the feminine correlation of the Spirit in the "economy" of salvation, inasmuch as the Spirit is closely associated both with the person and mission of Mary and with the church, the bride of Christ. We will return shortly to the Holy Spirit. Here we wish to note only that introducing a new name ("Mother") seems a mixed blessing and one that as such has no clear scriptural foundation.

Seventh, some critics have dismissed as deistic contemporary suggestions for renaming the trinity. It is hard to make this charge stick, beyond the case of "Source, Word, and Spirit." That triad might convey a sense of God as divine Spirit who created (Source) an orderly world (Word) and then left it alone to run according to its own internal causality (Spirit). Rather than the remote, noninvolved God of classical Deism, many of the proposed triads present a highly involved God but One in whom Feuerbach might have rightly detected not so much a revelation from/of God as the projection onto "God" of human desires and ideals operative among us during our varied pilgrimages of religious self-discovery. Sallie McFague's "Mother, Lover, Friend," a triad that she herself has coined, which avoids the biblical narrative, and which is to replace "Father, Son, Holy Spirit," looks suspiciously like a deity that personifies deep concerns about women, ecology, and world peace.[21] Earlier McFague had reiterated the charge made by others that male-dominated Christianity has fashioned for itself a male idol, the "triumphalist imagery" of God the Father, who undercuts human responsibility and proves increasingly dangerous, or at least irrelevant in the days of feminism, environmentalism, and global consciousness about peace.[22] As much as some other recommended new names for God, her "Mother, Lover, Friend" appears to propose a fresh role-model for implementing her (crucial) social and political agenda.[23] Is this to talk about the God of Jesus Christ, or is it to make God (or a god?) who will be supportive of our projected hopes and dreams? May we speak here of a clear example of religion reduced simply to an (attractive) social construct, and "God" becoming a mere reflection of what are judged to be the healthiest social relationships of today? Do we even detect an instance of idolatry in the creation of a new religion? Is she replacing the Johannine "God is love" with "love is God"? In any case in her triad ("Mother, Lover, Friend"), "Lover" and "Friend" fail to catch the singularity of the second and third persons of the trinity. While we have only one mother, we can enjoy many friends, and some people in the course of their lifetime have related to several or even many lovers. But Christians believe in only one individual Son of God and one individual Holy Spirit. We choose our friends and lovers, but we have no choice about our tripersonal God.

Our last paragraph has reported the detection of an alleged "male idol" and has raised the question of the triad ("Mother/Lover/Friend") being itself an instance of "idolatry." McFague's *Metaphorical Theology* does not permit us to avoid the question. She repeatedly brings up the twinned issues of idolatry and irrelevance (e.g., xi, 22, 28, 32, 43, 54), with the aim of presenting metaphors and models of God that are nonidolatrous and relevant for "contemporary sensibility" (6). She does not seem to use "idolatry" in the mainline sense of worshiping a false god or worshiping the physical image of a nonexistent deity. She does not want to impose a total ban on all talk of God the Father. She detects idolatry rather in two beliefs. The first is that of holding that the truth of "religious images" depends on their being "literal" (145). Here we insist that we understand the image of God the Father to be used linguistically in a metaphorical rather than a literal way. At the same time, we recall our position that we can also speak of God literally (e.g., "God is good" and "God loves each one of us"). This kind of "literalism" should not be dismissed as "idolatry" (xi). It may be unpalatable to those who endorse a neo-Kantian agnosticism about the Transcendent (or the transcendent?). But to dub such literal statements about God as cases of "idolatry" is to use that substantive in a way that is not recorded by the *Oxford English Dictionary* or any other standard dictionary of the English language.

The second situation in which McFague reaches for talk about idols and idolatry is "when one model of God" becomes "dominant—absolute or exclusive—at the expense of others" (126). One must ask here: What precisely is she criticizing? A "dominant" (others might say "primary," "normative," and "privileged") model of God as Father is one thing, an "exclusive" model (that absolutely rejects any alternative) is quite another thing. "Dominant" (along with its less pejorative synonyms) is simply not a synonym for "absolute" or "exclusive." If and only if "Father" proved to be a truly "exclusive" model might one start talking about an idol, in the sense of an immoderate or excessive attachment to one way of "imaging" the real God? But such is not the case. To take a mundane example, the concluding prayers in the 1974 Divine Office (= the Liturgy of the Hours According to the Roman Rite) for the first thirty-four "weeks of the year" address "Father" three times, "God and Father" once, "God our Father" once, but "Lord" thirteen times and "Lord (our) God" twelve times—not to mention "All-powerful" or "Almighty," "ever-living God" four times, "Almighty God" twice, and "God of power and mercy" once. (Since two of the thirty-four prayers contain a double address, and one a triple address, our statistics amount to thirty-seven models of address.) Some object to "Lord" as a divine title, as we noted on the first page of this chapter. But one conclusion comes through loud and clear from our example: "Father" is no *exclusive* model for God. Lastly, idolatry is presented by the Bible as a sin against God (e.g., Ex 20:2–5; Dt 5:6–9; Rom 1:25). Yet McFague assures us that sin is committed against human beings and the world, not against God.[24] How can anyone then lapse into genuine idolatry, if there are no sins against God? She is in no position to use persistently the charge of idolatry, a sin that she has abolished.

Apropos of the pressure to be "relevant" and conform to "contemporary sensibility," the question is: Whose sensibility? Is the whole world, even at the end of the twentieth century, so homogenized that we dare speak in the singular of the "contemporary sensibility"? Moreover, should our co-primary aim (along with eradicating idolatry) be that of making religious language "more relevant" to various groups who feel excluded by "traditional religious language" (xi)? Or should it rather be that of ensuring that our religious language is both as true to God as we can make it and as freshly communicative to *all* groups in the church and the world? In her 1987 book McFague's "relevance for contemporary sensibility" emerges as being "on the side of life and its fulfillment." There she asserts that "the main criterion for a 'true' theology is pragmatic, preferring those models of God that are most helpful in the praxis of being about fulfillment for living beings."[25] This all leaves us with the questions: What counts as valid fulfillment? Has God had anything to say about authentic "fulfillment for living beings"? McFague's neo-Kantian agnosticism does not permit any answers. She writes: "God is and remains a mystery. We really do not know: the hints and clues we have of the way things are— whether we call them experiences, revelation or whatever—are too fragile, too little (and more often than not, too negative) for much more than a hypothesis, a guess, a projection of a possibility that, although it can be comprehensive and illuminating, may not be true."[26] McFague's "God" is so epistemologically remote that little or nothing can be said for or against any divine names, and "arguments" about the deity can take place only in a Pickwickian sense.

To sum up: our ten principles, when used to monitor various moves from the scriptures to trinitarian theology, indicate that the three names of "Father, Son, and Holy Spirit" do not allow for substitutes. These particular metaphors, while not exclusive, enjoy a normative, irreplaceable status in naming the Christian God and organizing the basic beliefs of Christianity; they convey insights, fix historical references, and facilitate relationships that are unobtainable from other metaphors. God's identity and relation to the world are pinned down by and inseparably bound up with this language into which successive generations of Christians have been initiated. The Christian tradition (and scriptures) would cease to be *this* tradition (and *these* scriptures) if the metaphorical language for the tripersonal God as "Father, Son, and Holy Spirit" were to be replaced. The Christian tradition would not be interpreted but broken. Sharing the same history, the Christian community has its common, central way of naming God—three names that have come from its Founder and those apostolic persons who stood with him. These are the names by which it knows its God and is open to receive new life here and hereafter. So far this chapter has argued against eliminating the divine "Fatherhood" and the correlative "Sonship." What of the third person of the trinity, the Holy Spirit?

The Holy Spirit

The body of this chapter has fairly doggedly applied our ten principles to the question of naming God as "Father, Son, and Holy Spirit." In testing the move from the scriptures to a systematic theology of the trinity, we have attended largely, but not exclusively, to the Father and the Son. Something has been said about the Holy Spirit, to whom an appendix will be dedicated at the end of the book. But more should be added about using the scriptures in developing a systematic pneumatology. The key themes here seem to be: the personal character of the Holy Spirit, revealed and experienced in relationship (but not confusion) with the risen Christ and the Father; the "emergence" of the Spirit within the eternal life of the trinity; the functions of the Spirit in the "economic" mission.

When tackling the (emerging) personal character of the Holy Spirit (and other themes), one must obviously cope with the discontinuity that qualifies the scriptural testimony (seventh principle). Claims about convergent testimony (fourth principle) are made harder by striking silences in the scriptures: Amos, Isaiah, and Jeremiah, for instance, make no mention of God's Spirit as the source of their prophetic teaching. When we read and "hear" the scriptures (first principle), we come across images of wind, fire (e.g., descending tongues of flame at the first Pentecost), water, a descending dove (at Jesus' baptism), and a temple associated with the divine Spirit. Nevertheless, the Spirit remains much more elusive than the Son, for whom the scriptures yield a much richer language and far more titles. "Paraclete" (Jn 14:16, 26; 15:26; 1 Jn 2:1) stands almost alone over against very many NT titles for Christ. Active hearing of the scriptures (second principle) requires careful exegesis of such passages as 2 Cor 3:12–18: above all, vs. 17 that is often unreflectingly taken to identify the risen Christ with the Holy Spirit ("the risen Lord is the Spirit").[27] As vs. 17 echoes Moses' experience in Ex 34:34, no reference seems to be made to the risen Christ but rather to God identified as "the Spirit" by Paul in his commentary—something expressed well by the REB (even if this translation introduces here a striking addition): "the Lord *of whom this passage speaks* is the Spirit" (italics ours).[28]

Encouraged by Jungian theory with its images of the feminine as the transforming, life-giving principle, Gelpi follows others in retrieving an ancient, at times Gnostic,[29] idea about the Holy Spirit as "Divine

Mother" (215–38). While he regularly names the third person of the trinity as "the Holy Breath," Gelpi believes that the feminine ("Divine Mother") offers a needed personal image for the Holy Spirit. Belief in Jesus as supernaturally conceived through the power of the Holy Spirit creates, however, an immediate difficulty here. Jesus would have two mothers on earth: Mary of Nazareth and the Holy Spirit. At least as far as the economy of salvation is concerned, the Holy Spirit would also be "Mother" to the second person of the trinity—"God the Mother" along-side Mary as *Theotokos* or "Mother of God."[30] If we wish to assign alternate, biblically based names to the Holy Spirit, we could appeal to such texts as Jn 14:16, 26; Rom 8:15–16; 1 Cor 2:10–13; and speak of the divine Teacher, Communicator, and Intercessor. The title "Paraclete" (see above) denotes the Helper (or Intercessor) rather than the Advocate or Witness.[31]

To use the scriptures to call the Holy Spirit "Teacher," "Communicator," "Intercessor," and "Helper" is clearly to name the Spirit in a personal way. Only persons can be teachers, communicators, intercessors, and helpers. Even though Paul's letters are not fully clear on the distinct, personal existence of the Spirit, they point in that direction by speaking of the Spirit as "bearing witness" (Rom 8:16), crying out in prayer (Gal 4:4), and being "grieved" (Eph 4:30). This brings us to the key issue raised and answered in principle by the NT: the Holy Spirit as personal and equal to the Father and the Son. Are these biblical metaphors *merely* imaginative projections of human experience, or do they speak of the reality of God? Do these three metaphors—and, in particular, that of the Holy Spirit—tell us the truth about God? Our sixth principle (of metathemes and metanarratives) encourages us to point to recurrent patterns of the Spirit's activity, historical experiences that are attested by the scriptures and fix a true reference when we invoke the name of "the Holy Spirit."

In dealing with God's spirit (Hebrew *ruah;* Greek *pneuma*), the OT highlighted its power as "wind," the breath of life, or the divine inspiration that comes upon prophets. In pre-Christian Judaism "word," "wisdom," and "spirit" were practically synonymous ways for speaking of God's manifest and powerful activity in the world. When celebrating God's creative power the psalmist uses "word" and "breath" (or "spirit") as equivalent parallels: "By the *word* of the Lord the heavens were made, and all their host by the *breath* of his mouth" (Ps 33:6; see

Ps 147:18). The work of creation can be expressed in terms of God's *word* (Ps 33:6, 9; see Gen 1:3–31) or in terms of the divine *spirit,* as Judith's thanksgiving to God also illustrates: "Let your whole creation serve you; for you spoke, and all things came to be; you sent out your spirit and it gave them form; none can oppose your word" (Jdt 16:14 REB; see Ps 104:29–30). "Spirit" and "wisdom" are likewise identified: when God gives "wisdom," this is equivalently sending "the holy spirit" (Wis 9:17; see 1:4–5; 7:7, 22, 25). In short, like "word" and "wisdom," the "spirit" was a way of articulating the divine activity and revelation in the world. But James Dunn has rightly argued that, at the time of Jesus, the divine "spirit" or "Spirit" was not yet experienced and thought of in Judaism even as a *semi*-independent divine agent.[32]

The evidence marshaled by Dunn also establishes that the synoptic Gospels envisioned Jesus during his ministry as being driven, inspired, and empowered by God's Spirit (136–41). For Luke, in particular, Jesus was the paradigmatic Spirit-bearer (e.g., Lk 4:1, 14, 18–21; 6:19). Probably Jesus himself was also conscious of the Spirit in such terms (Mk 1:12; 3: 22–29; also perhaps 13:11). But he never seems to have unambiguously pointed to his deeds as signs of the Spirit's power.[33] In any case he is not credited with an awareness of the Spirit of anything like the same intensity as his consciousness of the God whom he called "Abba." In other words, the synoptics (and Jesus himself) described the divine Spirit in a fairly normal Jewish way: the dynamic power of God reaching out to have its impact on Jesus and through him on others. It took Jesus' resurrection and exaltation to initiate a *new, characteristically Christian* way of experiencing and thinking about the Spirit and the relationship of Jesus to the Spirit (the seventh principle of continuity/discontinuity).

First of all, the relationship between Jesus and the Spirit is understood to be transformed by the resurrection. Jesus now shares in God's prerogative as Sender or Giver of the Spirit. Paul speaks of the risen Christ as having become "a life-giving Spirit" (1 Cor 15:45). Yet he never quite says that Christ has sent or will send the Spirit. Luke and John say just that. Exalted "at the right hand of God and having received from the Father the promise of the Holy Spirit," Christ pours out the Spirit with its perceptible effects (Acts 2:33; see Lk 24:49). According to John, the Spirit comes from Jesus, is sent by Jesus or is bestowed by Jesus (Jn 7:39; 15:26; 19:30, 34; 20:22; see 4:10, 14). At the same time, neither for Luke nor for John does the sending or giving of the Spirit become merely Jesus' gift. He receives "from the Father" the promised Holy Spirit before pouring it out (Acts 2:33). John also talks about the Father giving the Spirit (Jn 14:16–17) or sending the Spirit (Jn 14:26), albeit, respectively, in response to Jesus' prayer and in Jesus' name. Even when John has Jesus promise to send the Spirit, the words "from the Father" feature prominently: "When the Helper comes, whom I shall send you from the Father, even the Spirit of truth, who proceeds from the Father, he will bear witness to me" (Jn 15:26). The Spirit is experienced as coming from the Father and the Son.

When referring to the Christian experience of the Spirit being bestowed, Paul picks up formulaic traditions to say that "God has sent the Spirit of his Son into our hearts" (Gal 4:6; see 3:5; 1 Cor 2:10). He also uses a divine passive which does not explicitly name the divine Giver or Sender: "the Holy Spirit has been given to us" (Rom 5:5); to each Christian "is given" some manifestation of the Spirit (1 Cor 12:7–8). Or else Paul writes of Christians "receiving" the Spirit without stating from whom they received it (Rom 8:15; 1 Cor 2:12, 14; Gal 3:2).

Nevertheless, Paul speaks not only of "the Spirit of God" (Rom 8:9; 1 Cor 2:11, 12, 14), but also of "the Spirit of Christ" or "the Spirit of God's Son" (Rom 8:9; Gal 4:6; see Acts 5:9; 1 Pet 1:11). The genitive is exquisitely ambiguous; it can be read both as a genitive of origin (the Spirit which comes from God/Christ), as a genitive of identity (the Spirit which is God/Christ), or as both. The second possibility leads to a further major reflection on the postresurrection function and understanding of the Holy Spirit.

Second, even though both Luke and John identify the Spirit as sent by the risen and exalted Jesus, they do not draw here a sharp distinction between the sender and the sent. Luke can move from cases of guidance by the ascended Lord (Acts 9:10–16; 18:9–10; 22:17–21) to cases of guidance by the Holy Spirit (Acts 8:29; 10:19; 16:6), without distinguishing very clearly between them. In fact, he reports at least once guidance by "the Spirit of Jesus" (Acts 16:7). (Does he mean "the Spirit which comes from Jesus" or "the Spirit who is Jesus"?) In John the coming of the Spirit (Jn 14:16–17, 25) seems to merge with the return of Christ himself (Jn 14:3, 18, 23, 28).

In Paul's letters the Spirit is not only *characterized by its relationship* to the risen and exalted Christ but in the experience of believers is almost *identified with* Christ (= the Spirit which is Christ or which is the presence of Christ). The Spirit witnesses to Jesus as divine Lord (1 Cor 12:3). The Spirit "in us" (Rom 5:5; 8:9, 11, 16; Gal 4:6) is practically synonymous with talk about our being "in Christ" (Rom 6:3, 11, 23; 16:11; 1 Cor 1:30; 3:1; 4:15; Phil 3:1; 4:1–2). Christians' experience of the Spirit merges with their experience of the risen Christ (1 Cor 6:11). The Spirit of God dwelling "in you" (Rom 8:9, 11) is, for all intents and purposes, equivalent to "having the Spirit of Christ" or Christ being "in you" (Rom 8:9, 10). This near functional identity allows Dunn to say not only that for Paul "the Spirit is the medium for Christ in his relation" to human beings, but even that *"no distinction can be detected in the believer's experience between exalted Christ and the Spirit of God"* (146).

Nevertheless, and this is our third point regarding the NT experience of the relationship Christ/Spirit, it is patent that neither Paul nor others finally identify Christ with the Spirit. Jesus was conceived through the power of the Holy Spirit (Mt 1:20; Lk 1:35)—a statement that cannot be reversed. It was the Word, and not the Spirit, that became flesh (Jn 1:14). It was the Son, and not the Spirit, who was sent "in the likeness of sinful flesh" to deal with sin (Rom 8:3), who acted in obedience to the missioning will of the Father (e.g., Mk 14:36; Rom 5:19; Phil 2:8), and who was not "spared" but "given up for us all" (Rom 8:32). Through his resurrection Christ, and not the Spirit, became "the firstborn" of a new eschatological family (Rom 8:29) and "the first fruits of those who have fallen asleep" (1 Cor 15:20).

It is the indwelling Spirit that helps Christians to pray "Abba" and witnesses to Christ (Rom 8:15–16; Gal 4:6; 1 Cor 12:3), and not an indwelling Christ who makes them pray like that and who witnesses to the Spirit. Finally, unlike the Spirit, it is the crucified and resurrected Christ who at the end will subject all things to his Father (1 Cor 15:24–28). The NT's story of Christ's mission, conception, death, resurrection, and its aftermath distinguishes him from the Holy Spirit.

In the last few pages we have put to work our fourth (see the convergence between Luke, Paul, and John), sixth, and seventh principles to characterize and identify the Holy Spirit, who first brings about the presence and activity of Christ (from his conception, baptism, and through his ministry to his resurrection) and then is sent by the Father and the Son to effect the sacramental rebirth of believers (Jn 3:3–8), their prayerful, saving access to the Father (Rom 8:14–17, 26–27; Gal 4:6), their being gifted with various charisms (1 Cor 12:1–31) and forming the living temple of the Church (1 Cor 6:19) in expectation of the resurrection to come (Rom 8:9–11). These references to the historical experiences of foundational Christianity fix the reference when we name God as "Father, Son, *and Holy Spirit.*" Christians understood the Spirit to have empowered Jesus (and the prophets before him) and to be "poured out" into believers and into the world.

Consensus (our fifth principle) cannot be easily mobilized here, as not all scholars agree that the NT presents God as tripersonal and not merely triune. Nevertheless, within the inherited confession of "one God" (1 Cor 8:6) their experience impelled the first Christians to distinguish between God as Father, Christ as Lord (or Son), and the Holy Spirit (e.g. Rom 1:1–4; 8:11, 14–16).

At the end of his Gospel Matthew puts on the lips of the risen Jesus a formula about baptism "in the name of the Father and of the Son and of the Holy Spirit" (Mt 28:19). Christians began by baptizing "in the name of Jesus" (Acts 2:38; 10:48; Rom 6:3; 1 Cor 1:13, 15; 6:11). Then at some point their experience pushed them into introducing the tripartite formula which has remained normative ever since. Another such formula turns up (much earlier) as a concluding benediction at the end of one of Paul's letters. It maintains the Holy Spirit in the third place but changes the order of the first two figures, names them differently ("Lord Jesus Christ" instead of "the Son" and "God" instead of "the Father"), and speaks not of their "name" but of "grace," "love," and "fellowship," associated respectively with the first, second, and third figure: "The grace of the Lord Jesus Christ and the love of God and the fellowship of the Holy Spirit be with you all" (2 Cor 13:14). In a summary of salvation history that can take different forms elsewhere in the Pauline correspondence (e.g., Gal 4:4–7), Christ is here associated with "God" and "the Holy Spirit" in bestowing spiritual blessings. "Grace" and "love" have characterized the divine dealings with human beings, who through faith and baptism share in the new fellowship created by the Holy Spirit. In earlier teaching Paul speaks in a different order and more succinctly of "Spirit," "Lord," and "God" (an order that reverses the first and third figures in Matthew's baptismal formula), and insists that spiritual gifts come from the one ("the same") divine source and should contribute to "the common good" (1 Cor 12:7). "There are varieties of gifts, but the same Spirit; and there are varieties of service, but the same Lord; and there are varieties of working, but it is the same God who inspires them all in every one" (1 Cor 12:4–6). These texts from Paul and Matthew (which certainly in the case of Mt 28:19 and probably in the case of 2 Cor 13:13 draw on a previous tradition) set Jesus as "the Son" or "the Lord" alongside (a) "the Father" or "God" *(ho theos)* and (b) "the Holy Spirit" or "the Spirit."

The order and the names (the Father, the Son, and the Holy Spirit) found in Matthew's baptismal formula became and remained standard for Christian faith. That formula, to put it mildly, does not clarify much about the relationship between the Father, the Son, and the Holy Spirit, or the relationship between the tripersonal God and humankind. To speak, on the one hand, of "the Father/the Son" and, on the other, of "the Holy Spirit" ("Holy" obviously through being "the Spirit of/from God") is to offer a very minimal identification of the Father, the Son, and the Holy Spirit in their relationship to each other and to human beings. In its own setting the Matthean baptismal formula is no less concerned than the Pauline benediction with the blessings that have come through Christ. Although we do not find in Matthew's formula, in Paul's closing benediction, or elsewhere in the NT anything like the later, full-blown doctrine of God as three (Father, Son, and Holy Spirit) in one and one in three, nevertheless the NT data provide a foundation and starting point for that doctrinal development. The doctrine of the trinity properly interprets the divine self-revelation attested by the scriptures and reaching its climax in the NT. Scruples over waiting for a full consensus (fifth principle) on the trinitarian face of NT revelation should not block our conclusions here.

In testing our ten principles' worth in any move from the scriptures, we have appealed to the value of six of them in the area of pneumatology; we should at least mention the relevance of the four remaining principles.

The Nicene-Constantinopolitan Creed, by confessing that the Spirit is to be "adored and glorified" together with the Father and the Son, embeds the three divine names in the larger whole of praise and worship. It sets any scriptural reflection on the Spirit firmly within a liturgical, traditional framework (principle three). As in the case of the Son, the Spirit's work in the economy of salvation is provisional and to be completed eschatologically. When we name God the Spirit, we cannot give anything like a complete, exhaustive account (eighth principle). As with the other divine persons, philosophical considerations must enter in when we attempt to draw on the scriptures and clarify our talk about the Spirit's being person-in-relationship within the deity and with the created world (ninth principle). Finally, inculturation (tenth principle) has its particular challenge here. Many, if not all, human cultures acknowledge in some way a pervasive, immanent divine "spirit." But the Christian modifier "Holy" sets the Holy Spirit apart as holy Mystery and divine person.

Even after deploying all ten principles in moving from the scriptural testimony on to systematic reflection, we still have to reckon with the personal invisibility and even anonymity of the Holy Spirit. What we will propose in an appendix about the Spirit's economic mission and distinctively personal presence "in, through, and under" the world, the believing community, and their scriptures remains vital if we are not to lose heart when pondering the elusive third person of the trinity.

5

Leadership and the Church's Origins

What do the scriptures indicate about the structure (or relative lack of structure) of the foundational church that Jesus and his first disciples left behind? Knowing what the church was originally can obviously help to clarify what it should be now. We assume that, by living their faith as a group and not as isolated individuals, the followers of Jesus were obeying the divine will. They were meant by God to do so. In other words, the church originated through the divine initiatives; by instituting with his disciples the church, Jesus properly expressed the saving revelation he was sent to communicate. The question we face here is: Originally was the church meant to be a completely egalitarian community, totally shaped by mutuality and reciprocity, and free of any kind of subordination to office holders and hierarchical organization? One can agree with Elisabeth Schüssler Fiorenza that "not the holiness of the elect but the wholeness of all is the central vision of Jesus."[1] But did this central vision of Jesus exclude any form of institutionalized authoritative leadership entailing leaders and those they led, as actually happened in the handing on to subsequent generations of a hierarchical organization (with a threefold ministry of bishops, priests, and deacons) that claimed to stand in an apostolic succession? Did that historical development betray Jesus' original dream (shared for a brief period by some or all of his first followers?) of a community of male and female disciples as co-partners variously and directly or personally empowered by the Holy Spirit to minister for the good of all? Did and does that hierarchical development necessarily involve male dominance in a patriarchal rule

101

and sexist culture that inevitably bring oppression by abandoning the vision of Jesus and his first disciples? Should then the whole Christian Church collaborate in restoring the earliest state of things, that normative first era which flourished without supervisory authorities and any official establishment—a church directly "governed" by the Holy Spirit? In short, what do the scriptures indicate about God's designs for the church, its ordering, and leadership? But first let us hear some challenging voices from the present and the past.

In her *Models of God: Theology for an Ecological, Nuclear Age* (Philadelphia: Fortress Press, 1987), Sallie McFague champions a radical, even total egalitarianism—what she calls a "nonhierarchical vision of Christian faith" and even an "antihierarchical" one (48), a vision that promises "fulfillment for all" (xii) by doing away with such "hierarchical dualisms" as "spirit/flesh, subject/object, male/female, [and] mind/body" (4) and bringing a "holistic, evolutionary, ecological vision that overcomes ancient and oppressive dualisms and hierarchies" (27). This interpretation of the world "as God's body" (xiii) seems to blur everything together in a journey back toward standard pantheism. But what of those who do not share McFague's "holistic" and, apparently, pantheistic sensibility (51), yet endorse her "nonhierarchical vision of Christian faith"? Was the proper, total egalitarianism of Christian life and ministry, a dream worthy of J. J. Rousseau, betrayed by the emergence of the hierarchical "dualism" of leadership roles: that is to say, by the "dualism" of the leaders exercising authority over the led? Did such a "deviation" leave behind the intended standard of foundational equality? Or was the leadership that developed with its continuity in ordained ministry legitimate, somehow authorized by Christ, and rightly exercised over those who accepted it?

According to one myth of Christian beginnings,[2] an original purity became corrupted in a story of decline *(Verfallsgeschichte)*. Subsequent human weakness and decadence spoiled the noble or even divine start the Christian movement enjoyed. This "myth" is no twentieth-century invention; we find it earlier, in perhaps surprising places like the *Leviathan* of Thomas Hobbes (1588–1679). In his version of church history as a story of decline, the simple, charismatic groupings of the earliest Christians gave way to hierarchical structures. The "consciences" of the first Christians "were free, and their words and actions subject to none but the civil power." "Out of reverence, not by obligation," converts "obeyed" the apostles, who were distinguished for their "wisdom, humility, sincerity, and other virtues." As the number of believers increased, "the presbyters" (who later on "appropriated to themselves" the name and role of "bishops") and, eventually, the bishop of Rome asserted their authority, promoted a sense of obligation toward them, and tied "knots" on "Christian liberty." Hobbes advocated the demolition of this "ancient authority" and a return to "the independency" of the earliest Christians: "there ought to be no power over consciences of men, but [only that] of the Word itself, working faith in every one" (4, 47).[3]

Where Robert Wilken writes of "the myth" of Christian origins, accuracy suggests speaking in the plural and of "myths." Some important writers like F. C. Baur (1792–1860) with his Tübingen school have elaborated a conflict model when interpreting Christian beginnings. In an Hegelian dialectic, divergent views of faith met in a struggle that produced the compromise synthesis of the Catholic Church out of the thesis of Gentile Christianity (espoused by Paul) and the antithesis of Jewish Christianity (represented by Peter). Baur saw the dialectical character of history exemplified by the Catholic resolution of conflicts at the start of Christianity, while he also endorsed some elements of a *Verfallsgeschichte* view by arguing that the pure Pauline gospel had already been partially corrupted by the time the inauthentic Pastoral Epistles were written.[4]

Both the "original purity" model and that of an "original conflict" have to face the question: Does the origin of something, *just by itself* and quite apart from its subsequent development (see Chapter 1 and our third, seventh, and tenth principles, in particular), tell us what something "really" is? Here the work of Robert Wilken comes into its own with his insistence on the *historical* nature of Christianity and the feature of change that inevitably belongs to any historical phenomenon.

Instead of pursuing this issue, however, this chapter aims at applying to the origins and development of authoritative leadership roles our ten principles. Do the scriptures, when interpreted in the light of these principles, support the conclusion that Christian life and ministry should be utterly egalitarian—a perfectly equal circle, so to speak, with everyone holding hands and in no way related in any kind of pyramid structure? Or do the scriptures, when so interpreted, vouch for what has been the belief of most mainline Christians: namely, that the basic discipleship and wholeness of all also need particular ministries, which include the hierarchical leadership of some that is handed on to successive generations?[5]

Principles One Through Five

The first principle, that of "hearing" and being "answerable" to all the scriptures, has its special significance when reflecting on authoritative leadership in the church. The Gospels present us with Jesus as *the* ideal model for all ministry and leadership; any subsequent ministerial roles, and certainly any such roles that are to be exercised with his authority, should be grounded in and shaped by the example of Jesus himself. A properly Christocentric approach to leadership requires this; the church's ministry should always represent Christ. Nevertheless, in this case as elsewhere, it is not enough to hear only the Gospels and what they report about the pre-Easter situation. Idealizing (or rather reconstructing in one's own way) the ministry of Jesus may lead to an unsympathetic suspicion toward other NT books that refuses to give them an expectant hearing, does not respect their inspired witness to Jesus and his emerging church, and overlooks the wider guidance of the Holy Spirit.

Such a negative attitude toward the full NT canon and history, particularly when the question of church ministry comes up, has expressed itself over many years. Earlier in this century, for instance, some writers detected in such books as Luke-Acts and the Pastoral Epistles a deterioration into "early Catholicism." In coining and promoting this negative term they pointed to what they claimed to have happened in first-century Christianity: a decline from the pure Gospel of Jesus and Paul that occurred with the fading of the hope for the *parousia,* and the emergence of a structured church dispensing salvation through ministerial ordination, institutionalized apostolic succession, set forms of doctrine, and reestablished law.[6] The thesis of "early Catholicism" enjoys at least the merit of accepting St. Paul as a reliable witness to genuine Christianity and not alleging that with the apostle a decline had already set in.

This thesis should be set in a wider context. In *From Synagogue to Church* (Cambridge: Cambridge University Press, 1992) James Burtchaell traces from John Wycliffe to Elisabeth Schüssler Fiorenza the thesis, expounded with secondary variations, that the earliest Christian

community had been "unorganized in structure, spontaneous in min
istries," and "free of authority figures or roles or offices" (1–179, at 179).
At some point (influenced or at least recorded by the early Paul, the later
Paul, Luke, the Pastoral Letters, the Johannine literature, Clement of
Rome, Ignatius of Antioch, or Irenaeus) a clerical takeover of authoritative officers that led to the monarchical episcopate began replacing and
stifling the egalitarian Spirit-led church and its charismatic order. Such a
reconstruction, as emerges from Burtchaell's critical survey, frequently
denies allegiance to a part, even to a large part of the NT books.[7]

If one respects the whole NT canon as authentically witnessing,
albeit in various ways, to an order, leadership, and mission that
emerged with Christ's authority and was substantially guided by the
Holy Spirit, what do we find? The Gospels report how Jesus chose out
of a wider group of his followers a core group of twelve to proclaim the
good news of the kingdom and to drive out demons (Mk 3:13–19). He
later dispatched them on a preaching and healing mission, with instructions about their *modus operandi* that obviously mirror not so much the
precrucifixion period as the situation of post-Easter itinerant missionaries (Mk 6:7–13, 30). At the end Jesus celebrated the Passover "with the
twelve" and Judas Iscariot is called "one of the twelve" (Mk 14:10, 17,
43 par.)—something that seems inconceivable unless the earthly Jesus
had already called that group into existence. Matthew, who calls this
core group both the "twelve disciples" and the "twelve apostles,"
repeats (and modifies) some of the instructions he finds in Mark and
adds others (Mt 10:1–11:1). When "sent" by Jesus, the twelve will
share in the authority he has received from God (Mt 10:40). In
Matthew's Gospel the twelve are not actually reported to have gone out
proclaiming the message of the kingdom; with the resurrection they
were commissioned (as "the eleven," after Judas' defection and sui-
cide) to make disciples of all nations, to baptize in the name of the
Father and of the Son and of the Holy Spirit, and to teach all that Jesus
had commanded them (Mt 28:16–20). Much of what we read here
comes, at least in its wording, from the evangelist Matthew, but for our
purposes one point is important. Talk in that closing scene of "the
eleven," as happens similarly in Lk 24:9, 37, would not be intelligible
unless that core group had already been created during Jesus' ministry.
The functions for that group involve some kind of leadership role—at
least in the work of preaching and healing.

Luke has Jesus himself give the name of "apostles" to the twelve (Lk 6:12–16), repeats practically all the instructions from Mark (Lk 9:1–5), tells of the trial mission of the twelve (Lk 9:6), adds a similar mission undertaken by a broader group of seventy-two disciples (Lk 10:1–12), and inserts Jesus' reaction to the joyful report of this latter group's success (Lk 10:17–20). Luke ends his Gospel with the risen Jesus commissioning "the eleven and those with them" for a worldwide mission (Lk 24:33, 47–49), for which they will be empowered by the gift of the Holy Spirit—a promise repeated by the risen Jesus to "the apostles" at the start of Acts (Acts 1:1–5). Luke's detail about the need for Judas' place to be filled (Acts 1:15–26) suggests that there were a group of twelve with an office to fulfill. For Luke the twelve (apostles) are *the* authoritative witnesses to the original Christian faith, above all as testifying to Jesus' resurrection from the dead and what it brings. Like Matthew (Mt 9:28) Luke draws from the Q, or sayings, source a promise about the twelve's future role in representing and judging "the twelve tribes of Israel" (Lk 22:30). Only "the twelve," in their function as representatives and judges, will sit on "the thrones," while all are called to "the banquet" in the new age (Mt 22:1–14 = Lk 14:15–24; see Mt 8:11 = Lk 13:29). Does a certain "hierarchical dualism" turn up in Jesus' metaphors of a "banquet" for all and "thrones" for some? One could well argue that he is speaking of twelve eschatological judges who will neither "judge" during their earthly lifetime nor hand on to others something of this office. Their sitting on thrones will occur with the eschatological gathering of all people around the coming Son of man.

Attentive reading of the Gospels shows, then, multiple witness for the fact that at some point in his ministry Jesus chose twelve disciples from among the wider ranks of his followers and gave them some kind of authoritative office and leadership role. Mark attests the original call (3:13–19) and subsequent mission of the twelve (6:7–13); Q reflects the existence of this core group (Mt 19:28 = Lk 22:30). Then they are "in place" to function as the key group receiving a foundational appearance of the risen Christ, a fact first attested by a kerygmatic formula in Paul (1 Cor 15:5) and subsequently narrated in varying ways by the Easter chapters of the Gospels.[8] The twelve are given by Christ authority to lead and teach in his name, an authority for which, as Luke and (in his own way) John indicate, they are empowered by the Holy Spirit.

Their apostolic mission shares in and comes from the mission of the Son and the Holy Spirit.[9]

Those who wish to "hear" the entire NT on the issue of leadership in the church also need to pay attention to what Acts and the Pauline letters indicate. In his first letter Paul distinguishes between those who "preside" and those who "defer" (1 Thes 5:12). A little later he notes how, within the whole "body of Christ," God has appointed various persons to be apostles, prophets, teachers, workers of miracles, healers, helpers, administrators, and speakers in various kinds of tongues (1 Cor 12:8–12, 28–30; see Rom 12:4–8). The apostle's language in 1 Cor 12 has encouraged some to envisage an exclusively charismatic church, a Spirit-filled community with no permanent institutions and ordained offices, a charismatic "pneumatocracy" as opposed to a hierarchical "christocracy." But in 1 Cor 12–14, does Paul intend to make permanent prescriptions for the church's order (by opposing charisms to institutions and offices or what is pneumatological and charismatic to what is christological and institutional)? Or does he intend rather to give some practical advice to the Corinthian community and help to solve particular challenges facing them?[10] A dramatic encounter with Christ (and not as such with the Holy Spirit) has made Paul himself an apostle who proclaims the resurrection of the crucified Jesus (1 Cor 9:1–2; 15:8–11; Gal 1:11–12, 15–17). The eight ministries of 1 Cor 12:28 become five in another, deutero-Pauline list: "his [= Christ's] gifts were that some should be apostles, some prophets, some evangelists, some pastors and teachers" (Eph 4:11). The list now includes the "evangelists" or official messengers/preachers of the good news (see Rom 10:8–17). The foundation of many local churches by apostles and others brought a shift in leadership, when pastors (called "overseers," "elders," and "deacons") took over from the missionary apostles, the other "evangelists," and the founders among whom had been the "pillars" of Gal 2:9. A range of NT sources reflects this movement from missionary to settled, pastoral leaders (Acts 20:17, 28; Phil 1:1; 1 Pt 5:1–4; the Pastoral Letters to Timothy and Titus), even if many details about the appointment of the latter, their leadership functions, and their relationship to the traveling missionaries remain obscure.

The Pastoral Letters, when recording a more developed organization of ministries, speak of "overseers" or "bishops" and their qualifications (1 Tim 3:1–7; see Tit 1:7–9), of the "elders" or "presbyters" to

be appointed by Titus "in every town" of Crete (Ti 1:5–6; see 1 Tm
5:17–20), and of the qualities of "deacons" (1 Tm 3:8–10, 12–13) and
apparently also of deaconesses (1 Tm 3:11).[11] There is some indication
of succession in teaching authority (2 Tm 2:2). Much is conveyed about
the teaching, preaching, defending sound doctrine against error, administration, and the domestic behavior expected from leaders. But apart
from some passing regulations concerning worship (1 Tm 2:1–2, 8) and
several references to the "laying on of hands" (1 Tm 5:22; see 1 Tm
4:14; 2 Tm 1:6), nothing further is said about the liturgical life of the
community and, for instance, about roles taken by these leaders (or others) in baptizing and celebrating the eucharist.

Hearing the whole NT canon on the issue of organization and
authoritative leadership supports at least this minimal conclusion: both
in the apostolic situation (reflected, e.g., by the authentic Pauline letters) and in the subapostolic situation (reflected, e.g., by Acts and the
Pastoral Letters) there was a measure of hierarchical organization in
communities which comprised the leaders (with their gifts and institutionalized offices) and the led (with their personal charisms), and were
not totally egalitarian.

Today, of course, some Christians hear, search, and read these
scriptures with radical suspicion; they play down the mission of the
Holy Spirit in guiding the foundational period of Christianity, denying
the authority of inspired scriptures to some or many NT books, and aim
at restoring the church according to the minicanon they accept. A sharp,
anti-Gnostic observation of Irenaeus may perhaps apply here: "When
the heretics are refuted from the Scriptures, they turn to accusing the
Scriptures themselves, as if there were something amiss with them"
(*Adversus haereses,* 3.2).[12] Irenaeus encouraged allegiance to the normative voice of the scriptures when facing the question of the church's
structure and other such critical issues. We return to him shortly.

Applying our second principle to the nature of the church as community and the issue of hierarchical organization, we can do so, as we
have seen, in three contexts: those of worship and practice, as well as
that of academic scholarship (which situates the reflections that have
just been developed). These three contexts work best here, we believe,
in a series of questions. First, does an "active hearing" of the whole
Bible which supports a hierarchical structure appropriate the scriptures
in ways that promote the liturgical praise of God and help community

worship? How would or does a completely egalitarian interpretation of the NT "perform" in the liturgy? Will it or should it result in the kind of common prayer practiced by the Society of Friends, or Quakers, who repudiate all hierarchical authorities? Second, what impact does a hierarchical reading of the scriptures have on the practice of Christian discipleship: that is to say, on generous fellowship and mission to the world? Will (and does) a totally egalitarian hearing of the NT produce, for example, far more shining examples of men and women who dedicate their lives to alleviating human suffering and oppression? Third, what judgment does intellectual integrity pass on nonhierarchical or antihierarchical versions of Christian origins? Let us push this question to a polemical extreme. How different are such latter-day readings of the NT from those of the very radical reformers of the sixteenth century, who dismissed Christianity's institutionalization as a sign of corruption, rejected the hierarchical leadership of the church and earthly authority of the state, aimed at a profound reconstruction of society and church, and with utopian confidence expected the Holy Spirit to mediate salvation directly to individuals? Does the NT support a community of equals in which direct charismatic endowments or charismatic leadership would rule out hierarchical office transmitted to subsequent generations? In other words, the three contexts (of worship, practice, and scholarship) which elucidated the sense of our second principle (see Chapter 1) could be fruitfully introduced when reflecting biblically on the nature of the church as community.

Hierarchical structure, in the sense of episcopal succession with bishops enjoying the sanction of apostolic authority, finds support from another source (our third principle): the notion of the "rule of faith" as developed by its second-century exponent, Irenaeus of Lyons. His championing of the rule of faith was intertwined with his recognition of (a) the canonical scriptures (in particular, the four Gospels), and of (b) the hierarchical ministry (in particular, the episcopal office held in apostolic succession), as the office of the apostles gave rise to the continuity of the ordained episcopal office. Consistency suggests that those who follow Irenaeus in (a) should follow him in (b). Those, however, who in various ways endorse Gnostic and other apocryphal texts (and hence reject position [a]) will hardly accept position (b). Irenaeus himself acknowledged an authoritative continuity in orthodox teaching of bishops succeeding one another and proclaiming the one faith and tradition

of the apostles. Far from being secret tradition, this rule of faith
belonged publicly, above all, to the great church, and their episcopal
succession could be traced back to the apostles—something Irenaeus
did for the see of Rome (*Adversus haereses,* 3.2). He criticized fiercely
the secret, antihierarchical, and antiapostolic position of the Gnostics:

> They oppose tradition, claiming to be wiser not only than the pres-
> byters [= the bishops] but even than the apostles, and to have dis-
> covered the truth undefiled. The apostles, they say, mingled with
> the Savior's words matter belonging to the Law;[13] and besides this,
> the Lord himself uttered discourses some of which derived from
> the Demiurge, some from the Intermediate Power, some from the
> Highest, whereas they themselves know the hidden mystery with-
> out doubt, contaminations, or admixture (ibid.).[14]

Those unsympathetic to the orthodox tradition will not ask either what
the emerging hierarchical structures contributed positively to Christian
faith, worship, and living, or how this development might have enjoyed
its early intimations in the biblical record. They maintain their posi-
tion(s) on what the church should be now solely on the basis of what
they think (or imagine?) the church to have been originally. At the same
time, those who endorse our third principle need to acknowledge that
the classic creeds of Christianity that provide essential frames of reference for interpreting and "practicing" the scriptures do not explicitly
endorse a permanent hierarchical organization. At best such an authoritative succession is conveyed implicitly through professing the church
to be "one, holy, catholic, and apostolic."

When we pass to our fourth principle, we allow the broadest and
most varied account of biblical witness to come to bear on the alternatives: either a completely egalitarian community in which all are co-
partners guided by the Spirit, or a communion of disciples that is, at
least in part, governed, sanctified, and taught by hierarchical leaders in
apostolic succession. We say "at least in part," since Christian history
repeatedly yields many men and women who have helped to lead, sanc-
tify, and teach others, without themselves being hierarchical leaders or
bishops in apostolic succession. We sampled above, when applying our
first principle, some of the relevant NT testimony. To deploy fully the
principle of biblical convergence would involve a full examination of
scriptural perspectives on authoritative leadership, based on personal,
charismatic gifts or on official, hierarchical organization. One would

need, for instance, to look carefully at relevant passages in the fourth Gospel, the Johannine letters, and the Book of Revelation.

"Contemporary consensus" (principle five) calls for a similar wide examination, this time of two fields of scholarship in particular. What conclusions do widely respected exegetes reach on NT ecclesiology and, above all, on the nature of leadership in the emerging church? Universal consensus can hardly be expected here. But that may not excuse us from examining seriously what biblical scholars conclude about the nature and leadership of NT churches.[15] The second group of scholars who seem particularly relevant here is formed by those engaged in bilateral and other conversations on church order in the light of the NT. The men and women officially appointed to share in such dialogues and produce joint statements do not, or do not normally, read the NT history as if the definitive church order belonged to the golden age of Jesus and his first disciples, so that any subsequent development and change could only be for the worse. In our experience most participants in such dialogues do not take the view that the original *"shape"* of the Christian community (during the pre-Easter and/or the immediately post-Easter situation?) or at least the *"shape"* of that community, as they reconstruct and reimagine it, should take precedence, and that contemporary church order should be radically remodeled according to their idealized reconstruction of the primitive ideals and state of affairs. In our experience they generally accept that the same Holy Spirit, who in a special way inspired a relatively few believers to write the scriptures, also gave some guidance to the very many post-apostolic Christians and their leaders in the church, or at least can be seen to have done so in her fruitful developments. Normally members of ecumenical dialogues provide a useful jury for those who wish to interpret and appropriate the scriptures in the area of church order and leadership.[16] Some argue that the NT does not single out *one* pattern of ministry as divinely ordained. The NT neither excludes nonepiscopal forms of leadership (e.g., government through elders) nor imposes for all times and places a threefold ministry of leadership (of "bishop/overseer," "elder/presbyter," and "deacon") that may enjoy an early intimation in the Pastoral Letters. Some Christians hold for an apostolic succession in a ministerial form but without episcopal succession. There appears, however, to be substantial consensus that the NT supports some organized ministry, some structured leadership, and not a

total egalitarianism in which individuals appeal straight to the Holy
Spirit in justifying their ministry and mission.

Principles Six Through Ten

When testing the biblical basis for ecclesial leadership, whether
official or charismatic, a sense of metathemes and metanarratives (principle six) encourages attending, for instance, to the exercise of authority not only in the ministry of Jesus but also prior to it and then later in
the post-Easter situation. What patterns are suggested by the offices of
priest, prophet, and king that recur in the scriptures and have been taken
up in Christian tradition? The pervasive biblical theme of priestly,
prophetic, and kingly authority has surely some relevance to the question of leadership in the Christian community. Matthew's Gospel seems
to use metanarratives about Moses and the exodus story to illuminate
the ministry of Jesus. Do any patterns for authoritative leadership
emerge from Matthean allusions to Moses? Paul, at least to some
extent, links his apostolic mission to the prophetic call of Jeremiah (Gal
1:15; see Jer 1:5). Christian art was to develop this metatheme by often
matching the twelve minor prophets with the twelve apostles. What
might such metanarratives that link the stories of Moses, Jeremiah,
Jesus, and Paul indicate about the exercise of leadership in the church?

Our seventh principle (continuity within discontinuity) bears on
the shift from the pre-Easter situation of Jesus and the post-Easter situation of Paul. Authoritative leadership continued to be justified by the
actions of Jesus in founding the Christian community, even while this
leadership was not to be exercised in exactly the same way. During the
visible, earthly mission of Jesus the twelve were given the authority of
the kingdom (Lk 22:29); Jesus spoke of a "banquet" for all and
"thrones" for some, a distinction that was to be roughly paralleled by
Paul's language of the one body of Christ and the various gifts, including those of church leadership (see above). The trial mission of the
twelve gave way to a definitive mission, when with Jesus' authority and
through the power of the Holy Spirit (Mt 28:16–20 par.) the apostles
and their associates began evangelizing the world and creating a worldwide fellowship of believers. Paul was authorized by the risen Jesus to
lead the way in this mission to the Gentiles (Gal 1:1–17). His and other
apostolic preaching centered on the resurrection of the crucified Jesus

(1 Cor 15:1–11). A pre-Easter trial mission for the kingdom was followed by a definitive mission that authoritatively proclaimed the Easter Mystery and a new life to be already shared now through baptism (Rom 6:3–4) and the Lord's Supper (1 Cor 11:23–26) that unite Christians with Jesus' victory over death. Our seventh principle allows one to see how the discipleship of all and the leadership of some were maintained through the diversity of two situations, for which the first Good Friday and Easter Sunday formed the watershed.

The crucifixion and resurrection realized and revealed the kingdom proclaimed by Jesus, yet it remained a kingdom still to be consummated. The eschatological provisionality abundantly attested by the NT affects or should affect everything in church life: worship, beliefs, standards of behavior, and patterns of organization (including hierarchical leadership and apostolic succession in ordained ministry). This eighth principle for appropriating the scriptures invites us to recognize the provisional nature of all human authority, including that of hierarchical leaders succeeding one another in the church. They belong to and lead a community that is a public sign of God's kingdom which will finally and fully come in and through Christ. This NT eschatological perspective on the church and her leadership must never be lost. The last thing we read in the scriptures about the twelve sets them within the eschatological context of the heavenly Jerusalem to come (Rv 21:14). To check a merely retrospective view that risks reducing apostolicity to mere episcopal succession, a risk encouraged by the way Irenaeus and later Eusebius of Caesarea left us lists of the occupants of the great dioceses, we need an "anamnesis" of the last days—an expectation of what is to come that rises above a mere memory of what has been.

How might our ninth principle (the Bible's dialogue with philosophy) work for the issue in hand? What would this dialogue suggest when debating with those who maintain total "egalitarianism" and exclude all forms of "subordination"? To argue that "subordination is never and nowhere acceptable" is to make an ultimate, philosophical statement about the way interpersonal arrangements should always be. One looks here for some clarity on the notions and reality of authority and subordination,[17] along with some philosophical reflections on church order. Could a realistic philosophy—and that is the question this chapter faces—envision the church not just as a community of disciples but as a community of *equal* disciples, which excludes any and all subordination to authority figures? Work in hospitals, theaters, cockpits of jet airliners, fire stations, military posts, and other scenes of human activity would turn dangerously chaotic if there was no one officially in charge. The functioning of surgeons, managers, directors, captains, chiefs, and generals obviously involves the subordination of those led to their leaders. In many areas of life we need someone in authority who gives orders (often requiring to be articulated after genuine and supportive dialogue) and takes final responsibility. Or is it *only religious* authority (that "hier-archy" in the proper sense denotes) to be ruled out, on the basis that any subordination whatsoever within Christianity has been excluded by Jesus and the Holy Spirit? In that case the argument about authority in the church moves from our ninth principle back to principles one through eight, as cited and applied above. Furthermore, to accept superiors and subordinates (*not* to be confused with masters and slaves) in "secular" affairs while excluding them in the "sacred" zone of religion would posit an extraordinary gap between the order of "nature" and that of "grace." Jesus is remembered, of course, as challenging natural family ties (Mk 3:31–35 par.) and such natural duties as that of burying dead relatives (Lk 9:59–60 par.). On the question of leadership did Jesus reject it completely and so take an extraordinary stand against such a "natural" way of organizing people? Rather than rejecting all leadership in his community, Jesus encouraged new ways for exercising authority—the greatest needed to become the least and the servants of all (Mk 10:41–45 par.). When reflecting on the post-Easter situation in any case it seems fanciful to hold that a worldwide church could be coordinated and even maintained in its communion if all authoritative leadership and subordination were to be banished. A point that is obvious to political philosophers and sociologists—that institutionalization is necessary for survival—sometimes seems to escape the attention of theologians and exegetes. Sociologists may go further here, by arguing that religious authorities and institutions can foster rather than thwart the spiritual lives of individuals and groups.[18]

Finally, cultural considerations (principle ten) come into play. The inculturation of the church's authority and ways of exercising it in obedience to Christ invites much discernment and perhaps painful self-criticism. Here we want also to remain alert to the temptation to absolutize or one-sidedly privilege some cultural values. Egalitarian, antihierarchical social politics appear at times to dictate the positions taken about church order. Cultural principles should not be substituted for responsive allegiance to Jesus Christ and what the inspired scriptures witness about his intentions for the disciples and their community. The risk of reinventing the origins of Christianity in the image of current fashions and values may not be overlooked, just as one should not blindly stay imprisoned in rigid and even dying cultural forms inherited from the past. The inculturation of the scriptural vision of church leadership is a challenging task. Easy claims about hierarchical organization necessarily issuing in male dominance and patriarchal rule call for testing. Is that assertion necessarily true at all times and in all cultures?

The stakes are obviously high when theologians seek to appropriate the scriptures on the question of fidelity to the directly willed church order. Christ's actions brought into existence the church as worldwide communion of disciples. Does or should this ecclesial communion exclude the institutionalized, hierarchical leadership of those who are consecrated and "missioned" (see Jn 10:36)? Or does it call for an institutional structure and authority that is legitimately transmitted, while remaining a fundamental fellowship with the tripersonal God that reaches beyond all merely human structures, arrangements, and authority? In answering this central question, the present chapter has proposed ways of interpreting and appropriating the scriptures in line with our ten principles. Here, as elsewhere, we invite challenges both to these principles and to the way we apply them. But first let us air one challenge coming from ourselves.

The question tackled in this chapter could be rephrased in terms of the *apostolic* origins and sign-value of the threefold ordained ministry and, in particular, of the episcopal office as it emerged in the second century and has continued ever since. Do bishops relate to the apostles in a way that resembles (but is not synonymous with) the relationship in which the apostles stood to Christ, so that bishops form a sign of continuity with the apostolic faith in Christ and witness to him that constitutes the church? Putting this question presupposes that one accepts that what comes from Christ through the apostles (in both the pre-Easter and post-Easter situation) makes the church to be his church. Hence it presupposes that one wishes to be "apostolic"—that is to say, that one wishes to transmit the faith, proclamation, church order, and commitment to service arising from the apostles. Thus the question

becomes: Is the church community, constituted by the proclamation of
the word, the celebration of the sacraments, and ministry to the world,
also genuinely apostolic in being served by an ordained ministry and
led by bishops? We say "also," because we must acknowledge the life
and worship of the *whole* community, maintained by the Holy Spirit, to
be the primary expression of "the faith that comes to us from the apostles" (First Eucharistic Prayer) and of the continuity in/of that faith. In
this sense of continuing to be apostolic in faith and life, apostolic succession is an attribute of the whole church and is wider than mere episcopal succession. That said, the issue remains: Do members of the
ordained ministry and successors in the episcopal office embody visi-
bly in structured forms the church's fidelity to the apostolic faith, witness, and life in fellowship? Do that ministry and office belong among
the necessary means for handing on and living the same apostolic faith
in "succession" or continuity? This chapter could have tried applying
our ten principles to apostolic succession in one of its major post-NT
signs and developments: episcopal succession. Instead, we phrased the
question more broadly: in terms of some kind of ecclesial leadership in
a hierarchical organization as opposed to a totally egalitarian community.

6

The Petrine Ministry as Easter Witness

In applying its ten principles, this book has thus far tackled unquestionably central issues: the divinity of Christ, his redemptive work, the naming of the trinity, and the basic structure of the church. Let us now add a fifth issue, one that is of lesser importance in the "hierarchy" of Christian truths but which has considerable significance for inner-Christian dialogue and unity: the Petrine ministry. What do the scriptures indicate about God's designs for the function of Peter? Obviously any discussion of the Petrine ministry and primacy bears on the role of the church leader with the major Petrine connection: the Bishop of Rome. But in this chapter we wish to limit our reflections to the place of Peter at the start of Christianity, using the Petrine function as a fifth case in applying our ten principles for the theological appropriation of the scriptures. In writing this chapter we are aware not only of being situated in a whole web of historical, cultural, and scholarly traditions, but also of separating ourselves from the assumptions and conclusions held by many of our readers. We hold, as will emerge, that witness to the crucified Jesus' resurrection offers the preferable key for interpreting and explaining the Petrine ministry—an approach that does not correspond to the cherished views either of those who champion this ministry or of those who reduce and even denigrate it.

Principles One Through Five

"Hearing" the scriptures (principle one) involves hearing *all* the relevant NT texts about the function of Peter. What has happened and continues to happen is that only some passages receive a hearing and are then questioned on their significance for the Petrine (and Papal) ministry; this has been the case with both those who maximize and those who minimize their impact. In other words there has been a widely shared tradition about the texts to be heard, a tradition that coexists with strong divergences as to what these texts witness to and even prescribe. On 17 October 1978 Pope John Paul II expressed this consensus when, in the first address of his pontificate, he cited three texts (Mt 16:18–19; Lk 22:31–32; and Jn 21:15–17) and stated: "We are completely convinced that all modern inquiry into the 'Petrine ministry' must be based on these three hinges of the gospel."[1] The first two of these three texts have their context in the pre-Easter situation: the first text promises Peter "the keys of the kingdom of heaven" and the power to "bind" and "loose"; the third establishes Peter as the pastor who must feed Christ's "lambs" and "sheep." These three classic passages that have featured so much in the defense of the Petrine/Papal primacy (as well as in debates about and opposition to that primacy) point to a Petrine function instituted by, or at least promised by, the pre-Easter Jesus (Mt 16:18–19; Lk 22:31–32). These and other Petrine texts from the ministry of Jesus have been repeatedly cited to legitimate the pastoral ministry of Peter (and of his successors) for the universal church. The first (Mt 16:18–19) and third (Jn 21:15–17) of the "big three" texts figure prominently in the First Vatican Council's teaching on the Petrine primacy (DS 3053), while the second (Lk 22:31–32) of those three texts turns up in the same Council's statement on the Pope's infallible magisterium (DS 3070). In its first common report on "Authority in the Church" (Venice 1976) the Anglican-Roman Catholic International Commission (ARCIC) mentioned only three biblical texts when it came to "conciliar and primatial authority" with their attendant "problems and prospects": Mt 16:18–19; Lk 22:31–32; Jn 21:15–17 (n. 24).[2] In its second statement on "Authority in the Church" (Windsor 1981) ARCIC listed a range of Petrine texts from the NT (nn. 2–9), paying particular attention to the "big three" texts, each of which is mentioned twice.[3] These three texts received the primary emphasis when John Paul II presented the Bishop of Rome's "ministry of unity" in his encyclical of 25 May 1995, *Ut unum sint,* even if the Pope at once adds: "It is also significant that according to the First Letter of Paul to the Corinthians the Risen Christ appears to Cephas and then to the

Twelve" (n. 91).[4] The 1981 Windsor statement from ARCIC had likewise remarked in passing on this "special appearance" of the risen Jesus to Peter, noting that it is also attested by Lk 24:34.[5]

What if we take up this possibility opened by Luke and Paul for interpreting the Petrine function: namely, an interpretation based on understanding Peter's primary (but not exclusive) role in the emerging church to be that of witnessing to the resurrection and of gathering the community through the power of his Easter message? At the end of the Emmaus story Luke quotes a traditional formula: "The Lord has risen indeed and has appeared to Simon" (Lk 24:34), a formula that converges with another tradition cited by Paul in 1 Cor 15:4–5 (Christ "has been raised" and "appeared to Cephas"). Seemingly Luke introduces the early formulation about the appearance to Peter so as to head off any impression that the Emmaus appearance is the primary one. Even before Cleopas and his companion return, Peter's testimony has brought to Easter-faith "the eleven" and "those who were with them" (Lk 24:33). The report from Emmaus and the later appearances of the Lord strengthen and clarify this faith, but do not create it for the first time. Luke has prepared his readers for the role of Peter as the agent of faith in the resurrection. This is the real thrust of Jesus' promise to Peter at the Last Supper: "For you I have prayed that your faith may not fail; and when you have come to yourself, you must lend strength to your brothers" (Lk 22:32). The primary appearance of the risen Lord to Peter enables the apostle to play just that role. He comes to himself and strengthens his brethren by the power of his Easter-faith.

Mk 16:7 seems to refer to this foundational appearance to Peter. Some scholars have also detected a version of this encounter in John 21, even if the narrative tells of seven others, above all the beloved disciple, being with Peter on that postresurrection occasion.[6] In the opening chapters of Acts, Luke presents Peter as the head of a "college" of Easter witnesses. A hint of such a collegial mindset comes from Paul, when he appeals to the common preaching of the resurrection (1 Cor 15:11) after listing Peter as the first witness to the risen Lord (1 Cor 15:5). Peter does other things: e.g., taking the initiative to find a substitute member of the twelve after the death of Judas (Acts 1:15–26), conferring with John the gift of the Holy Spirit (Acts 8:14–17), working miracles (Acts 3:1–10; 5:15–16; 9:32–42), playing a key role in the admission of Gentiles into the church (Acts 10.1–11:18; 15:1–29). But the major function of Peter is that of being, "with the eleven" (Acts 2:14) and "all" the other first Christians (Acts 2:32), *the* public witness to the resurrection of Jesus from the dead. For Luke he is the example *par excellence* of an authoritative eyewitness (to the risen Lord) and minister of the word (Lk 1:2).

Various writers have "heard" the NT on the Easter prominence of Peter, only to develop this theme in unsatisfactory ways. In his *Jesus* Edward Schillebeeckx reconstructs matters as follows: Peter undergoes a conversion experience, becomes the first to "see" the truth of Jesus' resurrection (albeit without him or anyone else seeing the risen Jesus himself), and leads others to accept this truth.[7] The thesis of Schillebeeckx recalls earlier writers, often liberal German Protestants, who reduced all the Easter encounters or experiences to that enjoyed by Peter.[8]

In *The Gnostic Gospels* (New York: Random House, 1979) Elaine Pagels objects to the whole doctrine of Christ's bodily resurrection because it functions as a means of social control and ideological repression. It "serves an essential [or essentially?] *political* function: it legitimizes the authority of certain men [= the Popes of Rome] who claim to exercise exclusive [*sic*] leadership over the churches as the successors of the apostle Peter. From the second century, the doctrine has served to validate the apostolic succession of bishops, the basis of papal authority to this day" (6–7; italics hers). Three pages later she writes of the theory "that all authority derives [simply or only partly?] from certain apostles' experience of the resurrected Christ, an experience now closed forever" (10). She assures her readers: "Even today the pope traces his [ordination]—and the primacy he claims over the rest—to Peter himself, 'first of the apostles,' since he was 'first witness of the resurrection'" (11). There is much to question and challenge here. First, that "certain apostles' experience of the resurrected Christ" and, in particular, Peter's experience of the risen Jesus, served "an essential political function" by legitimating papal authority down through the centuries is highly dubious. When texts were produced to legitimate that authority, they were regularly the "big three": Mt 16:18–19; Lk 22:31–32; Jn 21:15–17. John 21 has been pressed into service as part of a promise-conferral scheme—the primacy promised in Matthew 16 was conferred in John 21—and not precisely to maintain that the very appearance of the risen Jesus to Peter validates the authority of Peter and his successors. Inside the Roman Basilica of St. Peter the "big three" texts tower over the congregation. The key "appearance-to-Peter" texts (Lk 24:34 and 1 Cor 15:5) are notable for their absence, a fact remarked on years ago by Erich Seeberg.[9] Obviously the popes have not been so interested in linking their primacy to Peter precisely as the "first witness of the resurrection." Would that Pagels were right and that official claims for a succession to Peter's function had taken more, or at least some, notice of his Easter experience and ministry! Second, one should distinguish between an encounter with the risen Christ and "the whole doctrine" of his bodily resurrection. That doctrine drew on and included much more than simply the appearances of the risen Jesus: e.g., it drew on (and modified) previous Jewish beliefs about resurrection, and included notions about the nature of the risen bodiliness that St. Paul for one did not propose as if they were implied by the appearance of Jesus to him. He did not directly use what he reported in 1 Cor 15:8 when fashioning his subsequent argument about the risen "spiritual" body (1 Cor 15:35–54). Third, the doctrine of Christ's bodily resurrection (which includes the witness to his appearances) has served some "political function." But its function has gone quite beyond any function that was merely political and this-worldly.[10] Fourth, even Pope Boniface VIII did not claim to exercise as successor of the apostle Peter exclusive leadership over the churches. If he made such a claim, he should have tried to abolish the office of bishops, suppress rectors of great churches, and in general remove all kinds of local and national leadership in Christendom. Fifth, the way "the apostolic succession of bishops" has been validated has regularly ignored any reference to Christ's bodily resurrection and the postresurrection appearances. In his accurate and very standard entry on "apostolic succession" for the *New Catholic Encyclopedia,* 15 vols. (New York: McGraw-Hill, 1967) F. A. Sullivan makes no reference at all either to the resurrection of Jesus or his postresurrection appearances (i, 695–96). When its 1993 Canterbury statement on "Ministry and Ordination" explained what the two traditions hold, the Anglican-Roman Catholic International Commission did not list Christ's bodily resurrection and Easter appearances among the "essential features" that belong to "apostolic succession" (n. 16).[11] In 1982 the Faith and Order Commission of the World Council of Churches published its long-awaited paper on "Baptism, Eucharist and Ministry." In expounding "Succession in the Apostolic Tradition" (nn. 34–38), that commission made no reference in its main text to the bodily resurrection and appearances of Christ; a commentary added to n. 34 referred in passing to the apostles' "witness of the life and resurrection of Christ."[12] We could go on naming further individual theologians and official reports to establish our negative conclusion. The exposition and validation of the apostolic succession of bishops (and of the church as a whole) has hardly, if ever, been connected with Christ's bodily resurrection and Easter appearances. The evidence does not support Pagels' assertion.[13]

Some scholars have "heard" resurrection overtones in the NT testimony to the Petrine ministry (e.g., Schillebeeckx, Seeberg, and Pagels), but have done so in less than satisfying ways. The NT allows us neither to separate Peter from the other Easter witnesses, nor to isolate Peter's experience of the risen Jesus from other NT data that relate him to the pre-Easter and post-Easter Jesus, nor to reduce the Petrine function simply to Easter witness. Pheme Perkins has rightly commented, for instance, on an early tradition associating Peter with the composition of Mark's Gospel: Papias' account of how Mark came to be written shows that Peter "was felt to be a living link to the words and deeds of Jesus."[14] A decade earlier Perkins published a major work on the resurrection of Jesus, *Resurrection: New Testament Witness and Contemporary Reflection* (London: Geoffrey Chapman, 1984). Yet in her 1994 book she does not make much of witness to the resurrection as *a*, let alone *the*, major key to the Petrine function. Peter as witness to the risen Jesus turns up rarely in *Peter: Apostle for the Whole Church* (3, 8, 33); he is presented as much or even more in such roles as an exemplary disciple (who eventually suffers martyrdom), founder, universal apostle, and shepherd. When all is said and done, "hearing" the scriptures and, in particular, the NT on the Petrine function will not and should not by itself decide one's primary approach to Peter's ministry. The other nine principles need to be deployed.[15]

Our second principle (the "active" hearing of the scriptures) encourages us to situate liturgically, practically, and academically an Easter vision of the Petrine function. (1) This vision looks well liturgically since it starts from Peter but points away from him to the resurrection of the crucified Jesus, the center of the church's sacramental life and *the* basis for praise offered together to God. To view the Petrine ministry primarily in terms of Easter witness is then to view it in a way that is liturgically congenial. (2) A vital Easter vision, either here or elsewhere, develops a practical desire to be agents of the risen Lord and to be engaged with him for the victory of life over death, justice over injustice, and peace over murderous strife. (3) This vision of the Petrine function, by focusing on the Easter mystery through which Jesus was revealed as the effective Messiah, Lord, and Son of God, expresses the truth at the heart of the Christian story. An "academic" account of the Christian story should prioritize Easter, since the events of the first Good Friday and Easter Sunday form the climax of the saving revelation of the tripersonal God. To prioritize Peter's role as Easter proclaimer has a further, theological advantage. Those who agree to set the (prophetic) service of the word ahead of the (priestly) sacramental ministry and the (kingly) shepherding and leading of Christ's flock will be predisposed to "hear" our version of the Petrine function as primarily (but not exclusively) involving the Easter word in witnessing to the resurrection. To sum up: a version of the Petrine ministry that centers on what the NT yields about his Easter witness has much to commend it in the three contexts that active hearing of the scriptures privilege—the liturgy, practical discipleship, and theological reflection.

The rule of faith, deployed in the classical creeds, forms the matrix for the interpretation and appropriation of the scriptures (principle three). The resurrection of the crucified Jesus stands at the heart of the Nicene-Constantinopolitan Creed and the Apostles' Creed. These creeds do not, to be sure, confess the Easter appearances as such, let alone name the great witnesses who saw the risen Lord and proclaimed his resurrection. But highlighting what the NT reports of Peter's role as Easter witness moves us to the center of our christological confession: the paschal mystery.

Our fourth principle, the convergence of biblical testimony, does not obviously support the case for prioritizing Peter's Easter witness. The NT does not contain a single, monolithic tradition about Peter. He can be depicted as fisherman or missionary (Mk 1:16–18; Lk 5:10), shepherd (Jn 21:15–17), rock (Mt 16:18; see Eph 2:20), repentant sinner (Mk 14:72), and martyr (Jn 21:18–19; see 13:36). The scriptural material about Peter offers a rich variety that does not appear to converge on one function, that of Easter witness as such. Nevertheless, we feel justified in relating the different traditions to this witness. In the opening chapters of Acts, Peter's missionary "fishing" takes the form of proclaiming the resurrection. The shepherding vocation comes from the risen Christ. Peter's role as "rock" receives its legitimation from the crucified and risen Jesus, who is the "living stone," the "cornerstone," and the "stone of scandal" (1 Pt 2:4–8). Peter's repentance comes with the passion, death, and resurrection of Jesus (Lk 22:61–62; 23:49; Jn 21:15–17); he will suffer martyrdom in the service of the risen Lord (Jn 21:18–19). In short, different Petrine traditions converge on the function of Easter witness. Without that witness they fail to make much sense.

The consensus of biblical scholars (principle five) does not show up as universal on the question of the Petrine responsibility for Easter witness. As we saw above, in her exegetical and historical study of Peter, Perkins does not attend a great deal to that theme. Nevertheless, a solid number of exegetes do. The judgment of R. E. Brown et al. (eds.), *Peter in the New Testament* (London: Geoffrey Chapman, 1973), still stands: "the important tradition about Peter having been the first of the major companions of Jesus' ministry to have seen the Lord after the resurrection" provided "very likely" the "original context or catalyst for much of the New Testament material about Peter" (165). In *Simon-Petrus: Geschichte und geschichtliche Bedeutung des ersten Jüngers Jesu Christi* (Stuttgart: Anton Hiersemann, 1980) Rudolf Pesch developed the theme of Peter as "witness of Easter-Faith" (49–50). Many other exegetes have over the years paid appropriate attention to that theme.[16]

Principles Six Through Ten

The principle of metathemes and metanarratives (principle six) appeals to single themes and extended narratives that rise above their original settings and recur, with appropriate developments and modifications, in new contexts. When explaining this principle, Chapter 1 names the resurrection of the crucified Jesus as the central metanarrative of the Bible. Stressing the Petrine function of Easter witness would have thus the advantage of recognizing his link with the chief narrative the scriptures yield for theological interpretation. His proclamation of the resurrection connects Peter with the central metanarrative of the whole Bible. As regards metathemes, we noted above six major images of Peter: as fisherman/missionary, shepherd, rock, martyr, repentant sinner, and Easter witness. Some of these images or themes enjoy a long biblical history (e.g., those of shepherds and repentant sinners). At times the OT prophets went on the equivalent of missionary journeys to bring God's word to the people; the theme and reality of martyrdom has its place in the OT history and literature, as well as in the NT (e.g., in the Gospels, Acts, and Revelation). The notion of "rock" enjoys certain variations, as when "apostles and prophets" are named as foundational stones for God's house and people (Eph 2:20), and the twelve feature as the foundations of the wall for the heavenly Jerusalem (Rv 21:14). These passages also bear on Peter's function as "rock" in being one of the apostles, the leader of the twelve, one of the original "pillars" (Gal 2:9), and as "Simon" who became "Peter" (Mk 3:16), the "rock" of Jesus' promise (Mt 16:18). In short, the six Petrine images are also equivalently biblical metathemes, and—as we have seen—they all relate to the Easter ministry of Peter.

Our seventh principle of continuity within discontinuity applies to the case of Peter. During the ministry of Jesus, Peter functions as a spokesman for the twelve (Mk 8:29; Jn 6:68–69). With James and John, he witnesses the raising of Jairus' daughter, Jesus' transfiguration, and the agony in the garden (Mk 5:37–42; 9:2–8; 14:33–42). According to Luke, Peter is sent with John to prepare the passover for Jesus and his disciples (Lk 22:8). Prominent at other points in the pre-Easter story (e.g., Mt 14:28–32; 17:24–27; 18:21–22; Mk 14:27–31), Peter changes dramatically with the resurrection of the crucified Jesus, assumes his leadership role, and effectively proclaims the reconciling forgiveness released by the Easter mystery and the associated gift of the Holy Spirit (e.g., Acts 2:14–42). The watershed of Easter does not invalidate or cancel what has been there in Peter's life through his closeness to Jesus and leadership of the twelve. One may also speak of some "continuity" between (1) Peter's pre-Easter denials, failures, and misunderstandings, and (2) his need in the post-Easter situation to learn and correct his behavior (Acts 10:9–48; Gal 2:11–14). Yet there is discontinuity here as well: what Peter now learns and corrects concerns very directly the mediation to others of Christ's salvation, something that does not touch quite so directly the shadow side of Peter's behavior in the pre-Easter context. Although there is obviously no complete break between the pre-Easter and post-Easter Peter, his new activity may not be reduced to the way he has operated during Jesus' ministry. After being sent on a trial mission with the rest of the twelve (Mk 6:7–13) to preach the kingdom to the Jews in the Holy Land (Mt 10:6 = Lk 7:2; see Mt 15:24), he is now commissioned to preach the resurrection of the crucified Jesus (and the new life it entails) to all Jews everywhere (Gal 2:7–8). Easter brings Peter the new, worldwide function of Easter witness as missionary, shepherd, and rock—an activity that eventually brings his final witness as martyr.

The future-oriented nature of divine revelation and salvation communicated through Jesus Christ (principle eight) leaves its impression also on the ministry of Peter and our theological reflections about it. His functions as rock, missionary, and shepherd are to be exercised for the sake of the present and future church and, even more broadly, for the sake of the coming kingdom of God. The goals of the Petrine function will be fully realized only when that consummation of all things comes, the climax of the Easter mystery to which the apostle witnesses. He proclaims a message that so far has received its full measure only in the risen Christ, "the first-born from the dead" (Col 1:18). Thus along with the eleven Peter is pictured in anticipation: the wall of the heavenly Jerusalem will have "twelve foundations, and on them the twelve names of the twelve apostles of the Lamb" (Rv 21:14).

The conceptual clarity that philosophy demands (principle nine) bears in particular on the biblical theme of Peter as Easter witness. What characteristics should we look for in a witness? How does witnessing and testimony work? What makes a witness credible? Philosophical contributions here can accompany the move from the simpler, prephilosophical material on the Petrine function (especially Lk 24:34; 1 Cor 15:5) to a clearer, theological statement of what such witness entails.[17]

It is insufficient here to recall the truism that most of what we know anyway comes to us through testimony. Of course, we constantly trust the word of others to acquire reliable beliefs and expand our knowledge about matters we shall not and simply cannot check for ourselves. As Easter witness, however, Peter testifies to an event that is not only extraordinary but also promises wonderful and everlasting benefits for those who accept his word and undertake a new way of life. Here, if anywhere, is a testimony that is far "bigger" than the witness himself, which aims to evoke a true and remarkably beneficial belief, and whose particular characteristics run counter to our general experience of what happens to the dead. Peter's report about meeting the risen Christ is obviously an astonishing piece of testimony about a divine action and very unlike things people then and now commonly experience.[18]

Lacking direct, perceptual information on the postmortem existence of the risen Jesus, we can only believe on the word of those who have claimed to have seen him (1 Pt 1:8). We rely on their testimony to what they have experienced firsthand. It is wise to recognize here the plurality of Easter witnesses and forestall an obvious objection to Peter's testimony: *testis unus, testis nullus* ("one witness is no witness"). This maxim does not apply in the present context, as Peter's Easter testimony draws corroboration from that of others. The collective witness coming from Paul, Mary Magdalene, and other early Christians bears on any critical response to the questions: Was Peter deliberately deceptive in his Easter witness? Was he blindly fanatical, honestly mistaken, or simply gullible about what he saw or thought he saw? In appraising Peter and finding him (and other Easter witnesses) to be credible, two things come into play.

First, we become personally related to these witnesses, even though they have long since departed from the visible scene. Their veracity and personal worth are at stake. Who they are and what they do support our belief in what they say. Impressed, for instance, by the utterly sincere and heroic quality of the conviction shown by Peter and Paul in living and dying for their testimony to Jesus' new postmortem existence, we trust their word, believe in them, and enter some kind of personal relationship with them. Hearing and believing a witness, especially about a matter of such importance as Jesus' resurrection from the dead, is an interpersonal act that differs from reading scientific instruments to confirm some general result from experiments about which we may have had our doubts. It also differs from checking scientific instruments to establish or confirm some scientific fact, as when a pilot reads an aircraft's altimeter to verify the height of a particular flight approaching a given airport on a particular day. In accepting the testimony of Peter and others to what happened once and for all to Jesus after his crucifixion and burial, we are not reading an instrument but hearing and accepting personal witnesses. Easter-faith, when coming "from what is heard" (Rom 10:17) about Christ, also involves our personal faith in those who testify to this unique good news.

Second, this witness changes those who accept their testimony. They do not receive the Easter testimony as if it simply were an astonishing report that they could accept and then, so to speak, walk away from. Here Karl Rahner's distinction between the role for us of Easter witnesses and the function of ordinary, secular testimony comes into play. As an example of the latter, I could have someone assure me that at midday last New Year's Day she saw a middle-aged man dive into the Tiber from the Ponte Cavour. Even though I was away in another part of Rome at the time, I could easily accept this testimony as credible and believe the witness, being encouraged to do so by similar sights I have earlier experienced in Paris when I saw people take similar plunges at high noon on New Year's Day. However, in the case of the first disciples' witness to the Easter appearances, I simply have never had such a personal experience. I was not there to be blessed by an appearance of the risen Christ in the period following his resurrection. My history has stationed me in a different place and time. From my own particular, historical experience I do not know what it is like to share in the origins of Christianity by seeing the risen Lord. Yet we today, Rahner argues, "do not stand simply and absolutely outside the experience of the apostolic witnesses," separated from them by an historical gulf that nothing can ever bridge. At a basic, primordial level we share with them (and indeed with all human beings) what Rahner calls the same "transcendental hope in resurrection," an orientation toward a total and lasting fulfillment of our existence. Like other "transcendental Thomists," Rahner finds this dynamic openness implicitly present in every exercise of human knowledge and freedom. Because of our primordial, transcendental hope, the apostolic witness to Jesus' resurrection does not bring us "something which is totally unexpected and lies totally outside of our experience." This Easter testimony comes to us as those who are insiders—not in the concrete, historical sense of having already had such a personal experience ourselves but in the transcendental sense of always, if implicitly, experiencing a thrust toward the full and permanent life of resurrection. Thus trusting the Easter witness of Peter and others differs from the case of accepting ordinary testimony to "merely secular" matters, where (1) we may have already enjoyed similar, if not identical particular experiences ourselves, and (2) accepting the testimony will not normally have much, if any, impact on the future course of our lives.[19] Accepting the testimony from Peter and the other Easter witnesses entails opening ourselves up to moving from a reliance on their testimony to a new way of life in which we may share something of the visionary's experience in the Book of Revelation. There the risen Christ himself is mysteriously experienced and testifies directly to his resurrection: "I died, and behold I am alive forevermore" (Rv 1:18).

Lastly, inculturation (principle ten) raises the question: How can we embody in various, particular cultures the theme of Peter's Easter witness? Faced with the one Peter and the many cultures, what can we express about the meaning of his word and witness for those cultures? What is it to appropriate and inculturate around the world the biblical testimony to the Petrine function? We remarked in Chapter 1 on the way meaning is at least partly a cultural phenomenon. What spiritual experiences and symbolic expressions can be brought into play to discover and translate the meaning of Peter's Easter function for different cultures? Obviously this task of inculturation will be closely associated with the task of inculturating the heart of the Easter message itself: Christ crucified and risen to join the Father in communicating the Holy Spirit to the world. This inculturation, even more than that for other aspects of biblical revelation, requires *both* insertion into *and* transformation of cultural values and symbols. Right from the first century of the church's history, witnesses like St. Clement of Rome found expressions of the resurrection in nature and human experience. Centuries later George Herbert in "The Flower" saw the pattern of his own spiritual life symbolized by the resurrecting power of spring in calling forth fresh growth. While *not equating* the resurrection with nature's new life in springtime, Herbert intended to insert the Easter message into the world around him. In "That Nature Is a Heraclitean Fire" Gerard Manley Hopkins, however, found the "comfort of the resurrection" in the way it reverses the "mortal trash" and "poor potsherd" of human existence. Herbert wrote of insertion, while Hopkins emphasized transformation in their literary inculturation of the message of Easter.

This chapter has set out what we take our ten principles to require when using the scriptures in reflecting on the Petrine ministry. As we observed at the end of Chapter 1, Christocentrism binds the ten principles closely together. By highlighting witness to the resurrection when interpreting the Petrine function, we obviously relate our priorities to the heart of the story and mystery of Christ: his crucifixion and resurrection from the dead. The role and responsibility that Peter had for the founding generation of the church derives from and centers on the very Easter mystery itself.

We expect the proposal we have made in this chapter, more than those made in previous chapters, to meet with resistance or simple silence. We can end by suggesting some reasons for such a reaction. First, in theology and elsewhere it is desperately hard to change commonly cherished ideas. As we have seen, the three texts (Mt 16:18–19;

Lk 22:31–32; Jn 21:15–17) have dominated expositions of and debates about the Petrine function. It is agreed, or more often quietly presupposed, that theological reflection about Peter should start from and center on these "big three" texts. It is uncommon to propose giving the priority to Lk 24:34 and 1 Cor 15:5. Second, our thesis depends on following the liturgy and building our theology of Peter around the resurrection of the crucified Jesus. Those many theologians who do not place the resurrection at the heart of their reflections will hardly turn around and do so when they come to the specific issue of the Petrine ministry. Third, we are encouraging a switch of symbols: away from assigning primacy to such Petrine symbols as "rock," "shepherd," and "fisherman" to acknowledging the centrality of the symbol of Peter as Easter preacher. Changes of symbols do not come easily, either in theology or elsewhere. Often it is easier to modify cherished ideas rather than cherished symbols. Fourth, we are championing an alternative biblical option, one found in Paul and developed by Luke. Many systematic theologians are still reluctant to let scriptural data call into question the positions that they have inherited from their teachers and their traditions.

7

On Not Misusing the Ministry of Jesus

Thus far this book has set out ten principles to guide the passage from the scriptures to systematic theology (Chapter 1). Subsequent chapters (Chapters 2–6) tested the value of these principles by applying them to some major theological issues. In this chapter we wish to address a recurrent phenomenon that can be found among theologians of very different standpoints: an appeal to the pre-Easter Jesus (generally the Jesus presented by the synoptic Gospels) as if this were the only or practically the only way to verify and legitimate theological positions about the trinity, the atonement, the church, the sacraments, and so forth.

This one-sided privileging of the significance of Jesus' public ministry tries to "get too much" out of the synoptic Gospels, as if the divine revelation through Jesus were completed with his life and death. This (normally tacit) presumption that nothing is revealed in the post-Easter situation obviously plays down the role of the Holy Spirit in illuminating the apostolic generation as to the meaning and implications of what they have experienced of Jesus (see Jn 14:26; 15:26; 16:13–14). This unilateral privileging of Jesus' ministry can hardly be compatible with hearing all the scriptures (principle one), biblical convergence (principle four), metathemes and metanarratives (principle six), and continuity-in-discontinuity (principle seven).

Different motives come into play to encourage this kind of "retreat" to the story of Jesus. Some seem prompted by the view, to be found both in the classical world and in the romantic movement, that antiquity is *a* or even *the* sign of truth. The older is presumed to be the better and the truer. What comes at the beginning guides us to the real truth of things; in our case it is the historical ministry of Jesus or rather what we know of it through the Gospels. Others hold that institutional Christianity, perhaps even as far back as St. Paul, has obscured the original message of Jesus. The "real" Jesus must be liberated from a Babylonian captivity within the church; and so scholars set about reconstructing his ministry and what can be known of it because only Jesus is "really" trustworthy. But what do we have at the end: the "real" Jesus or only Jesus as "recovered" by these exegetes and, one must add, often enough used to justify their particular religious and social agenda? Do they in fact finish up with an idol, the "Jesus" whom they have constructed and then declare to be authoritative, if not adorable? A further motive that appears operative is the desire to locate and establish the essence of Jesus (and perhaps also Christianity as well). Some strip off various "layers" and throw away everything except a core, which may be a wisdom message, apocalyptic proclamation, or some other version of the heart of the matter. At times this effort, as has often been remarked, can look like peeling an onion in search of a nonexistent core. Others again like Gerd Luedemann seem driven back to the ministry and message of Jesus because of difficulties they have over the Easter events and the (revelatory and salvific) impact of the resurrection. Thus Luedemann argues that in essence "*everything* that was finally recognized after Easter was already present" since "*all* the characteristics of the earliest resurrection faith" were already present "in the sayings and history of Jesus."[1] Motivation for the retreat to Jesus can vary. Let us provide some examples of what we are concerned about in misusing the data from Jesus' ministry.

The misuse turns up in popular discussion, when isolated texts battle with each other. One of us has heard the proposal to extend eucharistic hospitality to the nonbaptized on the basis of a saying from Jesus: "He who is not against us is with us" (Mk 9:40). In the debate this was then countered by another text: "Cast not your pearls before swine" (Mt 7:6). Notoriously the Gospels offer a supply of texts which can be similarly played off against each other. Talk of the unforgivable sin (Mk 3:28–30) may be counterbalanced by Jesus' injunction to forgive, even seventy times seven times (Mt 6:12, 14–15; 18:21–35). The special generosity toward the less-graced suggested by the parable of the laborers and its conclusion, "The last will be first" (Mt 20:1–6), may be offset by the saying at the end of the parable of the talents, "To every one who has more will be given, but from him who has not, even what he has will be taken away" (Mt 25:29). Jesus' encouragement to "buy a sword" to which the disciples respond by producing two swords (Lk 22:35–38) has, over the centuries, been taken as a general declaration of the right of Christians to bear arms, as support for the right of the medieval papacy to exercise both material as well as spiritual power, and as "proof" that Jesus encouraged armed revolution.[2] Such appeals to this Lukan passage can be "neutralized" by citing Jesus' beatitude about peacemakers (Mt 5:9), recommendation to "turn the other cheek" (Mt 5:39), rebuke to James and John who think that inhospitable Samaritans should be destroyed (Lk 9:51–56), promise that "losing" one's life for his sake will mean "finding" it (Mt 10:39), and warning that all who take the sword "will perish by the sword" (Mt 26:52). The severe words in the context of church discipline about recalcitrants being treated "like pagans and tax-collectors" (Mt 18:17) may be confronted with the way Matthew sees fulfilled in Jesus some words from Isaiah about "not breaking a bruised reed or quenching a smoldering wick" (Mt 12:20). Debates about "titles" summon up Jesus' injunction not to use the language of "teachers, fathers, and masters" (Mt 23:8–11), but "counter-texts" are obviously at hand. Jesus' own parables feature fathers (Mt 21:28–31; Lk 15:11–32) and masters (Mt 24:45–51 = Lk 12:41–48), and he speaks of "practicing and observing" what the scribes and Pharisees say—presumably as teachers (Mt 23:2–3). But all such use of isolated texts and "battles" between seemingly opposing sayings of Jesus simply does not handle the Gospel testimony appropriately. Such usage pays little or no attention to what the evangelists intended at stage three in the composition of their works, to stage two in the transmission and function of the "Jesus-material" in the early decades of Christianity, and to stage one and the question of such sayings coming from Jesus himself—in case we need to reflect on the significance of such words in the original setting of the ministry.

At this point it could be useful to give a couple of specific instances from those who theologically mistreat data from the ministry of Jesus. Elsewhere one of us has examined such misuse coming from John Hick.[3] Here let us take up another example, the work of Sallie McFague. To begin with, we wish to look at her treatment of Jesus' parables. They have frequently been simply neglected or at least played down as sources for Christology. To interpret "the work and person of Jesus" McFague herself takes as "central" the parables of Jesus and Jesus himself as parable or "paradigmatic figure."[4] Elsewhere she explains that "to see the story of Jesus as paradigmatic means to see it as illuminative and illustrative of basic characteristics of the Christian understanding of the God-world relationship." This story is "a [not *the*] classic instance, embodying critical dimensions of the relationship between God and the world."[5] Jesus is "a parable" of God's relation to the world, because he "manifests in his own life and death [but not also in his resurrection] that the heart of the universe is unqualified love working to befriend the needy, the outcast, the oppressed."[6] This language of Jesus as parable naturally raises the question: Is he absolutely unique and unsurpassably definitive in this function? Since McFague, as we have just seen, names Jesus as only "a parable," it is not surprising to find her commenting that he is "not ontologically different from other paradigmatic figures either in our tradition or in other traditions."[7] Her position on Jesus' limited role for revelation is logically applied to the question of redemption. She resists any idea that "salvation rests with one individual and in one past act" like Jesus' life, death, and resurrection.[8] In any case salvation comes across with strongly Pelagian tones when she explains that "salvation in our time must be the task of all human beings." This position is hardly surprising, since she takes sin to offend other men and women, but not God. Setting right a situation damaged by sin is a human task rather than primarily a forgiving and loving intervention on the part of God.[9] This "do-it-yourself" understanding of salvation seems to run parallel with a certain "do-it-yourself" approach to revelation. McFague invites us to conduct thought experiments with our new metaphors (and their accompanying concepts), doing now for our time what Paul and John did for their time.[10] This position seems hardly compatible with any normative role of Paul and John as authoritative witnesses to and inspired interpreters of any revelation that came through Christ. At the same time, the position is logical and coherent in its own terms. These apostolic witnesses can hardly be claimed to enjoy any authoritative control over our thought experiments, once Jesus himself is alleged to have no unique and absolute role as revealer.

Before leaving McFague's theological appropriation of Jesus' ministry, let us note two further unsatisfactory features. First, she rightly makes much of the preaching of the kingdom, but then goes further by claiming that the kingdom of God is "the root-metaphor of Christianity."[11] This root-metaphor "is a relationship of a certain kind. The key exemplar of this relationship is Jesus of Nazareth," who speaks of and demonstrates what the new relationship with God entails.[12] Beyond question, the metaphor of the divine kingdom bulks large in the synoptic Gospels, but it does not figure much in the Letters of Paul, the Gospel of John, and elsewhere in the New Testament. McFague's claim that the kingdom of God rather than God as Father is the root-metaphor of Christianity[13] does not match the NT testimony: kingdom-talk is largely confined to the synoptic Gospels, whereas the metaphor of God as Father occurs around 254 times in the NT and, as we saw in Chapter 3, comes across as the distinctive Christian way of speaking of and relating to God. Second, to highlight one key point in Jesus' proclamation of the kingdom—its entailing our new relationship to God— should not allow one to ignore other elements in that proclamation: for instance, the kingdom as saving gift from God's kindness and as the powerful reassertion of the divine authority. Second, despite anything said about Jesus' role as parable and exemplar, it hardly reveals anything at all of God; the relationship seems to be largely one-directional—from Jesus (and us) toward God. McFague represents Christians as holding "that there is a personal, gracious power [lower-case] who is on the side of life and its fulfillment, a power whom the paradigmatic figure of Jesus of Nazareth expresses and illuminates."[14] Yet this illumination illuminates very little about God, if McFague can then say that "theology is mostly fiction,"[15] that "we do not know what God's being is,"[16] and that she "makes no claims about the so-called immanent or intrinsic trinity."[17]

McFague one-sidedly privileges the ministry of Jesus for the very little that she wants to say about God, as "revealed" by Jesus as parable and exemplar. There are some other writers who also overstress the importance of that ministry but are more positive about what may be found there for Christian faith. A. J. B. Higgins, for instance, argues: "If it is important to understand early Christian beliefs about Jesus as recorded in the New Testament, it is even more important to attempt to discover how far these beliefs may have been derived from Jesus' own teaching and *consequently to what extent they were justified.*"[18] If Higgins means what he says, he holds that *the* (the only?) justification for early (and later?) Christian beliefs about Jesus is their derivation from Jesus' own teaching—which really comes to what he and other scholars think they can reconstruct of that teaching. Another example of such maximalizing of the Gospel record for faith comes from Joachim Jeremias. He apparently wished to base faith totally on what we can establish about the past facts of Jesus' life. Let us take something that Jeremias named as essential, Jesus' interpretation of his own death.

> The very heart of the kerygma, that "Christ died for our sins in accordance with the Scriptures" (1 Cor 15:3), represents an interpretation of a historical event: this death happened for us. But this raises the question whether this interpretation of the crucifixion of Jesus has been arbitrarily impressed upon the events, or whether there was some circumstance in the events which caused this interpretation to be attached to it. *In other words,* we must ask: Did Jesus himself speak of his impending death, and what significance did he attach to it?[19]

The implication of Jeremias' position must be clearly stated. If we cannot establish historically that Jesus himself attributed a redeeming significance to his impending death, this interpretation of the crucifixion deserves dismissal as "arbitrarily impressed." Nothing short of such proof would apparently satisfy Jeremias. Seemingly the only reason why he was ready to accept Jesus' death as having happened "for us" and "for our sins" was the actual demonstration that Jesus himself interpreted his coming death in that way.

Jeremias broadens the importance of the historical ministry of Jesus to the point of asserting that his "claim to divine authority" is "the origin of Christianity."[20] Silence is here maintained about any decisive, divine intervention in Jesus' resurrection from the dead. A few pages earlier Jeremias briefly mentions the resurrection but only to insist that the risen Christ was acknowledged to be identical with the earthly Jesus.[21] For Jeremias the astonishing, revelatory fact about Jesus was his claim to authority, not his rising from the dead!

It would be news to the apostle Paul that "the origin of Christianity" should be located elsewhere than in the fact that Jesus "died for our sins and rose again for our justification" (Rom 4:25). Paul frequently proclaims Jesus' death "for our sins" without bothering at all to remark, let alone insist, that statements from Jesus himself provide the required backing for this interpretation of the crucifixion. God's action in raising

Jesus from the dead, the gift of the Spirit, and the experience of the Gospel's spread supply the needed legitimation for Paul's proclamation. Further, it would be news for the apostle to learn from Jeremias that "we cannot understand the message of Paul unless we know the message of Jesus."[22] If so, Paul has rendered extreme disservice to his readers by rarely quoting or echoing the message of Jesus.

The case of McFague, on the "liberal" side, and of Jeremias, on the "conservative" side, illustrate appeals to the pre-Easter Jesus that try to base too much on reconstructions of what Jesus preached during his earthly ministry, almost as if divine revelation was not also communicated through his resurrection from the dead and the coming of the Holy Spirit.

Several years ago we published together an article on a theme that comes out of the ministry, "The Faith of Jesus," *Theological Studies* 53 (1992), 403–23, investigating the question of the kind of faith that Jesus may or may not have exercised during his earthly existence, and at the end pointing out that there is no contradiction between believing "in" the *risen* Christ and believing "like" the *earthly* Jesus. This article was reprinted in our *Focus on Jesus* (Leominster: Gracewing, 1996). Joseph Fitzmyer subsequently dismissed our investigation for its "futility" and its "failure" to clarify and realize certain relevant points. A detailed rebuttal of his criticism may serve to provide a sharper profile on the way we understand the synoptic Gospels to help us theologically, while not being the sole norm for Christian faith.

First, we were charged with "failing to make clear what New Testament writers outside the Gospels attribute to Jesus in what they call his 'faith' and what the Gospels may portray as his psychological awareness."[23] In fact, the *only* writer outside the Gospels whom we recognized as attributing faith to Jesus is Heb 12:2; the Gospels we dealt with were the synoptic Gospels. It is hard to know how we could have been clearer, as we offered *first* a section to which we gave the heading, "Outside the Gospels," and *then* a section to which we gave the heading, "The Synoptic Gospels."[24] At the time we thought we were indulging in too many headings and too much clarity in distinguishing between what we can glean from Heb 12:2 (in the context of the whole letter) and what the synoptic Gospels allow us to conclude.

Second, we were charged with attempting to "psychoanalyze" Jesus, as if like modern therapists we were hoping to recover a great deal, if not everything, about his interior life, including the interaction between the conscious and unconscious elements in his (human) mind. To psychoanalyze a person is a far more ambitious project that goes far beyond saying something in a modest and limited way about his psychology or interior dispositions. We actually drew encouragement for this latter task from a long document from the Pontifical Biblical Commission translated into English by Fitzmyer himself: "The cautious and nuanced claims" it made about Jesus' experience and "awareness of his filial relationship and redemptive mission," we wrote, "obviously involve some claims about his 'psychology.' "[25] We concluded that "not to know much about the 'psychology of Jesus' [= not to be able to psychoanalyze him] is not equivalent to knowing nothing at all."[26]

Third, a "failure to reckon with the three stages of the gospel tradition" was imputed to us by Fitzmyer, as if we were ignorant of the complexity of the sources and status of the sayings to be found in the synoptic Gospels. In an earlier work, one of us (O'Collins) had spent pages on the three-stage development that Catholic (and other) Bible scholars have endorsed for thirty years or more: the events of Jesus' life, the period of preaching and community transmission from the thirties into the sixties, and finally the composition of the Gospels by the evangelists themselves.[27] Our article clearly operated with that scheme of triple development, when we contrasted what we find in the Gospels, with what "comes from the tradition," and "what goes back to Jesus himself" or his "authentic sayings."[28] Obviously one can dispute some of the particular conclusions we reached, but it was simply inaccurate to accuse us of "failure" to work with the triple-stage framework for interpreting the Gospel material.

Fourth, we are charged with "glossing over" what supplies the basis, norm, and vitality for "the faith of Christians in the twentieth century." This is a surprising charge, as we were not writing an article about any such basis or norm for Christian faith today. From what we have stated earlier in this present chapter and in Chapter 1, we obviously agree with Fitzmyer that Christian faith and theology are not and should not claim to be "based solely on what exegetes or theologians can reconstruct as the inner dispositions of Jesus."[29] But our article was not examining the appropriate basis for Christian faith and theology as such. We were dealing with a particular and much more limited question, one that has been emerging in recent (rather than in traditional) works of Christology: Did the Jesus of history live by faith and, if so, in what sense? It would be a further question to examine what the recognition of Jesus' faith might mean for Christians in the twentieth century. Fitzmyer dismisses any faith exercised by the earthly Jesus as "really of little importance" for the faith of Christians today. The last lines of our article and our pastoral experience suggest otherwise; for many believers it is important and deeply encouraging that like them Jesus walked by faith and not by sight. But to hold a truly informed position here one would need to do something that neither Fitzmyer nor we have done: make a scientific survey of the rank-and-file Christians about this question.

This present chapter has aspired to correct a current, one-sided privileging of Jesus' ministry, as if what either ordinary readers or sophisticated scholars (on the left or the right) glean from the synoptic Gospels is and should be uniquely decisive in what we may know and believe as Christians. With some scholars this current trend looks like a latter-day reaction to Rudolf Bultmann and those who joined him in rejecting or at least ignoring any (theological) link between the faith and proclamation of the first witnesses and the Jesus of history. Bultmann refused to "ask behind" the kerygma and insisted on subjecting everything to the kerygma (as he understood it), as if it had no connection with Jesus. Against this view we join many others in holding what we know of Jesus' history is essential for faith. At the same time, this knowledge should not be allowed to assume the role of an exclusive norm. Christian faith may not exist without some historical knowledge (in particular, of Jesus), but it does not depend simply on such knowledge. We turn now to a practical agenda: the attitude systematic theologians should have toward textual criticism, translations, and commentaries.

8

Texts, Translations, and Commentaries

What are the biblical responsibilities for theological interpreters of the scriptures? In this chapter we want to illustrate and explore three areas of "practical" responsibility that systematic theologians enter whenever they draw on any wide spectrum of biblical sources. Some of the chief challenges facing them here can be expressed in three questions: (1) What is the original text of the passage? (2) How should it be translated into English (or into other modern languages)? (3) How should we explain the meaning of the text in its closer and wider context? In other words, how should theologians comment on a given passage, or what should they take over from biblical commentaries? Let us document on a variety of issues the tasks that texts, translations, and commentaries impose on systematic theologians.

Textual Challenges

To exemplify what theologians may have to face in making the scriptures work for them, we begin with some textual choices that affect Christology. Mark's Gospel opens with a quasi-title: "The beginning of the good news of Jesus Christ, Son of God." Nevertheless, while following this reading, the NRSV, the REB, and the NJB all note that the words "Son of God *(huiou theou)*" are missing in a few ancient authorities. What importance does this variant reading enjoy? If we decide against it and judge that the copyist responsible for those particular ancient witnesses simply omitted the two Greek words, then the original text of

Mark presents us with a complete pattern from chapters 1 through 15: the evangelist (as "omniscient" author) and his readers (1:1) know who Jesus is; a voice from heaven twice names him as "my Son" (1:11; 9:7); evil spirits call him "the Holy One of God" (1:24), "the Son of God" (3:11), or "Son of the Most High God" (5:7); and a human being (a centurion) names him as "God's Son" (15:39). A slight niggling doubt, however, clouds recognizing the full scope of this progressive disclosure of Jesus' divine identity. It is quite possible that one or more copyist expanded Mark's opening words by adding "Son of God." Yet even adopting the shorter reading for Mark 1:1, we see that much of the pattern remains intact — in the movement from a heavenly voice, through that of evil spirits to the confession coming under the cross from a human being. The longer reading of 1:1, however, shows the evangelist's hand more clearly: he and his readers know, right from the outset, the secret of Jesus' full identity which will be revealed in the story that follows.

The opening chapter of John's Gospel raises a textual issue which also bears on Jesus' divinity. John's prologue announces that the Word who was "God" from the beginning became flesh and dwelt among us as Jesus Christ (Jn 1:1–17). Should we follow the NRSV in its reading of the next verse? That translation gives us: "No one has ever seen God. It is God the only Son, who is close to the Father's heart, who has made him known" (1:18). Two recently acquired Bodmer papyri (p 66 and p 75) support this rendering, which was already more or less that of the NAB: "The only Son, God, who is at the Father's side, has revealed him." But it is not accepted by the NJB and REB, even though both of these versions recognize in their notes the way in which the reading adopted by the NRSV is attested by ancient witnesses. We are persuaded by the reasons B. M. Metzger gives for the reading accepted by the NRSV.[1] From a christological point of view, this means agreeing that Jesus is twice named as "God" (*theos* without the article or the anarthrous use of *theos*) at the start of John's Gospel (1:1, 18) — a naming that will recur at the end (20:28). This "inclusion" is strengthened if we follow the NRSV and the NAB, but it remains in place (1:1 being matched by 20:28) even for those who follow the NJB and REB by not accepting the second mention of "God" in 1:18. Just as with our example above from Mark's Gospel, not too much may be made of this debate about Jn 1:18. The recognition of Jesus' divine identity in the NT, as Chapter 2 above pointed out, does not stand or fall with the attribution of "theos," let alone with the number of times this happens outside John 1:1 and 20:28.

We have looked at two examples where the evidence for the text we prefer cannot be said to be blatantly compelling. We turn now to a case bearing on Christ's virginal conception, where the normally accepted criteria for choosing between conflicting readings decisively support the choice almost universally adopted. The NRSV follows the unanimous witness of the Greek manuscripts of the NT to the plural verb ("were born") by translating Jn 1:12–13: "To all who received him [the Word]...he gave power to become children of God, who *were born,* not of blood or of the will of the flesh or of the will of man, but of God." The 1966 Jerusalem Bible (but not the 1985 NJB) follows the witness of several early Fathers of the Church (notably Irenaeus, Tertullian, and Origen) in accepting the singular "he was born." But given the "consensus of all Greek manuscripts," we agree with the judgment of the editorial committee for the United Bible Societies' Greek NT that "the plural must be adopted."[2] This view is supported by four major commentators on John's Gospel: C. K. Barrett, *The Gospel According to St. John* (Philadelphia: Westminster Press, 2nd ed., 1978), 164; R. E. Brown, *The Gospel According to John I–XII* (Garden City, NY: Doubleday, 1966), 11–12; R. Bultmann, *The Gospel of John* (Philadelphia: Westminster Press, 1971), 59 n. 5; R. Schnackenburg, *The Gospel According to John,* I (New York: Seabury, 1980), 263–265. A more recent, thorough study by J. W. Pryor, "Of the Virgin Birth or the Birth of Christians? The Text of John 1:13 Once More," *Novum Testamentum* 27 (1985), reaches the conclusion that, while "puzzles remain," the "problems in accepting the singular far outweigh those in staying with the plural" (296–318, at 318).[3]

The plural reading ("were born") of Jn 1:13 should be followed by systematic theologians. At the same time, two observations from C. K. Barrett seem relevant for the theological reception of the verse: "The origin of [the singular reading] is readily understandable; the threefold negation (not of blood, nor of the will of flesh, nor of the will of a husband) seemed to correspond exactly with the church's belief about the birth of Jesus, and since the Virgin Birth [= the virginal conception] is nowhere expressly mentioned in John it was natural to introduce a reference to it here." Barrett adds: "The reading which refers explicitly to the birth of Jesus is to be rejected; but it remains probable that John was alluding to Jesus' birth, and declaring that the birth of Christians, being bloodless and rooted in God's will alone, followed the pattern of the birth of Christ himself."[4] Barrett's notion about the evangelist's "allusion" may be somewhat optimistic, but it is certainly more credible than Bultmann's brusque assurance that "the Fourth Gospel…not only does not contain the idea of the virgin birth, but (like Paul) excludes it."[5] In any case Barrett's suggestion about the origins of the reading in the singular ("was born") and the plausible reason for introducing that reading remind us of the way the church commonly accepted the virginal conception of Jesus. Thus a variant, which must yield to the unanimous voice of the Greek manuscripts, becomes itself a credible witness to tradition and the theological reception of John's Gospel.

The 1992 *Catechism of the Catholic Church,* when dealing with the virginal conception, broadly hints that it accepts the singular number in Jn 1:13 (#496, n. 147; n. 166). Perhaps this position could be justified along the lines of Barrett's commentary. Such a charitable interpretation, however, is made somewhat more difficult when *The Catechism,* in referring to the "mystery" of Christmas, follows the consensus of all the Greek manuscripts by apparently reading in the plural the disputed verb from Jn 1:13 (#526, n. 206). Consistency demands accepting either the singular or the plural reading, but not switching from one to the other.

Closely connected with the occasional challenge of determining the text in case of serious doubt is the question of punctuation that even more occasionally arises and affects the theological reception of the scriptures. As the oldest manuscripts of the NT lack systematic punctuation, modern scholars must insert the punctuation that seems appropriate. A classic case for Christology comes in Rom 9:5, where the punctuation is decided by one's conclusion as to whether Paul referred to Christ as "God *(theos)*." The apostle concludes his list of Israel's special privileges with a brief doxology or prayer of praise: "God who is over all be blessed forever." Another possible punctuation would present Paul's list as ending with a confession of Christ's divinity: "Christ, who is God over all, be blessed forever." For several reasons this punctuation (and the translation it entails) looks slightly less likely. First, while expressing the divinity of Christ in a variety of ways (e.g., through the titles of Lord, Son of God, and Wisdom), Paul reserves the title of "God" to "the Father." If *theos* (admittedly not *ho theos*) here in Rom 9:5 refers to Christ, it would be, together with Phil 2:6, an exception in the authentic Pauline letters. Second, the apostle directs his doxologies to God the Father (e.g., Rom 11:36; 16:27) and not directly to Christ (as does Heb 13:21). (This second argument must, however, face the objection that Pauline doxologies are always attached to what comes before. Here this would mean recognizing that the doxology is attached to Christ.)[6] Third, to name Christ as being "over all" would differ from his usually being "subordinated" to God the Father in the Pauline scheme (1 Cor 3:23; 11:3; 15:27–28). He is "sent" by the Father (Rom 8:3; Gal 4:4), who in Deutero-Pauline language is "above all" (Eph 4:6). (This third argument loses a little force when we recall two passages in the Letter to the Philippians. In the first [3:21] "the Lord Jesus Christ" has "the power which enables him *to subject all things to himself*"; in the second [2:6–7] he is not sent, but himself takes the initiative when coming into the world.)

Translations

Back in Chapter 1 we cited the old maxim "*caveat emptor* (buyer beware)" in connection with what are sometimes called euphemistically "the assured results" of biblical scholarship. This warning may prove even more timely in the area of translations. Here, as much as anywhere, systematic theologians and their students should remain on the alert about what they read and remember the warning expressed in another maxim, "No translation does justice to the original"; in its Italian version, *traduttore traditore*.[7]

One unsatisfactory feature of translations can come from their blurring the distinction between what the text says and what it is understood to mean, a blurring that turns translations into commentaries. A desire to explain the text clearly can lead to paraphrases and to supplying the readers with what the translators think the text should have said and/or meant. Prioritizing clarity and intelligibility can override fidelity.

Our opening example comes from the NEB when it renders 1 Tm 5:22 as "Do not be over-hasty in laying on hands in ordination, or you may find yourself responsible for other people's misdeeds; keep your own hands clean." The Greek text, which does not include words either for "in ordination" or "your own hands," ends by simply enjoining:

"Keep yourself pure." The NEB adds a footnote to offer the reader an alternative for the opening verse: "Do not be over-hasty in restoring an offender by the laying on of hands." Commentators on the letter recognize that the verse could refer to one of three practices: some kind of appointment to an official function, admission to baptism, or a reconciliation of penitents after they have performed an appropriate penance. But should a translation assume the role of a commentary by opting for one or other explanation? We are also concerned about the desire for elegantly balanced language, which seems to prompt the parallel: "laying on *hands*...keep your *hands* clean." A further point: normally one needs more English words when rendering a passage from the Greek. But here the desire to "bring out" the sense (at least as it has been understood by the translators) has led to twenty-five words being used to translate eleven words from the Greek. Those who revised this translation to produce the REB[8] rather drastically overhauled the NEB version of 1 Tm 5:22 and give us: "Do not be over-hasty in the laying on of hands, or you may find yourself implicated in other people's misdeeds; keep yourself above reproach" (twenty-four words and still more than double the number in the original Greek). By eliminating "hands" in rendering the final admonition the REB removes a connection the NEB gratuitously made between this closing admonition and the opening ("Do not be over-hasty in laying on hands in ordination" and "Keep your hands clean"). While correctly replacing the NEB's "responsible for" with "implicated in," the REB still (mistakenly, we believe) gives the impression that being implicated in "other people's misdeeds" could stem from being "over-hasty in the laying on of hands." All in all, the NRSV is more faithful here to the original: "Do not ordain anyone hastily, and do not participate in the sins of others; keep yourself pure" (seventeen words). By choosing "sins," this version keeps the classical translation for "hamartia." The REB, like the NEB, leaves one with one minor question: Why translate "hamartia" here with the somewhat fuzzier term "misdeed," when this same translation persistently renders it as "sin" in Romans? We are not arguing for a simple word-matching between the NT and current English as if we could always translate the same Greek words exactly the same way. But when we can do so (as here in the case of "hamartia"), why not do so? The major quibble we have with the NRSV arises from its decision to use "ordain"—a frank piece of commentary on the Greek ("do not lay hands on"), which is hardly offset by the note that reminds readers of what the original Greek says. The revised (1986) edition of the NAB leaves any such decision to the commentators by rendering the verse: "Do not lay hands too readily on anyone, and do not share in another's sin. Keep yourself pure."

A further example of translations becoming commentaries comes from Jas 5:15a–b: "The prayer offered in faith will save the sick man, the Lord will raise him from his bed" (NEB; eighteen words). No footnote warns the reader that the Greek text (thirteen words long) does not contain any equivalent for "from his bed." The translators for the REB, while properly dissatisfied with the NEB rendering, hardly do any better: "The prayer offered in faith will heal the sick man and the Lord will restore him to health" (eighteen words). The translation gratuitously adds "to health." The sequence of "heal" and "health" could easily (and falsely) imply that the Greek text contains a verb ("heal") and a noun ("health") that correspond. Moreover, the version rather clearly suggests that James 5 refers to a physical healing for the sick person — something that the Greek wording does not specify. Once again the NRSV proves more loyal to the original and less willing to turn translation into exegesis: "The prayer of faith will save the sick, and the Lord will raise them up." The use of the inclusive plural, incidentally, seems thoroughly justified, since the Greek text speaks in general of "anyone among you being sick" (Jas 5:14). The REB's talk of "the sick *man*" and the Lord "restoring *him* to health" (which matches the non-inclusive language of the NEB, "the sick man" and "the Lord will raise him from his bed") could be taken to imply either that women are not expected to fall ill or that, if they did, they could not expect to be restored to health and raised from their sickbed.

The NRSV does not, however, emerge so well when we turn to Heb 12:2a: "looking to Jesus the pioneer and perfecter of our faith." A footnote observes that the Greek original has no word corresponding to "our." Then why insert it? The NEB gives a similar, misleading impression that the faith in question is the faith his followers should exercise: "our eyes fixed on Jesus, on whom faith depends from start to finish." The REB corrects this impression and translates the passage: "our eyes fixed on Jesus, the pioneer and perfecter of faith." The REB, unlike the NEB in this verse, also allows the reader to pick up the echo between "pioneer of faith" (Heb 12:2) and "the pioneer of salvation" (Heb 2:10). But, returning to our main point here, let us observe how modern translations of Heb

12:2 have frequently added an "our" to "faith": "Jesus the pioneer and perfecter of our faith" (RSV); "Jesus, the Pioneer and Perfecter of our faith" (NIV); "Jesus who leads us in our faith and brings it to perfection" (NJB). The NAB originally rendered the phrase as "Jesus, who inspires and perfects our faith"; its 1988 revised NT version has shifted to calling Jesus "the leader and perfecter of faith." The reason for the frequent insertion of "our" seems to have stemmed from the widely shared reluctance to attribute faith to the earthly Jesus. In other words, a dogmatic presupposition appears to have predetermined not a few translations of Heb 12:2.[9]

At times, translations offer what can only be described as paraphrases. An example is provided by the NEB's rendering of 2 Cor 3:17a, which the REB also follows without any change: "Now the Lord *of whom this passage speaks* is the Spirit" (italics ours). The exegesis that prompts the addition of the italicized words looks correct: Paul is referring here in v. 17 to Ex 34:34, which reports Moses speaking with God and which Paul has recalled in earlier verses of 2 Cor 3. The translation adopted by the RSV, retained by the NRSV, and also found in the NAB ("now the Lord is the Spirit") is loyal to the Greek text, but has frequently been taken to indicate that Paul identifies the Spirit with the risen Christ—a piece of exegesis that we disputed in Chapter 4. The NEB and the REB skillfully head off such a misinterpretation. But should they do so in the translation itself, instead of leaving this task to a footnote or to the commentators? Should translators make something clear and precise when the original text is less clear and precise?

Before moving on from translations to commentaries, we want to encourage systematic theologians to watch out for three further phenomena: anachronisms, desymbolization, and some results of political correctness. Anachronisms may be relatively harmless as when the NJB translates Dt 24:5: "If a man is newly married, he must not join the army." "Joining the army" almost inevitably conjures up the recruiting procedures, training, and tours of duty characteristic of the military forces of modern nations, something quite different from what those male Jews experienced in the postexilic period. Theologically more serious issues arise with the NAB's translation of Rom 5:12 ("Through *one person* sin entered the world") and Rom 5:15 ("If by that *one person's* transgression the many died, how much more did the grace of God and the gracious gift of *the one person* Jesus Christ overflow for many";

italics ours). Using "person" here, particularly "the one person Jesus Christ," can mask the fact that the terminology of "one person" officially entered Christology only after much controversy at the Council of Chalcedon in 451. Even then, the concept of "person" was to undergo many centuries of development before reaching anything like what contemporary readers understand by the term. With this translation of Rom 5, the risk of anachronistic misrepresentation seems high indeed.

Biblical symbols like blood function as metathemes that recur in different scriptural contexts with important modifications. Three perspectives consistently emerge on blood: as a sign and symbol of deliverance and life, as a means for expiating guilt, and as a way for expressing and sealing friendship. These three perspectives make blood a central symbol/metatheme that climaxes with Jesus becoming "through his blood" the "means of expiating sin for all who believe" (Rom 3:25). Such symbolic metathemes, with their rich associations, evoke not just esthetic but also deep religious responses from the readers. A metatheme of great importance is obscured and even lost when recent translations show themselves reluctant to mention the blood of Jesus. We are thinking here not simply of *Good News for Modern Man,* the NT in *Today's English Version,* which repeatedly refuses to translate references to Jesus' blood and introduces the vaguer term, death. That version renders the first part of Col 1:20 as follows: "Through the Son, then, God decided to bring the whole universe back to himself. God made peace through his Son's death on the cross." The Greek text speaks here more vividly of "the blood of his cross." Major, scholarly translations can exhibit a similar, if not so thoroughgoing reluctance, to let the blood of Jesus move into English from the Greek original. Thus the NJB unlike the NAB ("the blood of his cross") translates the phrase in question from Col 1:20 as "his death on the cross." The NEB translates Rom 3:25a: "For God designed him [Christ Jesus] to be the means of expiating sin by his sacrificial death." The REB adopts practically the same wording ("For God designed him to be the means of expiating sin by his death") but moves things even further from the blood of Jesus by omitting "sacrificial." The NRSV faithfully translates the passage as "whom God put forward as a sacrifice of atonement by his blood," and so does the NAB: "whom God set forth as an expiation...by his blood." If we are permitted a pun late in this book, it seems to us the "death" and "sacrificial death" are more anemic expressions when compared with "blood" and "the blood of his cross." This is what the Greek texts say. Why make them more bland, especially when our twentieth-century media show clearly how powerful the symbol of blood still is? In any case refusing even here and there to translate *haima* as "blood" makes it impossible for Greekless students to track this powerful metatheme through the scriptures.

A desire for inclusive language has affected some translations of the Hebrew *ben adam,* the Aramaic *bar nasha,* and the Greek "ho huios tou anthrōpou." The NRSV renders Ps 8:4: "What are humans beings that you are mindful of them, *mortals* that you care for them?" (italics ours). A footnote observes that the original Hebrew speaks of "son of man" rather than "mortals." Where the prophet Ezekiel is repeatedly addressed as *ben adam* (from 2:1 through 47:6), the NRSV translates the phrase as "O mortal." The Aramaic text of Dan 7:13, "one like unto a son of man," becomes "one like a human being." But then the NRSV regularly renders the Greek *ho huios tou anthrōpou* as "Son of Man" (e.g., Mk 2:10, 28; 8:31), giving the phrase an even stronger titular flavor than the partly lowercase "Son of man" that the RSV adopted when translating the phrase in the Gospels. The NRSV rightly explains the *meaning* of the phrase in the psalms and the prophets. But can it claim to be true to what the original texts *say?* As this version of the Bible switches from "mortal," to "human being," and on to "Son of Man," less well-equipped readers cannot follow this metatheme through the scriptures. Any such tracking becomes even more problematic with *The New Testament and Psalms: An Inclusive Version,* and the translation offered in *The Five Gospels* coming from the Jesus Seminar. The first of these versions, Lk 9:58, renders as: "Foxes have holes, and birds of the air have nests; but the Human One has nowhere to lie down and sleep." The latter version translates Mk 2:27 as follows: "The sabbath day was created for Adam and Eve."[10] Is the desire for gender-inclusive language turning these translations into commentaries that censor retrospectively and falsely report past records? Is it making the text say what the translators wish it would have said?

These questions bring us back to one of the premises we set out in Chapter 1 and the appendix. Over hundreds of years the biblical writers drew on their languages and cultures to put down in writing what the Holy Spirit inspired them to record. Obviously these scriptural authors were not miraculously exempted from racist, national, patriarchal, sexist, and all other particular limits in the cultural horizons. To what extent is contemporary embarrassment over those past limits and defects at work when the *Inclusive Version* translates "sending his own Son" (Rom 8:3) as "sending God's own Child," "the power of darkness" (Lk 22:53) as "the power of evil," "sat at the right hand of God" (Mk 16:19) as "sat at the side of God," and "Our Father" (Mt 6:9) as "Our Father-Mother"? Such changes (or corrections?) in the language of the Bible suggest an attempt to rewrite the history and cultures out of which the Bible emerged — or at least a partial and misguided renunciation of the divine self-communication coming through specific human beings with all their limits and imperfections, sinful and otherwise. In these examples an overriding emphasis on equality between the sexes has led to replacing biblical metaphors with new ones (for instance, "Father-Mother" for "Father"), something that we argued against in Chapter 4 above.

Before leaving the question of translation, we should remind readers that we are addressing this question in the context of receiving the scriptures in systematic theology. Challenges differ when producing translations for those other contexts that we recalled under our second principle in Chapter 1: the liturgy and practice of Christian living. Here we have been concerned primarily with the academic context rather than with liturgical and popular usage. In passing from one language (in particular from one of the three biblical languages) to another, the desire to produce an accessible, idiomatic translation for liturgy and living can encourage many choices. But the more this happens, the less contemporary readers (and hearers) of these biblical versions may be able to encounter the original text and its message. One may espouse a double procedure here, by first converting biblical images into concepts and then putting these into supposedly equivalent images characteristic of a determined culture and the local language. Such a policy presupposes obviously a functional equivalence between the concepts of various cultures — something that cultural anthropology would vigorously query. Whatever our judgment on abstract concepts, we dare not lose sight of the privileged nature of biblical images. These particular images enjoy a unique place in the history of God's saving self-communication. Relentlessly replacing these images could reach the point of effectively cutting links with the biblical history of revelation and salvation.

Commentaries

In proposing our ten principles for the theological reception of the scriptures and then adding some reflections on the "practical" responsibilities of theologians, we cannot end without recalling the role of commentaries. Notoriously some systematic theologians consult commentaries and exempt themselves from reading the biblical text itself. In such cases the obvious result is that commentaries isolate theologians from the very works they should be receiving and interpreting. Commentators themselves do not, however, endorse such a practice; they consistently aim to help "bring out" the meaning of biblical texts and enable their readers to understand better those texts.

This "better" may be oriented precisely at the task of preaching. Commentaries written for preachers will not always yield much for theological study. Likewise, commentaries that view and expound the biblical texts through philological, social, and "historicist" spectacles will provide a wealth of lexical information, socio-cultural details, and historical references. But linguistic, literary, social, and archaeological data will not necessarily feed theology directly and significantly, above all when grappling with the message of John, Paul, and other outstanding biblical witnesses. Such "historicizing" commentaries, even if (or especially when?) they claim uncommitted neutrality, will, nevertheless, be informed in significant ways by a range of philosophical and theological preconceptions and assumptions. A kind of historical positivism, for instance, may be functioning here by presuming that the meaning of a work is to be found only in its origins or in its surrounding data and by refusing to ask: What might God wish to communicate through these texts?

Those commentaries that openly and seriously grapple with the theological material provide valuable resources, yet call always for close scrutiny. They have obviously crossed that imprecise line that "separates" exegesis from theology. What theological, philosophical, and historical presuppositions, characteristics, and agenda shape such commentaries? What community of scholarship, confessional affiliation, and commitment to the claims of the scriptural texts do these commentaries represent? Where do they focus: on the prehistory of the text, on the intentions of the author(s), on the text's final form in the canonical scriptures, on its postcanonical history (in the *Auslegungs-* or *Wirkungsgeschichte*), or on a mixture of these foci? In respecting the scriptures as theological literature and distilling for their readers the results of the best scholarly work, such commentaries must incorporate various emphases and concerns in their methodology. They may, for instance, want to distinguish fairly sharply between exegesis as the clarification of the biblical author's meaning and interpretation as a broader exposition that goes well beyond what the original authors intended.

In short, just as with editions and translations of the scriptural texts, commentaries and, for that matter, dictionaries call for some critical discernment. Here, no less than elsewhere, systematic theologians should scrutinize what they are buying—in the spirit of *"caveat emptor."* The best commentaries and dictionaries prove almost indispensable criticism and guidance for theologians. At the same time, nothing can substitute for a constant and serious exposure to the biblical texts themselves.

9

Critical Reassessments

At the end we want to review and critically reassess what we have written in the course of this book. To begin with, we consider it important to insist once again on the scope of our work. We have not aimed at writing any kind of history of modern hermeneutical theory as it has developed from Schleiermacher and Dilthey through to Heidegger, Gadamer, Ricoeur, Jauss, and beyond. Nor have we wanted to dedicate ourselves to the contemporary debate about biblical and theological hermeneutics with Werner Jeanrond, Sandra Schneiders, David Tracy, and others. Lengthy and critical examination of the serious and complex issues they raise about the theory of textual interpretation is obviously a worthwhile task. But we have engaged ourselves with a different project, one that is called for nowadays by the way biblical studies (still largely historically oriented) and systematic theology are normally taught separately. Courses exploring the theological use of the Bible seem remarkably rare, if not simply nonexistent. Our book aims to meet that need by proposing some principles for passing from the biblical texts to theological positions. Chapter 1 argues for those ten principles only briefly; we believe that trying out our principles on some major theological issues constitutes a more effective test of their validity. Current literature offers a vast amount of theoretical reflection on interpreting and receiving scriptural and theological texts. We have preferred to concentrate on practice, in the sense of offering some guidelines for those who wish to cross the bridge from the Bible to systematic theology. No writer that we know is doing just this; our ten principles may be meeting a real need and encouraging a more adequate use of the scriptures in theology.

In testing our principles we chose some questions in Christology, soteriology, doctrine of God, and ecclesiology. How do our general rules perform in theological practice? We could have tested our principles by also taking up issues in further areas like the doctrines of creation, grace, sacraments, and eschatology. That would clearly have been useful, but would have meant writing a book at least twice the length of this one. In doing that we would have been moving toward attempting a full systematic theology in light of our ten principles. We chose the particular theological questions we examined for two reasons. First, they are all major and controverted issues; to have tried out our principles on minor or relatively uncontroversial questions could rightly have been interpreted as failure in our theological nerve. Second, both of us have done research, teaching, and writing in the areas we took up; it seemed imprudent to wander into such areas of systematic theology as sacraments where we had no previous specialized knowledge.

In this closing chapter we want to go back over our ten principles, reflecting critically on them and on their application. Our first principle, *hearing the whole Bible,* must face the challenge expressed by Werner Jeanrond: "We may wish to know what strategies could help us to make sure that our listening is true listening and not a distorted or ideological listening."[1] One might respond here by asking: Can any strategies help us to be completely *sure* that our listening is true listening and not distorted or ideological listening? Before the final vision of God, can anyone enjoy such total assurance? Yet Jeanrond puts his finger on the need to scrutinize ourselves for those prejudices that can distort our listening, understanding, and interpretation. Neither he nor we are proposing something that is both impossible and undesirable: the misguided attempt to rid ourselves of all presuppositions, reading perspectives, and "pre-judices" when facing texts. But there are distorted and distorting prejudices: for instance, cherished ideologies that take precedence over any belief that the Holy Spirit who inspired the writing of the Bible can speak to us through it. This belief calls for a sympathetic rather than a suspicious approach to biblical texts. At the same time, the role of the human authors in the making of the Bible means that our "sympathy" for the texts should also be a critical one. We certainly do not want to take back our second principle about theologians being *critical self-aware* interpreters of the scriptures.

Even before they came to our first principle, the opening pages of

Chapter 1 may have put the nerves of some Christian readers on red alert by introducing the Roman Catholic canon of seventy-two books. Does hearing the whole Bible (principle one) mean hearing also what they view as the Apocryphal Books? Nevertheless, at least in some sense all readers of the NT are hearing those books: for instance, in the use made of the Book of Wisdom in the Pauline and Deutero-Pauline letters, Hebrews, and other parts of the NT. Moreover, the way the 1991 *New Oxford Annotated Bible* inserts between the OT and the NT the Apocryphal Books, also applying to them the Catholic title of Deutero-canonical Books, witnesses to the increasing sense in scholarly and ecumenical circles of the historical and religious status of those works for understanding and interpreting the NT and its setting. By following here the lead of *The New Oxford Annotated Bible,* we do not think we are simply writing as Catholics to Catholics. While encouraging a respectful hearing also for the Apocryphal/Deuterocanonical Books, we do not want, however, to exaggerate their importance. In this present work they hardly make an appearance, beyond a reference or two in the appendix on the Holy Spirit to follow. The example of "covenant" as a metatheme (principle six) might have prompted us to cite Sirach's account of seven covenants (Sir 44–47), and the appeal to convergent biblical testimony (principle four) in dealing with Jesus' divinity might have led us to refer to the Book of Wisdom. But in neither case did we do so. In any case, the importance of covenant as a metatheme does not stand or fall by our respectful hearing of Sirach; the recognition of Jesus as not merely embodying divine wisdom (lowercase) but being in person the divine Wisdom (uppercase) may be helped by the Book of Wisdom but it is certainly not decided by giving that text a "canonical hearing."

One reader of our manuscript (whose judgment came to us anonymously) moved beyond the particular question of the Apocryphal/Deuterocanonical Books to make the more general criticism: "Most of the time the Old Testament might just as well not exist [for O'Collins and Kendall]." The biblical index for this book will, we believe, tell another story. If we had chosen other topics from systematic theology like creation and sin, the OT would have been represented even more extensively. In what we have published together and separately (e.g., O'Collins, *Fundamental Theology* [Mahwah, NJ: Paulist Press, 1981], and *Christology* [Oxford and New York: Oxford University Press,

1995]), has shown, we believe, our steady conviction that a Christian theology that fails to make extensive use of the Hebrew scriptures, the first part of our biblical canon, will remain seriously deficient.

Our other principles call for some further reflection and specifications. Appropriating the scriptures *within the living community of faith* (principle three) follows on what we noted in Chapter 1 when expounding the various contexts for theology. Just as legal texts belong in courts of law and dramatic texts enjoy their vitality on the stage but remain a dead letter when they are not acted for an audience, so the scriptures enjoy their particular power when read publicly and appropriated in worship. The primary readers and hearers of the scriptures are the community of believers. Our third principle applies this belief to theology, an ecclesial rather than an autonomous activity. At the end of the twentieth century the invitation to interpret and theologically appropriate the scriptures within the living community of believers corresponds to a wider phenomenon: the new, worldwide sensibility about the need to participate and maintain communion not only with other human beings but with the whole of nature.

Biblical convergence (principle four) includes but goes beyond *metathemes and metanarratives* (principle six). When they recur and help to make one cumulative story of the scriptures, such themes and narratives do so in terms that are recognizably the same or at least similar. Thus the seven covenants recalled by Sirach differ in functions, circumstances, and beneficiaries, but as bonds of relationship and fidelity between God and human beings they all deserve the name of "covenant." But biblical convergence is not limited to the kind of linguistic links that undergird metathemes and metanarratives. Thus a wide variety of testimonies converge in witnessing to the divinity of Jesus. For such convergent testimony one does not depend here simply on the wisdom language which backs up confessing him as divine Wisdom in person.

In recommending the lead offered by the *consensus of centrist exegetes* (principle five), we are perfectly aware that truth cannot and should not be decided by a majority vote. At times such a consensus has proved to be wrong or at least a very dubious pointer to historical truth: for instance, in the past a more or less unanimous consensus supported the priority of Matthew but nowadays the overwhelming majority of exegetes agree that Mark's was the first Gospel to be written. The history of biblical scholarship shows how sometimes one scholar or a small group of scholars have eventually won the day over against an overwhelming majority. At the start of controversies over such matters as the Mosaic authorship of the Pentateuch, the existence of Q, or a sayings-source, and the priority of Mark, an appeal to a consensus would have led away from what is now generally accepted as the truth. Our fifth principle recommends to theologians a prudential rule of thumb and discourages them from doing two things. First, with the desire (or pretense?) of being in the vanguard of biblical progress, some theologians can endorse the highly speculative suggestions of the "latest" author about matters like the different stages in the development of the Q community. Any systematic theology built upon speculations that will probably elicit strong and persuasive criticisms from the exegetical guild is obviously misguided and collapses with the rejection of the exegetical conjectures it took on board. Second, on such issues as the historicity of Jesus' empty tomb one can find writers (both liberal and conservative) making an easy appeal to what they call "the majority opinion." On closer inspection it may well turn out that there are not very many who can be named as supporting this "majority opinion." Once again we are in no way arguing that a genuine majority vote decides or should decide such issues. But we are concerned about the way some writers can claim support from "the majority" or even "the consensus" when in fact no names are given and no such "majority" or "consensus" is there to be found.

Apropos of our sixth principle *(metathemes and metanarratives)* we are well aware of the way "metanarrative" can be wrongly understood to mean a grand theory that encompasses the whole of biblical reality from the beginning to the end. We are definitely not using the term in that way, as if some single, totalizing narrative or concept could hold together everything scriptural from the earthly garden of Genesis right through to the heavenly city of Revelation. We are not attempting to force everything into such a Procrustean bed. Even the metanarrative *par excellence,* the resurrection of the crucified Jesus, does not violently enforce that kind of uniformity in the Bible. We are also aware of a partial coincidence between metathemes and typology. Within the matrix of biblical history OT "types" have been understood to foreshadow NT "antitypes." The correspondence can work at the level of persons (the first Adam and Christ as the last Adam), things (the manna in the desert and the Bread of Life of John 6), and events (the ceremonies performed by the high priest

on the Day of Atonement and the covenantal sacrifice of Christ as interpreted in Hebrews). The antitype draws on the type for some of its meaning. The correspondence can be constituted by difference as well as by
resemblance. Thus Christ came to reverse the work of Adam who
brought sin and death (Rom 5:12–14; 1 Cor 15:22). All types and antitypes can be classified as metathemes, but not vice versa. Metathemes
like grace, love, and sin go well beyond identifiable examples of OT
types and NT antitypes.

To illustrate our seventh principle, *discontinuity within continuity,*
we took the example of the shift from the situation of the earthly Jesus
to that of the apostle Paul. Some have pushed to an extreme either discontinuity or continuity. Thus, on the one hand, Rudolf Bultmann
reduced to the status of mere *prolegomena* the synoptic Gospels (which
are the great witnesses to the ministry of Jesus) and privileged as the
main guides to a NT theology Paul and John, who are major witnesses
to the situation of the Easter kerygma. On the other hand, there are
those like John Hick and Joachim Jeremias who tip the balance too
much in the direction of the prepaschal Jesus. Our principle of disconti-
nuity/continuity implies here that, while the prepaschal Jesus is essential as revealer of God and mediator of salvation, the complete
revelation and salvation have not yet taken place. That completion
awaits the qualitatively new postresurrection situation. In terms of
Jesus himself, his prepaschal state does not coincide perfectly with his
postpaschal glory.

Our eighth principle promoted a sense of *eschatological provisionality* in the theological appropriation of the scriptures. This principle rests on the fact that the divine self-revelation that reached its
unsurpassable and definitive climax with Christ still awaits its final
fullness in the glorious manifestation of God at the end of time. In
brief, eschatological provisionality stems from the eschatological
nature of revelation.

The ninth principle about *dialogue with philosophy* has provoked
two major questions from a reader who prefers to remain anonymous:
"As O'Collins and Kendall obviously reject some philosophical view-
points, which philosophy do they propose for such dialogue? Aren't
they turning theology into philosophy and so distorting it?" The varied,
international experience which both of us have enjoyed has made us
value a wide range of philosophies: linguistic analysis, various forms

of existentialism, various forms of neo-Thomism, some strands of pragmatism, phenomenology, hermeneutical philosophy, some strands of idealism, personalism, Confucianism, and other Eastern philosophical traditions. We have learned at least something from all these forms of philosophical thought. Obviously we reject materialist philosophies that deny God and the spiritual dimension of human beings; at the same time one of us (O'Collins) drew much from debate and dialogue with one of its exponents, David Armstrong, who was his supervisor many years ago at Melbourne University. Neither of us has profited a great deal from process thought; it creates more problems with one's doctrine of God than it succeeds in solving.

We agree with our critic that "turning theology into philosophy" will automatically distort it. In fact, we offered one or two examples of (false) philosophical presupposition controlling theological conclusions. But we are not recommending a philosophical takeover. What rather is at stake is clarity in our theological positions. Those theologians who want to summarize the biblical story of divine communication by speaking of God's "symbolic self-communication" need to draw from some philosophical reflections on the nature of symbols and of communication. Otherwise they may speak less than properly and intelligibly when they call the prophets "symbolic persons" and write of the exodus as "the symbolic event par excellence." No adequate account of the scriptures bringing the word of God to human beings should bypass such questions as: What is word and language? What is it to be a hearer of the divine word? These are ultimate, primordial questions that philosophers also attend to. When theologians want to expound the biblical approach to "truth," they are well-advised to compare and contrast what they have to say with the rich philosophical approaches to truth. When they draw on Acts and other NT books to develop the theme of Christian testimony, they can enrich their own and others' understanding and interpretation by taking over some of the philosophical language and thought we recalled in Chapter 6. Right from the second century Christians have repeatedly and rightly taken advantage of some metaphysical concepts in their struggle for a little more clarity about accepting Christ as simultaneously a necessary (divine) being and a contingent (human) being. In pondering his personal preexistence, we neglect at our peril philosophical studies of time and eternity. In general, the Bible witnesses to historical particularities, while philosophies tend to operate

within a universal horizon. No theology that wishes to appropriate seriously the scriptures can abandon such historical particularities as the
election of the Jewish people, the ministry of Jesus, and his crucifixion;
yet all theology needs help from philosophers if it is going to communicate intelligibly with other disciplines in the public domain.

Our tenth principle *(inculturating the biblical testimony)* aims at
encouraging theology to be an all-embracing and thorough response to
the world and its various cultures. But it is an inculturation that will
regularly challenge "normal" value systems, customary views of reality, and accepted lifestyles. We do not want to make things easy for ourselves here by merely pointing out practices that are wrong in any
culture: for instance, killing aged parents or practicing female circumcision. The Bible witnesses to a countercultural faith that reshapes
whole perspectives on the nature and destiny of human beings and their
world. This faith collides with and dramatically criticizes many
aspects, for example, of the current Western culture that spreads everywhere its obsession with professional success, possessions, and good
health. What does true success mean in the light of Jesus' resurrection
from the dead? What do we really want to possess for all eternity? Is
there any good health that can compete with the life of the risen body?
Inculturating the biblical testimony also involves steadily applying
Paul's warning about not being "conformed to the pattern of the present
world" (Rom 12:2).

We ended Chapter 1 by showing how our ten principles entail
using the scriptures in a christological way. We could have enlarged
Chapter 1 by arguing at greater length for our principles. In fact, the
whole book could have taken the form of a fully deployed argument for
the ten principles, assigning a chapter to each one. But we preferred to
test their validity and helpfulness by applying them to specific questions. Is Jesus qualitatively unique and not simply different only in
degree from outstanding saints and prophets (Chapter 2)? Is divine love
the primary way to explain the *how* of redemption (Chapter 3)? Our
affirmative answer to the second question may well stir up some discussion and dissent among our readers.

In Chapter 3 we applied our first eight principles somewhat
briefly, being convinced that the most serious difficulties against a theology of redemption in the key of love arise in the philosophical area.
We know hardly anyone who does not agree that the divine love is the

why of redemption; God is motivated by utter love in bringing about our salvation. But does that love account for the *how* or the "mechanism" of redemption? Here we believe that a fully developed Christian philosophy can help one perceive that love is an ontological force, the most powerful force in the whole cosmos, as Pierre Teilhard de Chardin so beautifully acknowledged. We must also emphasize something which consistently emerges from our analysis of the different dimensions of love: this Christian philosophy of love (both divine and human) finds its main foundation in the biblical testimony. This is perhaps *the* example for those who insist on the intertwining of Christian theology and philosophy. Let us also recall that we are not belittling liberation and expiation as biblically based and important statements of the *how* of redemption. What we have argued for is the primacy of love in a scriptural account of our salvation.

A crucial item for our discussion in Chapter 4 is the distinction between simile and metaphor. A simile uses language in its customary sense to compare an aspect of something or someone with an aspect of something or someone else. In the case of Is 42:14 God's "loud" intervention is likened to a woman gasping or panting in the pangs of birth. Metaphor extends the use of language beyond the "ordinary" meaning(s) to generate new perspectives on reality by asserting an identity between two subjects (and not merely a comparison of two aspects): "Joanna is the lion of her netball team; God is Father to the people" (see Dt 32:6). In this latter statement we encounter some crucial information about God that turns up in the OT and then gets developed in the history of Jesus and the founding generation of Christianity.

In Chapter 5, when discussing the biblical evidence for church leadership and authority, we spent less time on its major presupposition: Jesus founded and in some sense intended to found a distinct and enduring community. That was also a major presupposition for the following chapter which argued for Easter witness as the best, primary key to the Petrine ministry. We predict, incidentally, that some reviewers will want to characterize or even dismiss that latter chapter by naming it as "very Roman Catholic in ethos" or "veering toward Catholic apologetics." To mount a little defense ahead of time, let us point out how a whole line of Protestant authors — Adolf von Harnack, Eric Seeberg, Oscar Cullmann, Willi Marxsen, and Gerd Luedemann, to name just a few — have written on Peter and done so precisely in the context of the resurrection. So far from this topic being "very Roman Catholic," Catholic authors have tended to play it down or simply avoid it.[2] In proposing a new, Easter approach to the Petrine ministry, are we pushing "Catholic apologetics" if we take a line that differs rather markedly from the usual Catholic reliance on the three classic texts about Petrine authority (Mt 16:18–19; Lk 22:31–32; Jn 21:15–17)—the texts that, as we documented, remain the cornerstone of the view of that authority taken by Pope John Paul II? In short, let our proposal about Peter's Easter testimony be discussed on its own merits (or demerits) and not put aside by labeling it as typically "Roman Catholic."

As much or even more than other works that we have co-authored, we expect this book to draw criticism. But we welcome all serious evaluation, both positive and negative. In proposing our ten principles and applying them to controverted issues, we have ventured out over open ground. We will be enormously grateful for any constructive help toward correcting and refining the ten principles that we have developed and applied.

An Appendix on the Holy Spirit

The opening pages of Chapter 1 restated the traditional doctrine about the biblical texts being written under a special impulse from the Holy Spirit—what Dionysius the Pseudo-Areopagite called "the power granted by the Spirit to the scripture writers" (*Divine Names* 1.1.1). Can we say anything further about this divine activity? In any case, does the traditional axiom about all three persons of the trinity being always involved inseparably in every external action *(opus ad extra)*[1] mean that biblical inspiration is simply "appropriated" to the Holy Spirit and is not strictly "proper" to the Spirit? One very similar question must be asked about the traditional Christian conviction that the Holy Spirit guides the subsequent hearing and interpretation of the Bible by the community and individuals. When we speak of the Spirit "confirming" the witness of scriptures[2] or speak of reading the scriptures "in" the same Spirit through whom they were written,[3] are we referring to a divine action that is "proper" or special to the Holy Spirit? Can we clarify this double activity traditionally attributed to the Spirit, that of first inspiring the composition of the scriptures (the passage from word to text) and then of illuminating their appropriation (the passage from text to word) in successive reading communities? Our primary effort here will be to clarify this "double activity," but we will also suggest reasons for seeing it as "proper" to the Spirit.

Much theological writing about divine activity yields little help toward responding to our questions.[4] A. I. C. Heron pays some attention to the role of the Spirit in the writing and reading of the scriptures—

what he calls "the third central Reformation theme: *the activity of the Spirit in relation to the Word in Scripture*" (105; italics his).[5] But those who publish books about the Holy Spirit do not take up the question of the Spirit's involvement in the writing and reading of the scriptures.[6] Even in the NT itself, when Paul lists the gifts of the Spirit (e.g., 1 Cor 12:4–11), he does not mention as such the gift of being an inspired writer. Those theologians and philosophers who explore God's interaction, whether extraordinary or ordinary, with creation normally reflect on divine activity in relation to the world without any special reference to the Holy Spirit. Those who treat the question of biblical inspiration usually relate this charism to the foundation of the church, compare and contrast it with prophetic inspiration, and, while recognizing the plus-value of the scriptures as peculiarly revelatory and salvific, elaborate the relative autonomy enjoyed by the sacred authors. At times they recall the traditional language about these authors being God's living instruments in the composition of the books of the Bible, but have little or nothing to say about how this collaborative, effective causation or double agency works.[7] How can the divine agent (the Holy Spirit) and the human agents (the biblical writers) be fully active and really cooperative in one specific event? Let us take up biblical inspiration as proper to the Holy Spirit and then offer some reflections in response to the central challenge raised by this appendix: Can we clarify even a little the special divine causality at work in the writing and reading of the scriptures?

Obviously the "proper" role we maintain in the writing of the scriptures depends upon and fits into the broader, "proper" role we ascribe to the Holy Spirit for the whole life of the church, for individual Christians, and indeed for all human beings and their world. The Spirit has a special, "proper" mission in the "economy" of salvation that is not strictly as such shared by the other two persons of the trinity. The divine activity *ad extra* of the tripersonal God is common *qua* activity to all three persons, but takes place according to a trinitarian pattern: from the Father, through the Son, and in the Spirit. In every exercise of God's creative power, the distinction of the three persons is somehow manifested: the Father's proper role as unoriginated, the role of the other two divine persons in their origins, and all three persons in their intradivine rationality. In his treatise written to Ablabius *(Quod Non Sint Tres Dei)* St. Gregory of Nyssa classically formulated this distinction revealed in (common) trinitarian activity: "We are not told that the Father does anything by himself in which the Son does not cooperate; or that the Son has any isolated activity apart from the Holy Spirit.... Every activity originates from the Father, proceeds through the Son, and is brought to perfection in the Holy Spirit."[8] Within the order of creation and redemption the divine persons are distinct and distinctively present.

Then the temporal missions of the Son and Holy Spirit, which correspond to their eternal missions or "comings-forth" within the eternal life of the trinity, have visible effects in time; something happens in history that constitutes the *terminus ad quem* of each temporal, "economic" mission. Here the "term" or objective effects within the network of finite, created beings are special or proper to the Son or the Spirit. Thomas Aquinas points to the example of the incarnation: all three divine persons were involved in bringing it about, but the "term" or visible point of arrival, the Incarnate Son of God with his mission, is peculiar to the Word.[9] Only the Son assumes a human existence and actualizes—or rather is—the personal being of Jesus. The "economic" mission of the Spirit is likewise "proper," the self-communication of God in love and as Love: the Spirit who vivifies the church aims not only to bring all human beings to accept the presence of God in Christ but also to "christify" the universe. Men and women make up the perceptible "term" of this activity, to the extent that they let themselves be opened to the power of love (the Spirit's mission), and in that love relate through Christ (the Truth and Revelation of God) to the ultimate foundation of all life (the Father).

It is within this whole ecclesial and cosmic mission that the function of the Spirit vis-à-vis the scriptures should be interpreted. If the causality of inspiration is a common work *ad extra* of the trinity, the "term" of biblical inspiration, the visible and tangible scriptures with their special truth-revealing and life-bestowing power, is "proper" to the Holy Spirit and a kind of "real symbol" of the Spirit's presence. Here an analogy with the incarnation may be pressed into service. Given their distinct "terms" or outcomes, we say that just as the Word alone "became flesh," so the Spirit alone inspired the scriptures.[10] The Son of God unites in his own person a physical, individual humanity; in a similar way the Spirit takes up and relates in a particular way to various physical objects: the whole church, graced individuals, and the inspired (and inspiring) Bible. While sanctifying human beings, the Holy Spirit also makes the scriptures "holy" (Rom 1:2; 7:12; 2 Tm 3:15). Just as

Christ's visible humanity is hypostatically united to the Son of God, so the humanly composed and distributed scriptures also belong in an intimate, distinctive way to the Holy Spirit. In both cases the tangible effect or "term" of a common divine action is united in the proper or special way, respectively, to the Word of God and the Spirit of God. This "high" account of the Holy Spirit's relationship to the scriptures— almost "real presence" in the scriptures—throws further light on our first principle: faithful hearing of the scriptures entails loving attention to the Spirit of Love present in those texts.

If one agrees that the work of the Holy Spirit in *first* making the scriptures and *then* continuing through them to illuminate and shape life constitutes part of the Spirit's special "economic" mission and "proper" activity (or even if one continues to insist that this activity is only appropriated to the Spirit), can we offer any insights into how this double activity is exercised? We face this question, drawing some encouragement from the fact that very few effects in our world result from a single cause. The double agency (of the Holy Spirit and the sacred writers, and then of the Holy Spirit and the illuminated readers or hearers of the scriptures) does not seem to pose an overwhelming difficulty. Where the NT cites passages from the OT and attributes their formation to the Holy Spirit (Mt 22:43–44; Acts 4:25–26; 28:25–27; Heb 3:7–11; 10:15–17), the human authorship is also mentioned (except in the last two instances). The Holy Spirit and the human writers or readers act together in a single event: in the former case for the production of a biblical text and in the latter case for the actuation of some religious experience "inspired" by the scriptures. The massive challenges lie elsewhere: nothing that we say about divine action can possibly be an adequate description; modern philosophy has not come up with any agreed theory of (personal) action. Moreover, some accounts of divine action exclude not only the direct inspiring of the scriptures but any other particular, divine actions such as the incarnation and the resurrection.[11] Let us take a stand here.

First of all, we recognize that in speaking of God's activity we refer to a personal, incorporeal agent of a radically different kind from any or all temporal, created agents whether personal or nonpersonal. The invisible, direct actions of God are unlike any created causality and, in particular, very different from that exercised by corporeal, personal agents like ourselves. The primary, omnipresent, nonembodied

Agent, God, is located and active everywhere, acting from within and independently of our observation. We human beings normally act from without, and through movements of our body; as corporeal agents we are open to observation (the great exception being our mind/body interaction). Human activity's closest analogy to divine action comes in the way we bring about changes in our world by our intentions and decisions (which we then translate into action). The divine intentions as such immediately cause effects, without any need to be translated into action by some bodily movement. Moreover, by maintaining such special divine actions as biblical inspiration and the incarnation, we are certainly not proposing that God comes on the scene to act for the first time. Nothing exists or happens without God's creating and sustaining activity. By creating and sustaining everything in existence, God already acts through the founding relation of creation to be always dynamically and intimately present everywhere, to everything, and in every situation of creation. God causally contributes to every occurrence. We are speaking rather of special situations in which God is differently engaged and intentionally produces various, qualitatively distinct effects; particularized interactions of God bring about particular states of affairs at particular times and places within the created world. As regards the case in hand, the quality and nature of the effects (the initial "creation" of the Bible and the "sustaining" of its impact on subsequent generations) point to the Holy Spirit's effects rather than the cause that brings about these effects. Our greater clarity about effects holds true of created causality and, even more, of divine causality: right from the most basic divine causality at work in creating and then sustaining the universe we continually experience. Hence when naming the Holy Spirit as special, infinite Agent in the original composition and subsequent impact of the scriptures, we should expect that the precise way the Spirit brings about these effects through the finite, human agent will remain profoundly mysterious. This mystery is all the greater when we recall the radical asymmetry in the relationship between the Holy Spirit and the human agents.

We might appeal here to the mind/body analogy. The Holy Spirit brings about particular effects (the writing of the scriptures and religious experiences "inspired" by reading or hearing the scriptures) in a way that resembles the effects of the mind on the body illustrated in various bodily actions. In both the original composition and subsequent reading of the scriptures, the Spirit will normally be working through (not bypassing, still less violating) the processes of human writing and understanding, as the mind works in and through the body. The obvious limitation in this analogy stems from the fact that we are exploring a double agency between complete agents (the Holy Spirit, on the one hand, the human writers and readers of the scriptures, on the other). Our mind does not exist and act independently of our body. Add too another fact: the mind/body relationship remains at least somewhat mysterious. How far can it then illuminate the deeply mysterious relationship between the Holy Spirit and the writers (and readers) of the scriptures? We may be better advised to seek other analogies involving beneficial interactions between distinct persons: e.g., analogies from "within the circle" of Christian faith. When someone is baptized, two agents (the embodied and visible minister, and the risen, invisible Christ) collaborate in producing a common, good result. Divine and human agents are simultaneously active in bringing about in one event other spiritual results: e.g., pardon from sins (through the minister's words of absolution) and moments of revelation (when the human words of a preacher do convey the word of God).

These three examples remind us that in a real sense the divine "action" is the finite, often publicly observable effect: the altered behavior of the exorcised person, the shining joy of the forgiven sinner, and the newly graced discipleship of those who hear the word of God. This brings us to our second point. The classical adage "every agent brings about something similar to itself" *(omne agens agit simile)* suggests the various ways in which effects will have a special relationship to and consistently resemble their causes. In our case the Holy Spirit leaves a personal impression on the effects and is known through these effects: the books of the Bible and the religious impact those books have enjoyed ever since. The Spirit is actively present in these scriptures; they participate in the Spirit and lead successive generations to participate in the Spirit. What the Spirit has brought about as *sibi simile* (the biblical texts) in their turn make their readers and bearers "similar" to the Holy Spirit who continues to actualize the scriptural message. The classical adage we appeal to helps to illuminate both the original inspired passage from living word to written text, and the later endlessly repeated inspired passage from text to living word when readers experience the spiritual power and even the numinous quality of the scriptures.

Third, such direct actions of God as the Holy Spirit's inspiration of the scriptures, far from being random, arbitrary events, are related to a wider project that gives point and purpose to their occurrence: the future completion of all persons and things in Christ. Another adage, "The end commands all," proves its worth here. Both in inspiring the writing of the scriptures and then in guiding their interpretation and appropriation through the preaching, sacraments, and the whole life of the Christian community, the Holy Spirit does all this in view of the final goal: the progressive assimilation of the entire community to Christ. The scope of biblical inspiration is nothing less than that of lovingly promoting a dynamic movement toward full participation in the presence and truth of Christ and through him in the infinite Life that is God the Father. By means of the scriptures, the Holy Spirit witnesses in a special way to Christ, leads people to him, and "writes" his image on their hearts (2 Cor 3:3). It is this Christocentrism of the scriptures that points to their qualitative uniqueness—a qualitative uniqueness that emerges from their origin (in the special activity of the Spirit) and their goal (in the unique person of Jesus Christ).

Here we feel free to go beyond the explicit intentions of Paul when he wrote: "We have received...the Spirit which is from God, that we might understand the gifts bestowed on us by God. We impart this in words...taught by the Spirit, interpreting spiritual truths to those who possess the Spirit" (1 Cor 2:12–13; see 2 Pt 1:20–21; 1 Jn 2:20–21). Among the outstanding "gifts bestowed on us by God" are the scriptures. The Spirit in the scriptures speaks to the Spirit in believers, making it possible to "understand the scriptures and interpret" the "spiritual truths to which they witness"—above all, the Truth that is Christ himself. The ultimate aim of the scriptures is to make us live in the Spirit by praising and loving the Father through Christ.

Notes

Chapter 1

1. On revelation, tradition, inspiration, and biblical truth see W. J. Abraham, *The Divine Inspiration of the Holy Scriptures* (London: Oxford University Press, 1981); P. J. Achtemeier, *The Inspiration of Scripture: Problems and Proposals* (Philadelphia: Westminster Press, 1980); F. Alencherry, *The Truth of the Holy Scripture according to Vatican II and in Catholic Theology, 1965–92* (Rome: Gregorian University Press, 1994); R. F. Collins, "Inspiration," NJBC, 1023–33; H. Gabel, *Inspirationsverständnis im Wandel* (Mainz: Matthias-Grünewald-Verlag, 1991); G. O'Collins, *Fundamental Theology* (London: Darton, Longman & Todd, 1981); id., *Retrieving Fundamental Theology* (London: Geoffrey Chapman, 1993). On modern interpretation of the scriptures see R. Morgan with J. Barton, *Biblical Interpretation* (Oxford: Oxford University Press, 1988).

2. Those who endorse a low Christology (better described as mere Jesuology) are not in a position to develop an adequate theology of biblical inspiration. Taking a merely human view of Jesus, whom they do not acknowledge as the personal, preexistent Word of God "become flesh" (Jn 1:14), they cannot logically do much with the belief that through the collaboration of human authors the Holy Spirit produced a divinely inspired number of books, the Word of God in written form. In short, belief in the personal and written Word of God stand or fall together. Sallie McFague logically associates (and rejects) the two beliefs when she writes in *Metaphorical Theology: Models of God in Religious Language* (Philadelphia: Fortress Press, 1982): "I have not found it possible as a contemporary Christian to support an incarnational christology or a canonical scripture; nevertheless, I have found it possible to support a 'parabolic' Christology and Scripture as the Christian 'classic' "(x). She calls Jesus "a parable of God" (not the Parable of God) (e.g. 18, 44–54) who told us about and as "the key exemplar" demonstrated a new relationship with God (111). It is "illegitimate" to identify him with God; such incarnational Christology would be a form of idolatry, namely, "Jesusolatry" (18, 51). The historical

170

life of Jesus is not the life of God the Son, but only a "metaphor of God" (18) and not even "the" metaphor of God. She explains later in the book what she means by the Bible as a "poetic classic" (59–63), a theme to which we return shortly. Here let us simply observe that millions of "contemporary Christians" not only "find it possible to support" but also positively rejoice in "an incarnational christology" and "canonical scriptures." As the Second Vatican Council recognized, very many non-Catholic Christians "honor Sacred Scripture, taking it as the norm of belief and action" (*Lumen Gentium,* n. 16); "they affirm the divine authority of the Sacred Books," *Unitatis Redintegratio,* n. 21; see John Paul II's encyclical of 25 May 1995, *Ut Unum Sint,* nn. 12, 66.

3. See M. Goshen-Gottstein et al., "Scriptural Authority," ABD v, 1017–56; H. Graf Reventlow "Theology (Biblical), History of," ABD vi, 483–505. While recognizing the value of these two articles, we must observe the fact that the ABD does not carry a separate entry on biblical inspiration. See also W. Pannenberg and T. Schneider, eds., *Verbindliches Zeugnis, I, Kanon–Schrift–Tradition* (Göttingen: Vandenhoeck & Ruprecht, 1992). For the NT authors and their christological faith, the authority of the OT scriptures coincides with the authority of God. Thus they disclose their theology in a special way through citations from sacred scriptures. See H. Hübner, "New Testament, OT Quotations in the," ABD iv, 1096–104.

4. Even some who share our (high) belief in the Spirit and Christ can endorse a merely de facto, functional account of scriptural authority. *In Opening the Bible* (London: George Allen and Unwin, 1972) Thomas Merton writes: "The basic claim made by the bible for the word of God is not so much that it is to be blindly accepted because of God's authority, but that *it is recognized by its transforming and liberating power.* The 'word of God' is recognized in actual experience because it does something to anyone who really 'hears' it: it transforms his entire existence" (2). The alternatives proposed beg the question: we can *either* "blindly accept" biblical authority *or* "recognize in experience" its "transforming power." What of a third possibility: expecting *in advance* through the knowledge of faith that the Bible will speak to us with power because its transforming authority derives from persons (the Holy Spirit, Christ, and his apostles)?

5. See D. A. Lee, "Beyond Suspicion? The Fatherhood of God in the Fourth Gospel," *Pacifica* 8 (1995), 140–54.

6. F. Schüssler Fiorenza, "The Crisis of Biblical Authority: Interpretation and Reception," *Interpretation* 44 (1990), 353–68, at 360–61. The attempt to interpret the scriptures as "classic" texts goes back many years: see, e.g., J. Coventry, *Christian Truth* (London: Darton, Longman & Todd, 1975), 45, 66. In dialogue with T. S. Eliot, H.-G. Gadamer, F. Kermode, and others, David Tracy developed at length an interpretation of the scriptures as "classics" in *The Analogical Imagination* (New York: Crossroad, 1981).

7. On biblical authority see nn. 3 and 4 above; see also P. L. Culbertson, "Known, Knower, and Knowing: The Authority of Scripture in the Episcopal Church," *Anglican Theological Review* 74 (1992), 144–74; J. A. Keller, "Accepting the Authority of the Bible: Is It Rationally Justified?" *Faith and Philosophy* 6 (1989), 378–97; S. M. Schneiders, "Scripture as the Word of God," *Princeton Seminary Bulletin* 14 (1993), 18–35; J. R. Wright, "The Official Position of the Episcopal Church on the Authority of Scriptures," *Anglican Theological Review* 74 (1992), 348–61; 478–89. A further challenge to biblical authority comes from those who maintain (implicitly, if not blatantly) that the (best? most widely accepted?) critical historian "stands over" the scriptures as the authoritative interpreter; see C. M. LaCugna, *The Theological Methodology of Hans Küng* (Chico, CA: Scholars Press, 1982).

8. On the way some writers filter out in advance interpretative options that do not correspond to their agenda, see A. C. Thiselton, *New Horizons in Hermeneutics* (London: HarperCollins, 1992), 442–50.

9. See J. C. O'Neill and W. Baird, "Biblical Criticism," ABD 1, 725–36; D. Stuart, "Exegesis," ABD 2, 682–88; W. G. Jeanrond, "Interpretation, History of," ABD 3, 424–43; Pontifical Biblical Commission, *The Interpretation of the Bible in the Church*, translated in *Origins* 23:29 (January 6, 1994), 497–524.

10. On the Canon see J. A. Sanders and H. Y. Gamble, "Canon," ABD 1, 837–61; R. E. Brown and R. F. Collins, "Canonicity," NJBC, 1034–54.

11. On foundational and dependent revelation see O'Collins, *Retrieving Fundamental Theology*, 87–97.

12. See W. G. Jeanrond, *Theological Hermeneutics: Development and Significance. Studies in Literature and Religion,* ed. D. Jasper (London: Macmillan, 1991); B. Smalley, *The Study of the Bible in the Middle Ages* (3d ed.; Oxford: Basil Blackwell, 1983); A. C. Thiselton, *New Horizons in Hermeneutics,* passim.

13. London: Doubleday, 1992; in the United States the book is entitled *Jesus and the Riddle of the Dead Sea Scrolls* (San Francisco: HarperSan Francisco, 1992); see also G. O'Collins and D. Kendall, "On Reissuing Venturini," *Gregorianum* 75 (1994), 241–65.

14. New York: Macmillan, 1993; see reviews by R. B. Hays, *First Things* 43 (May 1994), 43–48; G. O'Collins, *The Tablet* (September 17, 1994), 1170.

15. See R. Bultmann, "Is Exegesis without Presuppositions Possible?" *Existence and Faith: Shorter Writings of Rudolf Bultmann,* trans. S. M. Ogden (New York: Meridian Books, 1960), 289–96; G. Ebeling, "The Significance of the Critical Historical Method for Church and Theology in Protestantism," in *Word and Faith,* trans. J. W. Leitch (Philadelphia: Fortress Press, 1963), 17–71.

16. London: SCM Press, 1975. Karl Rahner's 1961 essay, "Exegesis and Dogmatic Theology" (*Theological Investigations* v [London: Darton, Longman, & Todd, 1961], 67–73), encouraged systematic theologians to do exegesis in a scholarly way but did not propose principles to guide their use of exegetical results. In his *Biblical Exegesis and Church Doctrine* (New York: Paulist Press, 1985) Raymond Brown related biblical scholarship to official doctrines and dogmas rather than to the work of systematic theology.

17. This self-claimed freedom to make texts mean what "I want" continues to show up, for example, when some modern writers expound Easter texts from the New Testament: see G. O'Collins, *The Resurrection of Jesus Christ: Some Contemporary Issues* (Milwaukee: Marquette University Press, 1993), 6–10.

18. See anonymous editorial "What's Wrong with Deconstructionism," *American Philosophical Quarterly* 29 (1992), 193–95; and A. C. Thiselton's critical evaluation of J. Derrida in *New Horizons in Hermeneutics,* 103–32, 472–74, 582–92.

19. U. Eco, *Interpretation and Overinterpretation* (Cambridge: Cambridge University Press), 23.

20. In "Dei Verbum" (Dogmatic Constitution on Divine Revelation) Vatican II cites, in fn. 25, the words of St. Ambrose: "When we pray we address God; when we read the divine words, we listen to him" (*De officiis ministrorum* 1.20.88). This also applies to theologians.

21. See D. N. Fewell and D. M. Gunn, "Narrative, Hebrew," ABD iv, 45; R. Majercik et al., "Rhetoric and Rhetorical Criticism," ABD v, 710–19; J. I. H. McDonald, "Rhetorical Criticism," in R. J. Coggins and J. L. Houlden (eds.), *Dictionary of Biblical Interpretation* (London: SCM Press, 1990), 599–600; R. C. Tannehill, "Narrative Criticism," ibid, 488–89.

22. *God Encountered* (Collegeville, MN: The Liturgical Press, 1993), 95. Sallie McFague calls "worship" the "primary context...for any discussion of religious language" (*Metaphorical Theology,* 2), but rightly goes on to include the other two contexts that this paragraph summarizes.

23. On this text from Matthew, see R. E. Brown, *The Death of the Messiah* i (New York: Doubleday, 1994), 836–39.

24. From the almost limitless literature on the scriptures, the creeds, and the tradition see E. Lanczkowski et al., "Glaubenbekenntnis(se)," TRE xiii, 384–446; O'Collins, *Fundamental Theology,* 161–91; F. E. Vokes et al., "Apostolisches Glaubensbekenntis," TRE iii, 528–71.

25. R. E. Brown (*Catholic Biblical Quarterly* 42 [1980], 421–23) in his review of E. Schillebeeckx, *Jesus: An Experiment in Christology,* trans. Hubert Hoskins (New York: Seabury, 1979) regrets Schillebeeckx's one-sided reliance on N. Perrin, S. Schulz, T. J. Weeden, and others—that is to say, on what F. Kerr (*New Blackfriars* 60 [1979], 549–52) calls the "extremely fragile

and arguable hypotheses of his favourite exegetes." In their reviews R. H. Fuller (*Interpretation* 34 [1980], 293–96, at 293) and A. E. Harvey (*Journal of Theological Studies* 31 [1980], 598–606, at 604) also note the way in which Schillebeeckx, even if he claims to be doing his own exegesis, in fact follows the debatable and even quite dubious views of certain exegetes.

26. See J. Ashton, "Abba," ABD i. 7–8.

27. London: SCM Press, 1990, 142.

28. On this exegetical debate, as it developed from 1970 to 1993, see W. M. Becker, *The Historical Jesus in the Face of His Death* (Rome: Gregorian University Dissertation, 1994), 105–160.

29. On the "rule" of "scriptura sui ipsius interpres" see the 1647 *Westminster Confession of Faith*, 9.

30. J. Barr, *The Semantics of Biblical Language* (Oxford: Oxford University Press, 1961); B. S. Childs, *Biblical Theology in Crisis* (Philadelphia: Westminster Press, 1970).

31. See J. Blank, *Paulus und Jesus* (München: Kösel Verlag, 1968); D. Wenham, *Paul: Follower of Jesus or Founder of Christianity?* (Grand Rapids, MI: Eerdmans, 1995). In what follows we attribute to Jesus what seems to go back historically to stage one (his earthly ministry) and not merely to stage three (the redactional work of Mark and the other evangelists).

32. See O'Collins, *Fundamental Theology,* 24–31; see also the warning here about making too much of the differences between philosophy and theology and even alleging a hard and fast separation. On the relationship between philosophy and theology see I. Dalferth, *Theology and Philosophy* (Oxford: Blackwell, 1988); R. Fisichella, "Oportet philosophari in theologia," *Gregorianum* 76 (1995), 221–62, 503–34, 701–28; T. V. Morris (ed.), *God and the Philosophers: The Reconciliation of Faith and Reason* (Oxford: Oxford University Press, 1994); C. Stead, *Philosophy in Christian Antiquity* (Cambridge: Cambridge University Press, 1994).

33. *Thomist* 54 (1994), 699–703, at 703.

34. Some idea of the vigorous philosophical debates on time and eternity that went on through the 1980s, in the decade before Kuschel published the original (German) version of his book in 1990, is provided by B. Leftow's *Time and Eternity* (Ithaca, NY: Cornell University Press, 1991) and A. G. Padgett's *God, Eternity, and the Nature of Time* (New York: St. Martin's Press, 1992).

35. L. Wittgenstein, *Philosophical Investigations,* n. 124, trans. G.E M. Anscombe (3d ed., New York: Macmillan, 1969), 49e.

36. M. F. Wiles, *God's Action in the World* (London: SCM Press, 1986), 89.

37. G. D. Kaufman, "On the Meaning of 'Act of God,' " *Harvard Theological Review* 61 (1968), 175–201, at 185, n. 10.

38. W. P. Alston, *Divine Nature and Human Language: Essays in*

Philosophical Theology (Ithaca and London: Cornell University Press, 1989), 211; see 208–13 for further criticisms of Kaufman's position.

39. For some further points that can fill out our tenth principle see M. Dhavamony, "The Christian Theology of Inculturation," *Studia Missionalia* 44 (1995), 1–43; the whole issue is devoted to "Inculturation: Gospel and Culture."

40. *Moralia sive Expositio in Iob, Dedicatio,* iv, PL 75. 515.

41. Some of the difficulties to be faced by theologians being helped in their appropriation of the scriptures by philosophers are reflected in the often painful exchanges between philosophers and NT scholars reported by T. P. Flint and E. Stump (eds.), *Hermes and Athena* (South Bend, IN: University of Notre Dame Press, 1993); review by H. Meynell in *New Blackfriars* 76 (1995), 127–139.

42. "Prefaces to the Old Testament," trans. C. M. Jacobs, *Luther's Works,* xxv (Philadelphia: Muhlenberg Press, 1960), 236.

Chapter 2

1. See J. Hick, *The Metaphor of God Incarnate* (London: SCM Press, 1993), 2, 4–5, 36, 150.

2. G. W. E. Nickelsburg, "Son of Man," ABD vi, 137–50, at 149. For a superior treatment of the historicity of the Son of man sayings see R. E. Brown, *The Death of the Messiah* i (New York: Doubleday, 1994), 506–15.

3. See G. O'Collins, *Christology* (Oxford: Oxford University Press, 1995), 87.

4. Ibid., 87–90.

5. Ibid., 62–66, 140–41.

6. Ibid., 136–52.

7. See J. Hick, *The Metaphor of God Incarnate,* 16–46.

8. See J. D. G. Dunn, *Christology in the Making* (London: SCM Press [2nd ed., 1989]), 114–21; N. T. Wright, *The Climax of the Covenant* (Edinburgh: T. & T. Clark, 1991), 56–98.

9. See J. A. Fitzmyer, *Romans,* The Anchor Bible 33 (New York: Doubleday, 1993), 548–49.

10. The Pontifical Biblical Commission, *The Interpretation of the Bible in the Church* (Vatican City: Libreria Editrice Vaticana, 1993), 81.

11. R. W. Funk, R. W. Hoover and the Jesus Seminar, *The Five Gospels: The Search for the Authentic Words of Jesus* (London: Macmillan, 1993), 4, 7.

12. See G. O'Collins, "The Incarnation Under Fire," *Gregorianum* 76 (1995), 263–80, at 264–65; reprinted in G. O'Collins and D. Kendall, *Focus on Jesus* (Leominster: Gracewing, 1996), 30–46.

13. J. Mackey, *Jesus the Man and the Myth* (London: SCM Press, 1979), 242, 247.

14. J. Hick, *The Metaphor of God Incarnate*, 26; see 19, 150.

15. See G. O'Collins, "The Incarnation Under Fire," 265–67.

16. With insignificant variations this translation of Ti 2:13 appears in the NIV, NJB, NRSV, and REB, with the NRSV indicating in a note the possibility of translating the final words as "of the great God and our Savior Jesus Christ." The 1990 Catholic Study Bible edition of the NAB, which contains a revised translation of the NT, translates the final words as "of the great God and of our savior [lower case] Jesus Christ," indicating in a note another possible translation: "of our great God and savior [still lower case!] Jesus Christ."

17. *Summa Theologiae*, 1, 2, 3; see also 1, 3, 1–8.

18. In "St. Augustine's Account of Time and Wittgenstein's Criticism," J. McEvoy writes: "Eternity is not spread out in time; it is not time extended to infinity, in a form of everlastingness; it is unchanging, simultaneous presence, and there exists no parallel in God to the successive states of motion or experience that characterize time" (*Review of Metaphysics* 37 (1984), 547–77, at 554). See also B. Leftow, *Time and Eternity* (Ithaca, NY: Cornell University Press, 1991).

19. See B. Hebblethwaite, *The Incarnation* (Cambridge: Cambridge University Press, 1987).

20. See G. O'Collins, "The Incarnation Under Fire," 276–77.

Chapter 3

1. See, e.g., von Balthasar, *Love Alone,* trans. A. Dru (New York: Herder and Herder, 1969), and *Word and Revelation: Essays in Theology,* trans. A. V. Littledale and A. Dru, 2 vols. (New York: Herder and Herder, 1964–65).

2. See M. L. Taylor, *God Is Love: A Study in the Theology of Karl Rahner* (Atlanta: Scholars Press, 1986).

3. See G. Gutiérrez, *A Theology of Liberation,* trans. C. Inda and J. Eagleson (Maryknoll, NY: Orbis, rev. ed., 1988); id., *The God of Life,* trans. M. J. O'Connell (Maryknoll, NY: 1991); id., *Las Casas: In Search of the Poor of Jesus Christ,* trans. R. R. Barr (Maryknoll, NY: 1993).

4. C. E. Gunton, *The Actuality of the Atonement: A Study of Metaphor, Rationality, and the Christian Tradition* (Edinburgh: T. & T. Clark, 1989); J. McIntyre, *The Shape of Soteriology* (Edinburgh: T. & T. Clark, 1992); B. Sesboüé, *Jésus-Christ l'unique Médiateur,* 2 vols. (Paris: Desclée, 1988–91). Apart from a few remarks about the "story of love" (ii, 30–31) and the "logic of love" (ii, 150–51), Sesboüé has little to say explicitly about love in the whole

drama of salvation. In *Christ: The Christian Experience in the Modern World*, trans. J. Bowden (London: SCM Press, 1980), E. Schillebeeckx sets out the Christian experience of salvation and grace that has come from Jesus. He recognizes that Johannine theology represents Jesus to be "the witness of God-in-Love" (305), and he dedicates some pages to the OT theme of *hesed* (93–100). Yet love does not feature in what Schillebeeckx calls "the most important subjects" (912–13). In Gunton's *Actuality of the Atonement* love makes no appearance as such either in the chapter titles or in the section-headings for the seven chapters. It turns up in the index of subjects under "God" and the subheading "love." The index provides three references, but ignores some others (e.g., 20, 87, 92, 106, 136, 151, 157). Gunton explores the atonement and reconciliation in terms of the metaphors of the battlefield, justice, and sacrifice. "Language that is customarily used of religious, legal, commercial and military relationships is used to identify a divine action towards the world in which God is actively present remaking broken relationships" (46). But what of love relationships and speaking of God as experienced in the historical relationship of love with human beings? Gunton knows that one of his key terms (and one that describes the work of love in calling into being the community of love), "reconciliation," can be "overused and often trivialized" (177). Perhaps he thinks that the case is even worse for "love."He rightly criticizes some "objective"and "exemplarist"forms of atonement theology (156–60). He may be presuming that all atonement theologies in the key of love will be "purely exemplarist"and "merely subjective." But we believe that the account of love that we offer below avoids such weaknesses. Some defend Abelard's version of atonement against such charges; see R. E. Weingart, *The Logic of Divine Love* (London: Clarendon Press, 1970). We leave, however, the case of Abelard to the judgment of historical scholarship, arguing rather that our analysis of the divine love which (with its creative and re-creative power) overcame evil presents this love as every bit as ontologically real as and infinitely more objectively effective than the sinful human actions that put Jesus on the cross. Apropos of Jesus "governing" from the cross with "incomparable sweetness," St. Francis de Sales remarked that "nothing is so strong as love; nothing also is so sweet as its strength" (*Treatise on the Love of God,* trans. H. B. Mackey [Westminster, MD: Newman Press, 1949], 30[=1.6]). Yet we recognize that ever since Descartes, Pascal, and others promoted the view of love as a subjective property and an individual's passionate feeling, it has become somewhat more difficult to think of love as being also an ontological force and cosmic power, even if Teilhard de Chardin and others have continued to champion such a view. We shall see later how St. Paul describes the new Christian community as embodying the real power (and claim) of God's love that has created it. Victor P. Furnish calls love "the life force" of the Christian community (*The Love Command in the New Testament* [Nashville and New York: Abingdon Press, 1972], 197).

5. Trans. G. W. Bromiley (Grand Rapids, MI: William B. Eerdmans, 1994). Years ago in his *Jesus—God and Man,* trans. L. L. Wilkins and D. A. Priebe (London: SCM Press, 1968) Pannenberg developed briefly "the life in love" entailed by Jesus' call to the kingdom of God (232–35, 256–58). But love did not appear when Pannenberg went on to expound the saving significance of Jesus' death (258–80); both in the 1960s and later he was interested only in the place of the commandment of love in Jesus' ministry and not in love as illuminating the way in which the saving power of Jesus' death and resurrection operates. The first volume of his *Systematic Theology,* trans. G. W. Bromiley (Grand Rapids, MI: William B. Eerdmans, 1991), concludes with a section on "the love of God" (422–48), but the focus is mainly on the mutual love of the trinitarian Persons.

6. C. Spicq, *Agape in the New Testament,* trans. M. A. McNamara and M. H. Richter (3 vols.; St. Louis and London: B. Herder, 1963); see also K. Romaniuk, *L'Amour du Père et du Fils dans la Sotériologie de Saint Paul* (Rome: Pontificio Istituto Biblico, 1961).

7. See G. O'Collins, "In the End, Love," in J. P. Galvin (ed.), *Faith and the Future: Studies in Christian Eschatology* (Mahwah, NJ: Paulist Press, 1994), 25–42.

8. Among modern works on the philosophy of love (and related aspects of love) see R. Brown, *Analyzing Love* (Cambridge: Cambridge University Press, 1987); V. Brümmer, *The Model of Love: A Study in Philosophical Theology* (Cambridge: Cambridge University Press, 1993); J. Edwards, "Charity and Its Fruits," *Ethical Writings,* ed. P. Ramsey (New Haven: Yale University Press, 1989), 123–397; M. Fisher, *Personal Love* (London: Duckworth, 1990); B. Casper, "Liebe," *Handbuch philosophischer Grundbegriffe,* H. Krings et al. (eds.) iii (Munich: Kösel-Verlag, 1973), 860–67; G. Faggin, "Amore," *Enciclopedia Filosofica* i (Florence: Lucarini, 1982), col. 222–31; P. Gerlitz et al., "Liebe," TRE xxi, 121–91; H. Kuhn et al., "Liebe," *Historisches Wörterbuch der Philosophie,* J. Ritter and K. Gründer (eds.) v (Basel/Stuttgart: Schwabe Verlag, 1980), col. 290–327; C. S. Lewis, *The Four Loves* (London: G. Bles, 1960); M. Nédoncelle, *Vers une philosophie de l'amour et de la personne* (Paris: Aubier, 1957); D. L. Norton and M. F. Kille, *Philosophies of Love* (Totowa, NJ: Rowan and Allanheld, 1983); C. Osborne, *Plato and the God of Love* (Oxford: Clarendon, 1994); G. Outka, *Agape: An Ethical Analysis* (New Haven: Yale University Press, 1992); J. Pieper, *About Love,* trans. R. and C. Winston (Chicago: Franciscan Herald Press, 1974); S. J. Pope, *The Evolution of Altruism and the Ordering of Love* (Washington, DC: Georgetown University Press, 1994); K. D. Sakenfeld and W. Klassen, "Love," ABD iv, 375–96; I. Singer, *The Nature of Love* (3 vols.; Chicago and London: Chicago University Press, 1984–87); id., *The Pursuit of Love* (Baltimore and London: Johns Hopkins University Press, 1994); A. Soble, *The Structure of Love* (New Haven:

Yale University Press, 1990); E. C. Vacek, *Love, Human and Divine: The Heart of Christian Ethics* (Washington, DC: Georgetown University Press, 1994); D. D. Williams, *The Spirit and the Forms of Love* (Washington, DC: University Press of America, 1981). On the theology of love see G. Newlands, *Theology of the Love of God* (London: Collins, 1980).

9. Raymond Lull (c. 1233–c. 1315) frequently appealed to this principle; in justifying the incarnation Thomas Aquinas also referred to the self-communicatory quality of the good (*Summa Theologiae* 3a.1.1 resp.; see also 1a. 5.4 ad 2um; *Com. In 1 Sent.* 34.2.1 ad 4um).

10. See I. Singer, *The Nature of Love* ii, 19–126.

11. On the mutuality of love see Thomas Aquinas, *Summa Theologiae,* 1a 2ae.28.2 resp.

12. Brümmer, *The Model of Love,* 171.

13. On joy as an effect of love see Lk 15:7, 10, 23, 32; Augustine, *De Civitate Dei* 14.7; Thomas Aquinas, *Summa Theologiae* 1a 2ae.25.2c; 2a 2ae. 23.3 ad 2um; 28.1.

14. See, e.g., Gerasimos Santas, *Plato and Freud: Two Theories of Love* (Oxford: Basil Blackwell, 1988), 186–87.

15. Augustine, *Tractates on the Gospel of John* 26.4.

16. In *2 Sent.* 35.1.2c Aquinas offers the lapidary observation: "ubi amor, ibi oculus (where there is love, there is vision)."

17. G. Marcel, *Homo Viator,* trans. E. Craufurd (London: Victor Gollancz, 1951), 57–63.

18. We are perfectly aware that the NT never uses the term *erōs* for love, whereas at least one member of the *agapē* family (noun, verb, and adjective) turns up in every NT book, for a total of 341 occurrences in all. Nevertheless, the issue of need-love and gift-love has to be faced—a classic example of how philosophy pushes forward a question that silence on the part of biblical language might allow us to overlook.

19. *Confessions,* 1, 1.

20. This closing line of Dante's *Divine Comedy* echoes, of course, Aristotle's cosmic presentation of love: the unmoved Mover "moves by being loved" (*Metaphysics* 1072b3).

21. Aristotle, *Nichomachean Ethics* 9.4.1166a31; 9.9.1169b6; Thomas Aquinas agrees that "likeness is a cause of love" (*Summa Theologiae* 1a 2ae.27.3). Aristotle also speaks of such "unequal" friendships as those between rulers and subjects or parents and children (*Nichomachean Ethics* 8.7.1158b11–20).

22. D. Kendall and G. O'Collins, *Scottish Journal of Theology* 47 (1994), 511–18.

23. M. Klein, *The Psycho-Analysis of Children,* trans. Alix Strachey (London: Hogarth Press, 1973).

24. *Summa Theologiae* 1a 2ae.29.3.

25. J. J. Rousseau, *Émile,* trans. B. Foxley (London: Dent, 1974), 259–72.

26. "The Anniversary," *The Oxford Authors: John Donne,* (ed.) John Carey (Oxford: Oxford University Press, 1990) 102–3.

27. These two poems are found in H. Gardner (ed.), *The Faber Book of Religious Verse* (London: Faber and Faber, 1972), 38, 56–60.

Chapter 4

1. Like others (including some radical feminists), R. M. Frye points out, however, that the biblical references to God as Father were not culturally imposed; the sacred authors were well aware of "cults worshiping the Great Mother, along with other divinities of both sexes" ("Language for God and Feminist Language: Problems and Principles," in A. F. Kimel (ed.), *Speaking the Christian God: The Holy Trinity and the Challenge of Feminism* (Leominster: Gracewing, 1992), 27–43, at 27.

2. C. W. Bynum, *Jesus as Mother: Studies in the Spirituality of the High Middle Ages* (Berkeley: University of California Press, 1982); see G. O'Collins, *What Are They Saying About The Resurrection?* (New York: Paulist Press, 1978), 95–102. After examining some references to Jesus or God as Mother, Bynum remarks: "The theme of God's motherhood is a minor one in all the writers of the high Middle Ages except Julian of Norwich." She herself queries giving the theme "more emphasis than it deserves" (168, see 3).

3. The reference in the Psalms to God's motherly protection of the faithful (who are under the "shadow" or "shelter" of the divine wings) may refer—or may also refer—to the wings of the cherubim at both ends of the ark of the covenant; God was believed to be invisibly enthroned above the cherubim (1 Sm 4:4). In this context one should also note how some deities in the ancient Near East were pictured as winged.

4. See G. O'Collins, *Christology* (Oxford: Oxford University Press, 1995), 116–21.

5. Elizabeth Achtemeier argues, however, that such "female language for God" would "open the door" to identifying God with the world and identifying God with the processes of nature ("Exchanging God for 'No God,'" in A. F. Kimel [ed.], *Speaking the Christian God,* 1–16, at 8–9). Colin Gunton agrees: "As the history of religion and some of the excesses of feminist religion demonstrate, the logic of the female deity is a logic of pantheism" ("Proteus and Procrustes: A Study in the Dialectic of Language in Disagreement with Sallie McFague," in ibid., 65–80, at 76). See also what A. C. Thiselton, drawing on the work of Achtemeier and Susanne Heine, has to say about "goddess-

language" and "an unduly *immanental* notion of God as a presence which animates earth and nature" (*New Horizons in Hermeneutics* [London: Harper-Collins, 1992], 456–60, at 456; italics his).

6. R. R. Ruether, "The Female Nature of God: A Problem in Contemporary Religious Life," in *Concilium: God as Father*, J.-B. Metz and E. Schillebeeckx (eds.) (Edinburgh: T. & T. Clark, 1981), 61–66, at 61; italics ours. J. A. DiNoia cites studies to show that there is "no evidence that societies in whose religions goddesses were prominent had a social structure any less patriarchal than those with male deities" ("Knowing and Naming the Triune God: The Grammar of Trinitarian Confession," in A. F. Kimel [ed.], *Speaking the Christian God*, 162–87, at 181–82). J. M. Soskice points out that "religions are not patriarchal simply by virtue of styling their deities as 'fathers' but rather by underwriting social patterns that privilege men over women. This could be the case in a religion that used no personal stylizations for God of any form" ("Can a Feminist Call God 'Father?'" in ibid., 81–94, at 91).

7. E. A. Morelli denies that we can "attribute to woman *qua* woman a specific conscious access to God. To do so would be to assert that woman is not quite human, or that there are two distinct human natures" ("The Question of Woman's Experience of God," in A. F. Kimel [ed.], *Speaking the Christian God*, 222–36, at 236). What one might or might not attribute to woman *qua* woman is, of course, very different from all that women have experienced (and suffered) as a matter of fact in past history and continue to experience (and suffer) in the diverse cultures of the contemporary world.

8. Without referring explicitly to the two key Pauline passages, Johnson observes much later that, thanks to the Holy Spirit, Christians were "free to address God in an intimate way as Abba" (141).

9. R. E. Brown, *The Death of the Messiah* 1 (New York: Doubleday, 1994), 174.

10. See P. Widdicombe, *The Fatherhood of God from Origen to Athanasius* (Oxford: Clarendon, 1994).

11. On Jesus' use of "Abba" see R. E. Brown, *The Death of the Messiah*, 1, 172–75; G. O'Collins, *Christology* (Oxford: Oxford University Press, 1995), 121–25.

12. J. M. Soskice, *Metaphor and Religious Language* (Oxford: Clarendon Press, 1985), 15.

13. Some (e.g., Sallie McFague in *Metaphorical Theology* [Philadelphia: Fortress Press, 1982]) wish to ban as "idolatrous" any literal reference of language to God, granting only that through metaphors we can speak of God in ways that are true, but never literal (4–7, 28). William Alston "lapses" into such idolatry in his *Divine Nature and Human Language* (Ithaca: Cornell University Press, 1989) when he refers language literally to God (e g., 39–63). It is worth remarking here that neo-Kantian agnostics do not have a monopoly on

metaphorical theology. In his *The Actuality of the Atonement* (Edinburgh: T. & T. Clark, 1989) Colin Gunton shows himself at ease with metaphors and is no agnostic.

14. *Divine Nature and Human Language* (Ithaca and London: Cornell University Press, 1989), 26.

15. See R. M. Frye, "Language for God," in A. F. Kimel (ed.), *Speaking the Christian God*, 20–21. Like other patristic authors St. Gregory Nazianzen firmly scotched attributing male sex to God the Father (*Orat.* 31.7).

16. P. Ricoeur, *Religious Perspectives* (New York: Harper and Row, 1967), 19. Ricoeur adds to this brief comment in a later book (*The Conflict of Interpretations* [Evanston: Northwestern University Press, 1974]) when he says: "The symbol invites us to think, calls for an interpretation, precisely because it says more than it says and because it never ceases to speak to us" (28). See also his *The Symbolism of Evil* (Boston: Beacon Press, 1967), 347–57.

17. For details see B. Sesboüé, *Jésus-Christ l'unique médiateur: essaie sur la rédemption et le salut*, i (Paris: Desclée, 1988).

18. See P. R. Eddy, "Religious Pluralism and the Divine: Another Look at John Hick's Neo-Kantian Proposal," *Religious Studies* 30 (1994), 1–12; G. O'Collins, "The Incarnation Under Fire," *Gregorianum* 76 (1995), 263–80.

19. R. M. Frye, "Language for God," in A. F. Kimel (ed.), *Speaking the Christian God*, 17–43; C. Gunton, "Proteus and Procrustes," in ibid., 65–80. In the same volume, J. A. DiNoia sets out the difficulties against the double-gendered talk of "Mother/Father" or "Father/Mother" ("Knowing and Naming the Triune God," 182–83), as well as against substituting new triads for the names of "Father, Son, and Holy Spirit" (ibid., 169–73).

20. See F. Asensio et al., *Salvation, Studia Missionalia* 29 (Rome: Gregorian University Press, 1980).

21. See S. McFague, *Models of God: Theology for an Ecological, Nuclear Age* (Philadelphia: Fortress Press, 1987), 181. McFague's triad recalls the opening lines from Chapter 9 of *Kangaroo,* where D. H. Lawrence examines the three relationships that a "sincere" man might pursue with his wife: "He can propose to himself to be (a) the lord and master who is honoured and obeyed, (b) the perfect lover, (c) the true friend and companion." Lawrence adds that "(a) is now rather out of date." Without realizing it, he was preparing for his triad "lord, lover, and friend" to be changed into McFague's "Mother, Lover, and Friend."

22. Ibid., ix, 17, 68–69; see her earlier *Metaphorical Theology* (Philadelphia: Fortress Press, 1982), 9, 145–92. In passing, this earlier book had already suggested "father, mother, lover, friend" (3, 20, 191) as metaphors for God. Elizabeth Johnson, while echoing McFague by criticizing the image of God the Father for having functioned idolatrously, nevertheless adds: "What is

rejected as an idol may yet return as an icon" (*She Who Is*, 39–40, see 282, n 57).

23. See G. Green, "The Gender of God and the Theology of Metaphor," in A. F. Kimel (ed.), *Speaking the Christian God*, 44–64, at 47–49. Going beyond Green's observations, we ask: can the transcendent God as such function as role-model? Role-models such as the incarnate Son of God, Mary his mother, and all manner of saintly men and women need to be immanent, or within our world, to function like that: as heroically responsive to God and dedicated to other human beings within their various life-situations. McFague complains that men have a role-model in God, "a model for defining their self-identity, in a way that women do not" (*Metaphorical Theology*, 150). But, *pace* some readings of Lv 11:44, Mt 5:45, 48, and Eph 5:1, can the nonincarnated God the Father operate as such a role-model for any believer? Has such an *imitatio Dei Patris* ever been seriously proposed in mainline Christianity? From the outset men *and* women were invited to practice an *imitatio Christi* and find a role-model in the incarnate Christ (e.g., 1 Cor 11:1; Heb 12:2). In any case McFague's neo-Kantian agnosticism makes it very problematic for "God," in whatever shape or form, to operate as a role-model.

24. S. McFague, *Models of God*, 54–55.

25. Ibid., x, 192, 196.

26. Ibid., 192.

27. D. L. Gelpi, *The Divine Mother: A Trinitarian Theology of the Holy Spirit* (Lanham, MD: University Press of America, 1984), 136. Elizabeth A. Johnson is another who, against the view of the better exegetes, takes it for granted that the "Spirit" of 2 Cor 3:17 is "Christ the Lord" (*She Who Is*, 211).

28. On 2 Cor 3:17 see V. P. Furnish, *II Corinthians*, Anchor Bible xxxii A (New York: Doubleday, 1984, 212–13; 234–36; R. P. Martin, *2 Corinthians, Word Biblical Commentary*, xl (Waco, TX: Word Books, 1986), 59, 62–63, 71–72, 73–74.

29. John Turner ("Sethian Gnosticism: A Literary History," in *Nag Hammadi Gnosticism and Early Christianity*, C. Hedrick and R. Hodgson, Jr. [eds.] [Peabody, MA: Hendrickson, 1983], 55–86) describes at length the theme(s) of divine triads. Apropos of the Spirit being considered as Mother, he refers to the Gnostic Sethian treatises reported by Irenaeus and says: "One might begin with the [already Christianized] Ophite system of Irenaeus (cf. *Haer*. I.30), where one finds the triad of beings, Man, Son of Man, and Third Male, the first two of whom, as suggested above, may have been conceived as androgynous. There is also a lower mother figure, the Spirit, who emits Sophia-Prunicos, who by gravity descends to and agitates the waters below, taking on a material body" (59–60). On the Holy Spirit as divine Mother see also R. Murray, *Symbols of Church and Kingdom* (Cambridge: Cambridge University Press, 1975), 312–20; A. Orbe, "La procesión del Espíritu Santo y el origen de

Eva," *Gregorianum* 45 (1964), 103–18; id., *La Teologia del Espíritu Santo. Estudios Valentinos* iv (Rome: Gregorian University Press, 1966), 69–116; E. Pagels, *The Gnostic Gospels* (New York: Random House, 1979), 51–53.

30. See J. Galot, "L'Esprit Saint et la feminité," *Gregorianum* 76 (1995), 5–29; Y. Congar, *I Believe in the Holy Spirit,* trans. D. Smith, 3 vols. (London: Geoffrey Chapman, 1983), i, 163–66; iii, 155–64. In 675 the Eleventh Council of Toledo warned against interpreting the incarnation and virginal conception in terms of the Holy Spirit as "Father" and so attributing two (divine) Fathers to one incarnate Son (DS 553).

31. In his explanation of "Paraclete" J. Ashton (ABD v, 152–53) quotes R. Brown as insisting that the role of the Paraclete (especially in Jesus' farewell discourse) is that of "teaching and revealing activities of Jesus."

32. J. D. G. Dunn, *Christology in the Making* (2d ed., London: SCM Press, 1989), 132–36.

33. In Mt 12:28 ("if it is by the Spirit of God that I drive out the devils") Matthew has changed "finger of God" in the original Q-saying (Lk 11:20) into the more theological expression, "Spirit of God."

Chapter 5

1. *In Memory of Her: A Feminist, Theological Reconstruction of Christian Origins* (New York: Crossroad, 1983), 121.

2. R. L. Wilken, *The Myth of Christian Beginnings* (London: SCM Press, 1971).

3. T. Hobbes, *Leviathan* (New York: Macmillan, 1962), 498–99.

4. H. Harris, *The Tübingen School* (Oxford: Clarendon Press, 1975); P. C. Hodgson, *The Formation of Historical Theology: A Study of F. C. Baur* (New York: Harper and Row, 1966). In *Orthodoxy and Heresy in Early Christianity* (Philadelphia: Fortress Press, 1971; original 1934), Walter Bauer produced a variant of the conflict model with his thesis that Christian "orthodoxy" was merely the position that prevailed over other, equally valid apostolic traditions. See W. Henn, *One Faith, Biblical and Patristic Contributions Toward Understanding Unity in Faith* (New York/Mahwah, NJ: Paulist Press, 1995), 64, 267–68, 273–75.

5. On various NT concepts of ministry see J. D. G. Dunn, *Unity and Diversity in the New Testament* (London: SCM Press, 2d ed., 1990), 103–21.

6. J. H. Elliott, "A Catholic Gospel: Reflections on 'Early Catholicism' in the New Testament," *Catholic Biblical Quarterly* 31 (1969), 213–23; R. Wilken, *The Myth of Christian Beginnings,* 146–47. See also K. Aland, *A History of Christianity,* i (Philadelphia: Fortress Press, 1984); J. D. G. Dunn, *Unity and Diversity in the New Testament,* 341–66.

7. In general, Burtchaell's own thesis about the authoritative offices of early Christianity receiving their shape from Judaism is attractive and fits into a widely endorsed view of Judaism being the religious matrix of Christianity. But particular items in his reconstruction of the evolution in the orders of overseer or "bishop," presbyter, and deacon have been seriously challenged: see, e.g., the reviews by A. E. Harvey in *Journal of Theological Studies* 44 (1993), 678–79, and R. Wild in *Catholic Biblical Quarterly* 56 (1994), 359–61.

8. In writing here of "a" and not "the" foundational appearance to the twelve, we wish — among other things — to respect the roles of Mary Magdalene and Peter as primary Easter witnesses. On Mary Magdalene see our "Mary Magdalene as Major Witness to Jesus' Resurrection," *Theological Studies* 48 (1987), 631–46; and on Peter see Chapter 6 of this present work.

9. R. Brown, *The Gospel According to John,* i (New York: Doubleday, 1966), cvi; D. Bartlett, *Ministry in the New Testament* (Minneapolis: Fortress, 1993).

10. See E. Nardoni, "Charism in the Early Church since Rudolph Sohm: An Ecumenical Challenge," *Theological Studies* 53 (1992), 646–62.

11. Acts reports "elders" alongside "the apostles" in Jerusalem (Acts 11:30; 15:2, 4, 6, 22–23; 16:4). When Paul visits Jerusalem for the last time, no "apostles" are mentioned but only "all the elders" alongside James (Acts 21:18). Acts 6:1–6 reports the appointment of seven to "serve" *(diakonein)* in the administration in the Jerusalem church. One of them (Stephen), however, works wonders and acts as an outstanding speaker (Acts 6:8–10) before being put on trial and martyred. Another (Philip) becomes a wandering preacher and miracle-worker (Acts 8:4–40).

12. PG 7, col. 846.

13. The Jesus Seminar has here provided a latter-day parallel by alleging that after Jesus' death his disciples mingled with his wisdom teaching eschatological utterances that they derived from their earlier contacts with John the Baptist; see R. W. Funk et al., *The Five Gospels* (New York: Macmillan, 1993), 4.

14. PG 7, col. 847; this is our own translation.

15. J. Roloff, *Die Kirche im Neuen Testament* (Göttingen: Vandenhoeck & Ruprecht, 1993); D. Stanley, *The Apostolic Church in the New Testament* (Westminster, MD: Newman Press, 1965); F. M. Young, "On episcopos and presbyteros," *Journal of Theological Studies* 45 (1994), 142–48; R. Brown, C. Osiek, P. Perkins, "Early Church," *The New Jerome Biblical Commentary* (Englewood Cliffs, NJ: Prentice-Hall, 1990), 1338–50.

16. See "Baptism, Eucharist, and Ministry," Faith and Order Paper No. 111 (Geneva: World Council of Churches, 1982); Anglican-Roman Catholic Commission, *The Final Report* (London: SPCK and Catholic Truth Society, 1982).

17. See S. I. Benn, "Authority," in P. Edwards (ed.), *Encyclopedia of Philosophy* i (London: Collier Macmillan, 1967), 215–218; L. Krieger, "Authority," in P. P. Wiener (ed.), *Dictionary of the History of Ideas* i (New York: Charles Scribner's Sons, 1973), 141–62; J. Miethke et al., "Autorität," TRE v, 17–51; W. Veit et al., "Autorität," in J. Ritter (ed.), *Historisches Wörterbuch der Philosophie* i (Basel: Schwabe, 1971), col. 724–33.

18. See J. F. McCann, *Church and Organization. A Sociological and Theological Enquiry* (Scranton: University of Scranton Press, 1993).

Chapter 6

1. *Origins,* 8: 19 (October 26, 1978), 292.

2. Anglican-Roman Catholic International Commission, *The Final Report* (London: SPCK and Catholic Truth Society, 1982), 64.

3. Ibid., 81–85. One finds the same emphasis on the "big three" texts in J. M. Miller, *The Shepherd and the Rock: Origins, Development, and Mission of the Papacy* (Huntington, IN: Our Sunday Visitor, 1995). He identifies the scriptural foundations for the Petrine ministry (12–49), notes the apostle's role as witness to the risen Lord (31–33), but makes little of it. The twenty-one theses on the Petrine ministry of the Pope with which he concludes his helpful study (346–70) refer to Christ's incarnation (365) and divine sonship (363) but include nothing about the ministry of proclaiming the resurrection. J. M. R. Tillard's *The Bishop of Rome* (London: SPCK, 1983), while being a valuable ecumenical work on Peter and the papacy, has little to say about Peter as Easter witness (112–13).

4. *Origins* 25: 4 (June 8, 1995), 69.

5. *Final Report,* 82.

6. See, e.g., R. E. Brown, "John 21 and the First Appearance of the Risen Jesus to Peter," in E. Dhanis (ed.), *Resurrexit* (Rome: Libreria Editrice Vaticana, 1975), 246–65.

7. *Jesus: An Experiment in Christology* (London: Collins, 1979), 354–90; see G. O'Collins, *Jesus Risen* (London: Darton, Longman & Todd, 1987), 115–17.

8. See, e.g., E. Seeberg, "Wer war Petrus? Bemerkungen zu J. Haller, *Das Papstum. Idee und Wirklichkeit,* in *Zeitschrift für Kirchengeschichte"* 53 (1934), 571–84, at 581.

9. "Wer war Petrus?" 583–84.

10. See. C. W. Bynum, *The Resurrection of the Body in Western Christianity,* 200–1336 (New York: Columbia University Press, 1995).

11. *The Final Report,* 37–38.

12. Faith and Order Paper No. 111 (Geneva: World Council of Churches, 1982).

13. The chapter (3–27) Pagels dedicates in *The Gnostic Gospels* to the resurrection ("The Controversy over Christ's Resurrection: Historical Event or Symbol?") contains other unsatisfactory elements. Why the alternative, historical event or symbol? Surely historical events (e.g., Christ's crucifixion) can also be thoroughly symbolic? Further, rather than respecting the earlier witness from the central protagonist himself (1 Cor 9:1; 15:8; Gal 1:12, 16), she takes the later, Lukan account of Paul's encounter with the risen Christ (Acts 9, 22, 26) as the primary version of that episode (6). She also puts that foundational encounter on the same level as Paul's later experiences as reported in Acts 18:9–10; 22:17–18 (10).

14. *Peter: Apostle for the Whole Church* (Columbia, SC: University of South Carolina Press, 1994), 185.

15. For more material on the NT evidence see G. O'Collins, "Peter as Easter Witness," *Heythrop Journal* 22 (1981), 1–18, especially 1–8; id., *Jesus Risen,* 161–68.

16. See G. O'Collins, "Peter as Easter Witness," *Heythrop Journal* 22 (1981), 1–18, at 1–8.

17. See E. Barbotin, *Le Témoignage* (Brussels: Culture et Vérité, 2d ed., 1995); E. Cattonaro and G. Giannini, "Testimonianza," in Centro di Studi Filosofici di Gallarate, *Enciclopedia Filosofica,* viii (Florence: Lucarini, 1982), col. 210–15; C. A. J. Coady, *Testimony: A Philosophical Study* (Oxford: Clarendon Press, 1994); R. Latourelle, "Testimony," in R. Latourelle and R. Fisichella, eds., *Dictionary of Fundamental Theology* (New York: Crossroad, 1994), 1044–60; G. Marcel, *The Philosophy of Existence* (New York: Philosophy Library, 1949), esp. 67–76; the 1972 number of *Archivio di filosofia* which was completely dedicated to "La Testimonianza." This last volume, which offers in 534 pages the proceedings of a 1972 colloquium run in Rome by Enrico Castelli, contains papers by such philosophers as Hans-Georg Gadamer, Emmanuel Levinas, Donald MacKinnon, Gabriel Marcel, Maurice Nédoncelle, Paul Ricoeur, and Xavier Tilliette, along with contributions from such theologians as Claude Geffré, Raymond Panikkar, and Karl Rahner.

18. In his helpful chapter on "Astonishing Reports" Coady also deals well with the stubborn and badly argued skepticism of David Hume; see *Testimony,* 179–98.

19. See K. Rahner, *Foundations of Christian Faith,* trans. W. V. Dych (New York: Seabury Press, 1978), 274–75; id., "The Resurrection and Human Experience," *Sacramentum Mundi* v, 329–31; G. O'Collins, *Jesus Risen,* 137–47.

Chapter 7

1. G. Luedemann, *The Resurrection of Jesus: History, Experience, Theology,* trans. J. Bowden (London: SCM Press, 1994), 181–82, italics ours; see reviews by G. O'Collins, *Gregorianum* 77 (1996), 357–59, and in *Theological Studies* 57 (1996), 341–43.

2. A good example of the teaching of the medieval papacy using these verses to support its claim to exercise both spiritual and material power is found in the bull *Unam Sanctam* issued by Boniface VIII in 1302 (DS 870–875). Boniface believed that the spiritual power (sword) is exercised by the priest, while the material power (sword) is exercised by kings and soldiers at the will and sufferance of the priest (DS 873).

3. See G. O'Collins, "The Incarnation under Fire," *Gregorianum* 76 (1975), 263–80, at 264–69.

4. *Metaphorical Theology* (Philadelphia: Fortress Press, 1982), 44, 45.

5. *Models of God: Theology for an Ecological, Nuclear Age* (Philadelphia: Fortress Press, 1987), 46.

6. Ibid., 55.

7. Ibid., 136.

8. Ibid., 54.

9. Ibid., 54–55.

10. Ibid., 56.

11. *Metaphorical Theology,* 27.

12. Ibid., 111.

13. Ibid., 146, 166–67.

14. *Models of God,* 192.

15. Ibid., xi.

16. Ibid., 195.

17. Ibid., 224.

18. *Jesus and the Son of Man* (London: Lutterworth, 1964), 9; italics ours. In his *Jesus: An Experiment in Christology,* trans. H. Hoskins (London: Collins, 1979) Edward Schillebeeckx seems to endorse a similar position when he maintains that "Jesus [=Schillebeeckx's reconstruction of Jesus] is the one and only basis for an authentic Christology" (82).

19. *The Problem of the Historical Jesus* (Philadelphia: Fortress, 1964), 13; italics ours.

20. Ibid., 21.

21. Ibid., 14.

22. Ibid.

23. J. A. Fitzmyer, *Scripture, the Soul of Theology* (New York/Mahwah, NJ: Paulist Press, 1994), 86–87; all subsequent references to this book come from these two pages.

24. "The Faith of Jesus," 411–16, 416–21.

25. Ibid., 415, n. 52.

26. Ibid., 416.

27. See G. O'Collins, *Interpreting Jesus* (London: Geoffrey Chapman, 1983), 41–45.

28. See "The Faith of Jesus," 416, n. 54; 417, nn. 56, 59; 421.

29. See also what one of us (O'Collins) wrote on the faith/history (including exegetical reconstructions) in *Foundations of Theology* (Chicago: Loyola University Press, 1971), 64–112, and *Fundamental Theology* (London: Darton, Longman & Todd, 1981), 156–60.

Chapter 8

1. B. M. Metzger, *A Textual Commentary on the Greek New Testament* (Stuttgart: Deutsche Bibelgesellschaft/United Bible Societies, 2nd ed., 1994), 169–70.

2. Ibid., 169.

3. A response to Pryor's case is not convincing: R. Robert, "La leçon christologique en Jean 1, 13," *Revue Thomiste* 87 (1987), 5–22; see also J. Galot, "Maternità verginale di Maria e paternità divina," *Civiltà Cattolica* 139 (1988), 209–22.

4. *The Gospel According to St. John*, 164.

5. *The Gospel of John*, 59, n. 5.

6. B. M. Metzger, *A Textual Commentary*, 461.

7. On translating the bible see H. G. Grether, "Versions, Modern Era," ABD, vol. 6, 842–51; J. P. Louw (ed.), *Lexicography and Translation* (Cape Town: Bible Society of South Africa, 1985); E. A. Nida, "Theories of Translation," ABD, vol. 6, 512–15.

8. R. Coleman, *New Light and Truth. The Making of the Revised English Bible* (Oxford: Oxford University Press, 1989).

9. On the case for recognizing the way the earthly Jesus exercised faith—a case which is also supported by a range of considerations from different passages of Hebrews—see G. O'Collins and D. Kendall, "The Faith of Jesus," *Theological Studies* 53 (1992), 403–23; reprinted in O'Colllins, *Christology* (Oxford: Oxford University Press, 1995), 250–68.

10. V. R. Gold *et al.* (eds.), *The New Testament and Psalms. An Inclusive Version* (New York: Oxford University Press, 1995); R. W. Funk *et al.*, *The Five Gospels* (New York: Macmillan, 1993).

Chapter 9

1. *Theological Hermeneutics. Development and Significance* (New York: Crossroad, 1991), 1.

2. For details see G. O'Collins, "Peter as Easter Witness," *Heythrop Journal* 22 (1981), 1–18.

Appendix

1. See, e.g., St. Augustine of Hippo, *Contra sermonem Arianorum,* CSEL, 691.58; 695.6; *Epistolae,* 164, PL 33, 716; St. Thomas Aquinas, *Summa Theologiae,* 1.45.6. William Alston, who explores one major function traditionally assigned to the Holy Spirit (see n. 4 below), nevertheless adds: "I want to avoid getting into controversies over which Person of the Trinity is doing a particular job at a particular time. I will adhere to the widely accepted principle that all Persons of the Trinity are involved in the external operation (external to the Godhead) of any Person" (*Divine Nature and Human Language,* 226). A central principle of trinitarian theology declares that in God everything is common except where a relation of opposition prevents this ("in Deo omnia sunt unum, ubi non obviat relationis oppositio"); see W. Kasper, *The God of Jesus Christ,* tr. M. J. O'Connell (New York: Crossroad, 1984), 375, n. 95. Such relations of opposition result from the eternal, inner-trinitarian "comings-forth" and relations, reflected in the "economic" missions of the Son and the Holy Spirit.

2. On the *testimonium internum Spiritus Sancti,* see J. Calvin, *Institutes,* 1.7; ed. J.-D. Benoit, i (Paris: J. Vrin, 1957), 92–99; and the 1647 *Westminster Confession of Faith,* 7.

3. See Vatican II, *Dei Verbum* (Dogmatic Constitution on Divine Revelation), 12; the remark goes back through Leo XIII to St. Jerome (see n. 9 to Ch. 3 of *Dei Verbum*). Occasionally Fathers of the Church, without excluding the role of the Spirit, attributed biblical inspiration also to the "Logos" or Christ the "Kyrios"; see L. F. Ladaria, *El Espíritu en Clemente Alejandrino* (Madrid: Universidad Pontificia Comillas Madrid, 1980), 23–26.

4. The following representative works on the divine activity rarely or never refer to the Holy Spirit: the twelve contributions to B. Hebblethwaite and E. Henderson (eds.), *Divine Action* (Edinburgh: T. & T. Clark, 1990), make very few references to the Holy Spirit (only 84, 90–91); the divine acts in relation to the world are treated otherwise, mainly in terms of "God"; T. V. Morris (ed.), *Divine and Human Action* (Ithaca: Cornell University Press, 1988), has only one reference to the Spirit (295); R. J. Russell et al. (eds.), *Quantum Cosmology and the Laws of Nature: Scientific Perspectives on Divine Action* (Vat-

ican City: Vatican Observatory Publications, 1993) has much to say about "God," the "Trinity" in general, or "economic and immanent" trinity. But specific references to the Holy Spirit are few (e.g., 266, 289–90, 383). The same is true of R. J. Russell et al. (eds.), *Chaos and Complexity: Scientific Perspectives on Divine Action* (Vatican City: Vatican Observatory Publications, 1995). O. C. Thomas (ed.), *God's Activity in the World: The Contemporary Problem* (Chico, CA: Scholars Press, 1983) brings in the Holy Spirit only once (129); K. Ward in *Divine Action* (London: Collins, 1990) has nothing as such to say of the Spirit, let alone of the Spirit's role in inspiring the scriptures. In *God's Action in the World,* Maurice Wiles never considers biblical inspiration and rarely refers to the Holy Spirit (32–33, 36, 57, 89); in all but the last case he does so only when reporting the views of others. In *Divine Revelation and the Limits of Historical Criticism* (Oxford: Oxford University Press, 1982), W. J. Abraham dedicates five of his nine chapters to various aspects of "divine action" and "divine intervention," notes "the subjective witness of the Holy Spirit in bringing assurance to the believer of the significance of Jesus," but adds at once, "It would take us too far afield to explore them in depth" (52). In *Divine Nature and Human Language,* W. P. Alston has much to say about divine action, spends one chapter on the Holy Spirit (223–52; see also 101, 112), but is concerned there almost exclusively with the Spirit's work in regeneration and sanctification.

5. *The Holy Spirit: The Holy Spirit in the Bible, in the History of Christian Thought and in Recent Theology* (London: Marshall, Morgan & Scott, 1983).

6. The following works on the Holy Spirit have nothing directly to say about the Holy Spirit's role in the writing and reading of the scriptures: H. Berkhof, *The Doctrine of the Holy Spirit* (Atlanta: John Knox Press, 1964); J. Moltmann, *The Spirit of Life,* trans. M. Kohl (London: SCM Press, 1992); J. Taylor, *The Go-Between God: The Holy Spirit in Christian Mission* (London: SCM Press, 1972). D. L. Gelpi, *The Divine Mother: A Trinitarian Theology of the Holy Spirit* (Lanham, MD: University Press of America, 1984), seems to relate the Holy Spirit to the writing of the scriptures only once and that in passing (16). Despite many glowing pages about the Holy Spirit, Elizabeth Johnson in *She Who Is* (New York: Crossroad, 1993) seems unconcerned with the Spirit's activity in forming the scriptures. The NT is cited as the "biblical narratives of origin" (141) or the "literary precipitate" of first-century Christian experience (198), but never as narratives written under the inspiration of the Holy Spirit, and even less as the normative, authoritative literature of Christianity. In *Life in the Spirit* (San Francisco: HarperSan Francisco, 1992) T. C. Oden dedicates a few pages to the Spirit's role in the writing and hearing/reading of the scriptures (67–75). But he does little beyond repeating Calvin's phrase about the *testimonium internum Spiritus Sancti* ("the interior witness of the Holy

Spirit") and such traditional convictions as that of the sacred writers being the Spirit's living "instruments" in the production of the scriptures. When briefly treating the inspiration of the scriptures in *God the Spirit,* trans. J. F. Hoffmeyer (Minneapolis, MN: Fortress Press, 1994), Michael Welker succeeds in putting more life into Calvin's language (272–78). Apart from a few remarks by J. Moltmann, "Die Gemeinschaft des Heiligen Geistes" (ii, 921–937, at 932–934), the 104 contributors to the two-volume *Credo in Spiritum Sanctum,* J. S. Martins (ed.) (Vatican City: Libreria Editrice Vaticana, 1983) had practically nothing to say about the Spirit's double activity vis-à-vis the scriptures (in inspiring first their writing and then their ongoing appropriation).

7. The excellent entry on "Inspiration" by R. F. Collins, in R. E. Brown, J. A. Fitzmyer, and R. E. Murphy (eds.), *New Jerome Biblical Commentary* (London: Geoffrey Chapman, 1989), illustrates how little is explained by such traditional theories as causal instrumentality and concursive action (1023–33, at 1028, 1031–32, 1033). In *The Divine Inspiration of Holy Scripture* (Oxford: Oxford University Press, 1981), W. J. Abraham has little to say about the Holy Spirit, even less in the second half of the book (59, 68, 72, 103) when he develops his own constructive proposal about divine agency and inspiration. In *The Uses of Scriptures in Recent Theology* (Philadelphia: Fortress Press, 1975), D. H. Kelsey refers only briefly to the present reality and function of the Holy Spirit (93–94)—a silence "expressed" by the fact that the index includes no reference to the Holy Spirit. P. J. Achtemeier has more to say about the Holy Spirit in his *The Inspiration of Scripture: Problems and Proposals* (Philadelphia: Westminster Press, 1980).

8. "Quod Non Sint Tres Dei," *Gregorii Nysseni Opera,* ed. W. Jaeger, iii.i (Leiden: E. J. Brill, 1958), 47–48.

9. *Summa Theologiae,* 3.3.1–4.

10. This proper role of the Holy Spirit gets masked when the Second Vatican Council in *Dei Verbum* introduces this analogy but leaves the activity of inspiration unspecified as "God's words": "God's words, expressed through human language, have taken on the likeness of human speech, just as the Word of the eternal Father, by assuming the flesh of human weakness, took on the likeness of human beings" (13).

11. This is the position of Maurice Wiles in *God's Action in the World,* a work that would be more appropriately entitled *God's Non-Action in the World.* The view taken is that God is restricted to uniform action. Acting uniformly and impartially in all events in the world, God does not interact with the natural-historical causal nexus in such particular ways as those required by belief in the special inspiration of the scriptures. With all variety in the divine activity excluded, the interpretation of God's activity becomes attenuated to the point that we wonder why Wiles bothers to assert any divine activity at all.

Index of Names

Biblical Index